Kitchens

Kitchens

A Professional's Illustrated Design and Remodeling Guide

Chase M. Powers

McGraw-Hill

New York   San Francisco   Washington, D.C.   Auckland   Bogotá
Caracas   Lisbon   London   Madrid   Mexico City   Milan
Montreal   New Delhi   San Juan   Singapore
Sydney   Tokyo   Toronto

Library of Congress Cataloging-in-Publication Data

Powers, Chase M.
    Kitchens : a professional's illustrated design and remodeling
guide / Chase M. Powers.
      p. cm.
    Includes index.
    ISBN 0-07-050713-9 (hardcover : acid-free paper). — ISBN
0-07-050714-7 (paperback : acid-free paper)
    1. Kitchens—Remodeling. I. Title.
TH4816.3.K58P68 1996
643'.3—dc21
                                              96-46929
                                                CIP

McGraw-Hill

*A Division of The **McGraw·Hill** Companies*

pbk   1 2 3 4 5 6 7 8 9 0 DOC/DOC 9 0 1 0 9 8 7 6
hc   1 2 3 4 5 6 7 8 9 0 DOC/DOC 9 0 1 0 9 8 7 6

ISBN 0-07-050714-7 (PBK)
ISBN 0-07-050713-9 (HC)

*The sponsoring editor for this book was Larry Hager, the editing supervisor was
Sally Glover, and the production supervisor was Suzanne Rapcavage. It was set in
Souvenir by McGraw-Hill's desktop publishing department in Hightstown, N.J.*

Printed and bound by R. R. Donnelley & Sons Company.

 This book is printed on recycled, acid-free paper containing a minimum of
50% recycled, de-inked fiber.

McGraw-Hill books are available at special quantity discounts to use as premiums and
sales promotions, or for use in corporate training programs. For more information,
please write to the Director of Special Sales, McGraw-Hill, 11 West 19th Street,
New York, NY 10011. Or contact your local bookstore.

This book is dedicated to my best friends; they know who they are.

Contents

Introduction

Kitchen remodeling is, as you may know, a very lucrative business. One of the best home-improvement investments a homeowner can make is in kitchen remodeling. This fact alone makes selling kitchen jobs easier than selling many other types of remodeling work. Not only is kitchen remodeling popular with and financially rewarding for homeowners, it can produce better-than-average profits for professional remodelers.

This book is written for people who make their living as builders and remodelers. The purpose of this book is to make professional contractors aware of where and how they can make more money with fewer hassles. If you take the time necessary for a thorough understanding of kitchen remodeling, you can specialize in the trade and become known for your outstanding kitchen designs and workmanship. Once you've achieved this status, you can name your price and still have customers on a waiting list.

My experience as a builder and remodeler is extensive. I've spent most of my adult life remodeling kitchens and bathrooms. In addition to remodeling, I've built numerous new homes. I believe a kitchen is one of the most important rooms in a house, and many homebuyers and homeowners agree with me. If you're skeptical, take a look at the magazine racks in a local bookstore. Check out the titles aimed at home repair and remodeling. You will see that a majority of these magazines center around kitchens and bathrooms. There's a reason for this. Consumers are willing to pay handsome prices to get the kitchens they desire.

If you are not currently making considerable profits as a kitchen remodeler, you're missing a golden opportunity. Many styles of kitchens are popular. However, there is one trend in particular that you should pay attention to. I'm referring to the demand for large, eat-in kitchens. The public desire for these kitchens is extremely high. Again, just skim through some magazines and you will see that what I say is true. Homeowners are looking to the past for kitchen designs and decorations. Even homeowners who are not interested in period kitchens like the concept of a contemporary family kitchen similar in size to the large kitchens of the past.

This book has many unique aspects. First, *Kitchens: A Professional's Illustrated Design and Remodeling Guide* is not a how-to guide for homeowners. This book is written by a seasoned professional for contractors of all skill levels. Whether you are about to remodel your first kitchen or your hundredth kitchen, this book is a valuable guide to saving time, selling jobs, and making more money. This book takes you from the beginning to the very end of a job. You can use the illustrations as idea generators for your customers. The guide contains valuable suggestions that can improve your business tactics and steer you around the common obstacles faced by professional remodelers. The personal examples in the book can give you the strength needed to complete profitable remodeling jobs. Let me give you an example of what you can expect from this hands-on approach.

The first chapter is aimed at helping you with design issues. Many remodelers who do a fine job working within their trade have trouble with design plans. It's not mandatory that you design your own plans, but it certainly helps if you and your customers can share the excitement of creating custom layouts.

In the second chapter, I look at some popular kitchen styles. This discussion should help you understand some of the intricacies of specialty kitchens. After reading this chapter, you will have a basis on which to build your own designs.

The book next delves into a discussion of various aspects of the remodeling business. Chapter 3 examines the methods used to obtain accurate cost estimates. Job bids are discussed in Chapter 4. In Chapter 5, you can learn valuable negotiating techniques that will help you find big savings. A contractor must be able to make quick decisions. Chapter 6 helps you understand both the importance of and techniques needed to make take these sometimes difficult measures.

By the time you get to Chapter 7, you're heading into the hands-on aspects of kitchen remodeling. For example, Chapter 7 shows you the ropes for ripping out an existing kitchen. Plumbing is covered in Chapter 8, and electrical work is the subject of Chapter 9. In Chapter 10, I look at the aspects of HVAC systems that you may deal with in the course of your remodeling career. Chapters 11 through 15 discuss the subjects of specific remodeling options such as flooring, lighting, and fireplaces.

If you want to get into the business of kitchen remodeling, you owe it to yourself to read this book. Take a few moments to skim through the pages. It shouldn't take long for you to see how unique this book really is. I believe that once you've had time to read it, you will agree that *Kitchens: A Professional's Illustrated Design and Remodeling Guide* could be a powerful step toward a prosperous future in kitchen remodeling.

The right plan

Chapter 1

THE CRUCIAL first step in kitchen remodeling is settling on the right plan. In fact, all successful remodeling jobs begin with a well-thought-out plan. Whether you are designing new construction or planning a major remodeling job, your plan of attack will have a heavy influence on the success of the job and on your customer's happiness with the finished product.

During my long career as a professional remodeler, I've found that customers who wish to have their kitchens remodeled often fall into one of two categories. One group merely wants to upgrade the existing kitchen layout. The second group wants exotic custom work that requires more space than allotted. Both groups need a professional remodeler to explain what they can and cannot do or what they should and should not do.

This book is all about large, eat-in kitchens. Our goal is to convert existing kitchens into more spacious and efficient kitchens. For some jobs this will mean knocking out walls to combine dining and kitchen areas. A few customers will want additions built onto their homes to accommodate a more spacious family atmosphere. But many customers will want you to convert the space they have so that it merely appears larger. Obviously, your job as a contractor and guide to homeowners requires a lot of thought and effort. All kitchens can be reworked to make them more efficient and to provide a new look. You will be instrumental in helping your customers obtain the kitchens of their dreams.

Efficiency

Efficiency is essential if a kitchen is to be enjoyable to work in. Small kitchens can be a bit more difficult to arrange than larger kitchens for maximum comfort. However, smaller kitchens lend themselves to a greater degree of efficiency (Fig. 1-1). In order to design a pleasant, efficient kitchen, you must consider many components, such as cabinets, organizers, and accessories.

Figure 1-1

Beam ceilings with high windows offer more light. The additional natural lighting pays dividends in a kitchen where a lot of wood is present. Harris-Tarkett, Inc: Longstrip—The American Collection—Oak Mojave Wheat.

People

As a contractor, you must consider how many people are going to be in a kitchen at the same time. People require space. If a kitchen is poorly laid out, traffic patterns can be a serious problem. For example, putting an island counter in a small kitchen can create a traffic obstacle. Inconveniences such as dodging other people and taking turns getting to cabinets and appliances while carefully maneuvering around the island counter create frustration and a lack of appreciation for the kitchen. The same kitchen without the island cabinet would have a lot more floor space in which to move. This extra space would allow more activities to occur in the kitchen simultaneously. When you plan a layout, take into consideration the expected traffic flow of people in and through the kitchen.

Appliances

Large appliances are a part of every functional kitchen. A refrigerator and range are standard. Usually a dishwasher is tucked under the cabinet. A separate cooktop, trash compactor, or small freezer may also be included. The space necessary for the specific models of the desired appliances must be a factor in planning a kitchen remodeling job.

I've found that when homeowners begin to concentrate on remodeling their kitchens, they often draw up rough sketches of how they envision the new kitchen. Frequently they measure their existing appliances as a guide in making their layout. You must keep in mind that the new kitchen will probably have new appliances. The new appliances might not be the same size as the ones used in your customer's sample drawing. If you plan your remodeling scheme by the measurement of the existing appliances, what are you going to do when your customer decides to buy a new, larger refrigerator that doesn't fit in the space you have left for it? It only takes a fraction of an inch to keep an appliance from sliding into its designated space.

During your planning stage, consult the customer regarding the appliances to be used in the new kitchen. Based on your discussion with the client, make a list of all the appliances with which you expect your customer to equip the new kitchen. Once you have completed a list of the major appliances, create a list of small appliances, such as toasters, microwave ovens, and so on. Will any of these small appliances be mounted under wall cabinets? How many of them will take up counter space? Can you find creative ways to keep these small appliances out of the way when they are not in use? This type of advance planning will help you create a better kitchen.

When you consider the locations for appliances, keep kitchen work habits in mind. Would you want to walk to one end of the kitchen to get to the refrigerator and then have to walk all the way back to get to your range? You probably wouldn't. It is almost guaranteed that your customers wouldn't want to either.

Professional kitchen planners often refer to work triangles. A work triangle has its apex at the kitchen sink and its base corners at the range and the refrigerator. This model represents a person standing at the sink and then turning to get to either the range or refrigerator. Island-style kitchens (Fig. 1-2 and 1-3) often have very effective work

Figure 1-2

Island kitchen with abundant storage space. Note wood finish on front of dishwasher. Wellborn Cabinet, Inc.

Figure 1-3

Island kitchen with many outstanding features. High windows allow plenty of light. Arched window over kitchen sink creates a special elegance, as does the wooded range hood. Desk area is a nice touch. An island with this much counter requires electrical outlets. Wellborn Cabinet, Inc.

triangles. If the distance in the triangle is too short, the result is usually congestion. When the distance is too long, time and energy is lost during routine kitchen duties. Ideally, the triangle distances should range between 4½ feet to 5 feet for optimum kitchen efficiency and smooth traffic flow.

Although the theory behind a work triangle design is solid, work habits and lifestyles, not to mention design features, can blow the triangle theory out of the water. The key to creating your customer's ideal kitchen is to design it with that individual customer's needs in mind. Looking at hundreds of kitchen plans can help you make decisions about the design plan for a job. However, the plans designed by other remodelers should be used as guides to be studied, not rules to be followed.

Organized storage

Storage facilities are always a concern in a kitchen. When most people think of kitchen storage, they think only of storage in general terms. To design an efficient kitchen, you must break storage needs down into smaller categories. For example, there will be a need for food storage with daily access. Another area should be for foods that may not be used for days, or even weeks, at a time. Yet another area must be dedicated to the concealment of dishes and glasses. Pots and pans can be hung in plain view, but this is also considered a storage facility. When designing storage facilities, always plan on using cabinets made of quality construction (Fig. 1-4).

As the lives of people have become more hectic, product manufacturers have worked to produce items that make a busy

Figure 1-4

Good-quality cabinet construction. The wood triangles are used when attaching a countertop.

schedule easier to maintain. As a result, frozen meals, dishwashers, microwave ovens, and even cabinet organizers are now common in American households. Kitchens can be designed to meet the demands of two or more cooks. Husbands and wives with opposing schedules often prepare individual meals at staggered times. This situation can result in some conflict if tools, appliances, and fundamental kitchen needs are not planned carefully. Take enough time before starting your job to make sure your plan will meet the long-term needs of your customer.

Lighting

Lighting plays a vital role in the enjoyable use of a kitchen. A single ceiling light and a fluorescent tube over the kitchen sink are the relics of another time. Now we use under-cabinet, recessed, and track lighting to provide artificial light in kitchens. Skylights and large, garden-style windows are used for natural lighting. A list of the top ten enhancing features of a kitchen is sure to include good lighting.

Odds and ends

Important odds and ends, such as fire extinguishers, intercoms, and ventilating systems should also be considered during the planning stage. Make a list of everything that you would include in a perfect kitchen. Pore over your notes and add to them daily. After several days, review the list and begin to delete and reorganize items as needed. You will be surprised by how many little things you might have overlooked had you not listed them.

The nuts and bolts

No kitchen plan is complete without the nuts and bolts of the job. These include plumbing, electrical work, heating and air conditioning, floor coverings, and so forth. Some aspects of kitchen remodeling, such as cabinet type and placement, are obvious topics of conversation. On the other hand, the relocation of plumbing pipes for the new sink location may elude the inexperienced contractor or customer. While almost any of these nuts-and-bolts concerns can easily be taken care of in the middle of a large-scale remodeling, it pays to have your work planned and to stick with your plan.

Many smaller aspects of a remodeling job go unnoticed in the initial planning stage. Some of these items are important, and others have very little bearing on the finished job. For example, let's say that the new kitchen will have a refrigerator-freezer with a built-in ice-maker. The old refrigerator doesn't have this modern convenience. The ice-maker will need a water source. How will you get water to the appliance? If you address this issue early, you will not have a problem. You simply install a saddle valve tap on the cold water pipe under the kitchen sink and route the quarter-inch tubing to the back of the appliance. Even if you overlook this chore in the rough-in stage, it should be a simple matter while there is still unfinished access beneath the kitchen floor or a path for routing the tubing through the base cabinets. This is a oversight that probably won't spoil your plans, but there are others that could. Let me give you an example of a more serious complication due to an oversight.

Assume that you are adding an island cabinet in a new kitchen. The island will house an indoor grill that will have to be vented to the outside. In this type of situation, the vent from the grill goes into, and usually under, the kitchen floor as it travels to an outside wall. During rough construction, this is not a problem. You could cut out a path in the subflooring and route the duct between the floor joists. Then you would use new subflooring and floor covering to conceal the work. However, if you have finished your major remodeling and are just putting the grill into place when you discover the need for venting, you could have serious trouble rectifying the situation. If there is no access below the kitchen floor, there is no way to get the vent out. Trying the procedure mentioned for the rough-in stage would be disastrous at the close of a job. This is a perfect example of why you must think and plan ahead.

Comfort

All large kitchens should share one asset—comfort. An eat-in kitchen is meant to be more than a place where you toss salad or bake bread. It is a room that should exude warmth and comfort, a room that will entice you to linger in it. Now maybe your customers don't want kitchens that they will call their favorite rooms in their houses, but most people enjoy the family atmosphere that large kitchens provide.

Imagination

As you look through this book, you are going to see dozens of examples. While this book contains many suggestions for creating great kitchens, I want you to remember that the possibilities are limited only by your own imagination. As an example of the multitude of design options available to both you and your customers, I close this chapter with a look at a small sampling of available cabinet options (Fig. 1-5 through Fig. 1-24).

Figure 1-5

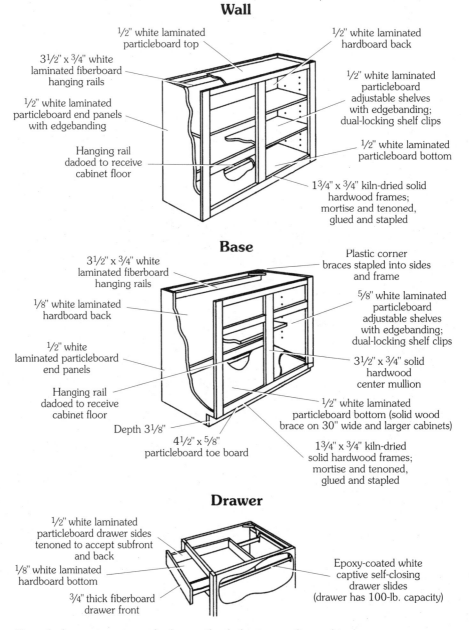

Wall

½" white laminated particleboard top

½" white laminated hardboard back

3½" x ¾" white laminated fiberboard hanging rails

½" white laminated particleboard adjustable shelves with edgebanding; dual-locking shelf clips

½" white laminated particleboard end panels with edgebanding

½" white laminated particleboard bottom

Hanging rail dadoed to receive cabinet floor

1¾" x ¾" kiln-dried solid hardwood frames; mortise and tenoned, glued and stapled

Base

3½" x ¾" white laminated fiberboard hanging rails

Plastic corner braces stapled into sides and frame

⅛" white laminated hardboard back

⅝" white laminated particleboard adjustable shelves with edgebanding; dual-locking shelf clips

½" white laminated particleboard end panels

3½" x ¾" solid hardwood center mullion

Hanging rail dadoed to receive cabinet floor

Depth 3⅛"

½" white laminated particleboard bottom (solid wood brace on 30" wide and larger cabinets)

4½" x ⅝" particleboard toe board

1¾" x ¾" kiln-dried solid hardwood frames; mortise and tenoned, glued and stapled

Drawer

½" white laminated particleboard drawer sides tenoned to accept subfront and back

⅛" white laminated hardboard bottom

Epoxy-coated white captive self-closing drawer slides (drawer has 100-lb. capacity)

¾" thick fiberboard drawer front

Detailed cross section of what to look for in quality cabinets. Wellborn Cabinet, Inc.

Diagonal corner peninsula

Figure 1-6

36" high diagonal corner peninsula
3 doors
2 adjustable shelves

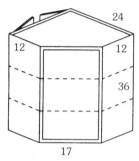

18" rotating shelves

18" round spin tray

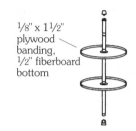

$^1/_8$" x $1^1/_2$" plywood banding, $^1/_2$" fiberboard bottom

30" high diagonal corner peninsula
3 doors
2 adjustable shelves

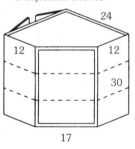

18" rotating shelves

18" round spin tray

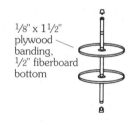

$^1/_8$" x $1^1/_2$" plywood banding, $^1/_2$" fiberboard bottom

Details for appliance cabinets, wall cabinets, microwave cabinets, and return-angle wall cabinets. Wellborn Cabinet, Inc.

Figure 1-6 (continues)

Figure 1-6

Diagonal corner appliance cabinets

60" high diagonal corner appliance garage

18" rotating shelves   18" round spin tray

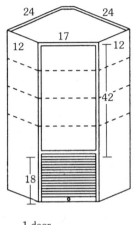

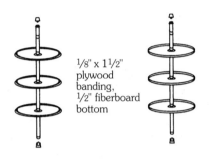

1/8" x 1 1/2" plywood banding, 1/2" fiberboard bottom

1 door
3 adjustable shelves

54" high diagonal corner appliance garage

18" rotating shelves   18" round spin tray

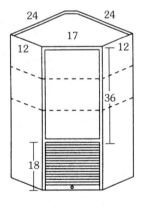

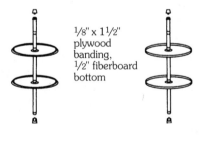

1/8" x 1 1/2" plywood banding, 1/2" fiberboard bottom

1 door
2 adjustable shelves

Figure 1-6 (continued)

Diagonal corner appliance cabinets

Figure 1-7

48" high diagonal corner appliance garage

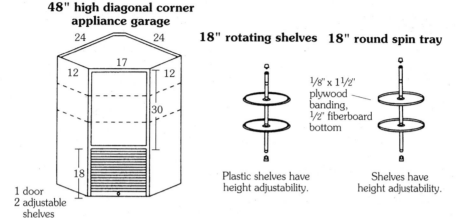

18" rotating shelves   **18" round spin tray**

⅛" x 1½" plywood banding, ½" fiberboard bottom

Plastic shelves have height adjustability.

Shelves have height adjustability.

1 door
2 adjustable shelves

Wall tambour cabinets

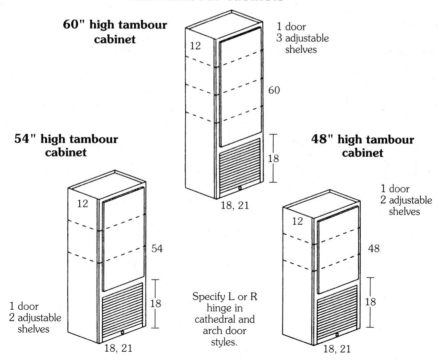

60" high tambour cabinet

1 door
3 adjustable shelves

54" high tambour cabinet

48" high tambour cabinet

1 door
2 adjustable shelves

1 door
2 adjustable shelves

Specify L or R hinge in cathedral and arch door styles.

Diagonal corner peninsula cabinets that give customers superior storage in a small space. Wellborn Cabinet, Inc.

Figure 1-7 (continues)

Figure 1-7

42" high microwave cabinet
2 doors
1 adjustable shelf
1 17¼" deep removable shelf.

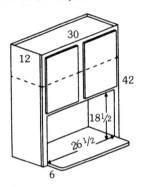

36" high microwave cabinet
2 doors
1 17¼" deep removable shelf.

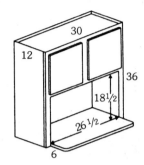

48" high microwave cabinet
2 doors
1 adjustable shelf
1 17¼" deep removable shelf.

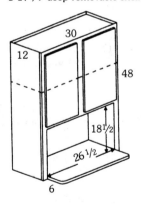

Base/wall return angle
2 doors
2 fixed shelves

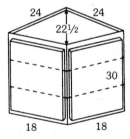

Inside angle 140°.
Outside angle 220°.
Square doors standard.
Ends not finished.

Figure 1-7 (continued)

Corner base cabinets

Figure 1-8

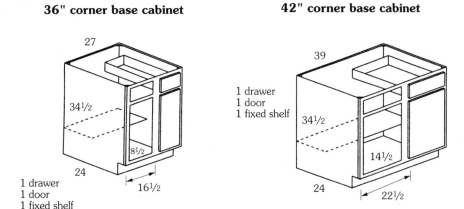

36" corner base cabinet

27

34½

8½

24

16½

1 drawer
1 door
1 fixed shelf

42" corner base cabinet

39

1 drawer
1 door
1 fixed shelf

34½

14½

24

22½

39" corner base cabinet

33

34½

11½

24

19½

1 drawer
1 door
1 fixed shelf

45" corner base cabinet

45

1 drawer
1 door
1 fixed shelf

34½

17½

24

25½

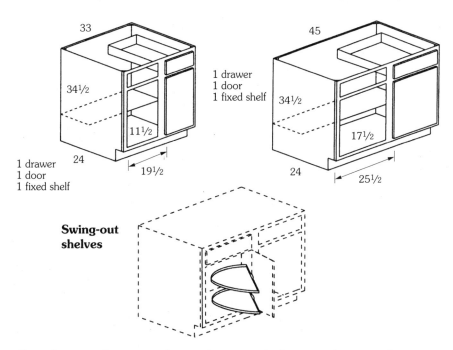

Swing-out shelves

Specifications for corner base cabinets with drawers, doors, and even swing-out shelves. Many accessories are available, as shown, to get more usable space out of cabinets. Wellborn Cabinet, Inc.

Figure 1-8 (continues)

Figure 1-8

Base accessories

Silverware tray

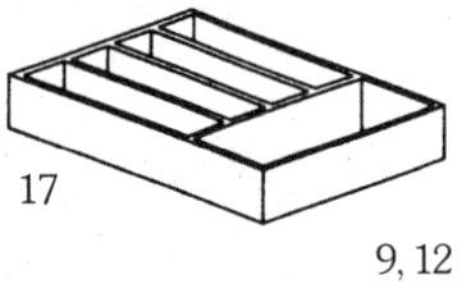
17
9, 12

Silverware divider

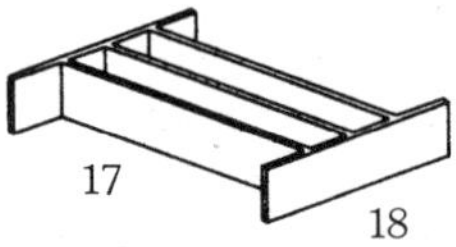
17
18

Drawer spice rack

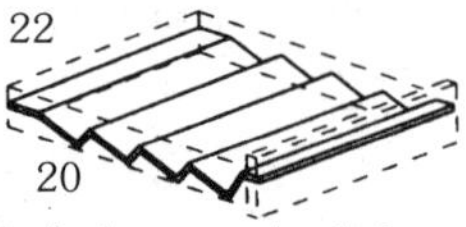
22
20

White high-density polyethylene. May be trimmed.

Silverware tray

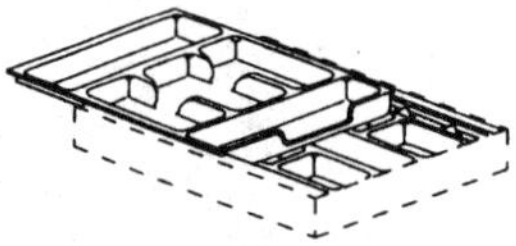

Double-tiered white tray. Guides have epoxy-coated sides. Top drawer integrates with bottom drawer by sliding back to reveal bottom drawer. Side flanges may be trimmed. Back of drawer must be removed for tray to be functional.

Interior drawer		
Min. height	Width	Min. depth
3 1/2"	12 1/4 to 14 3/4"	17 1/4"

Utensil drawer kit

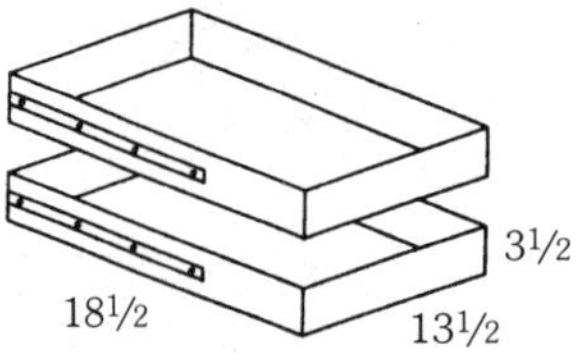
3 1/2
18 1/2
13 1/2

Slides are 3/8" oak. Bottom is 3/16" plywood. Kit includes 2 shelves and guides for installation.

Sliding shelf kit

2 shelf units and hardware

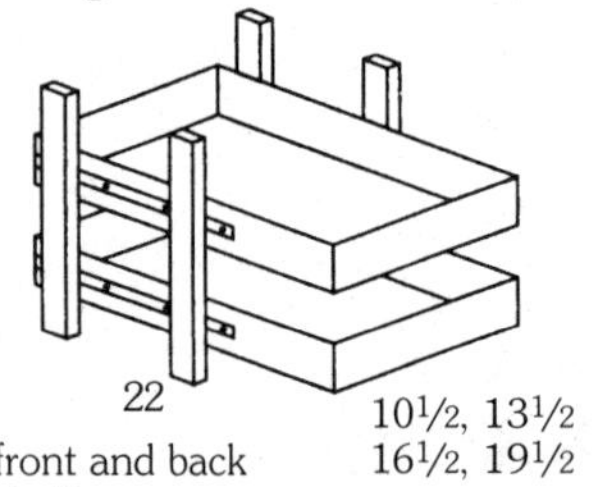
22
10 1/2, 13 1/2
16 1/2, 19 1/2

5/8" oak sides, front and back
3/16" hardwood bottom.
Adjustable wooden mounting brackets.

Single roll-out shelf

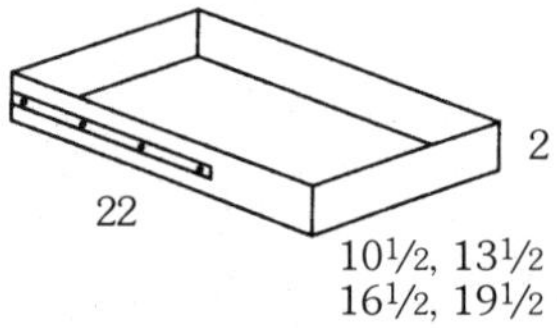
2
22
10 1/2, 13 1/2
16 1/2, 19 1/2

One shelf and guides for installation.
1/2" laminated particleboard sides.
1/4" oak front. Bottom is 1/8" hardboard.

Cutting board

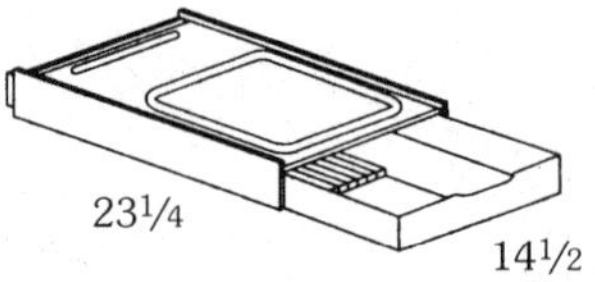
23 1/4
14 1/2

Includes cutting board, knife divider and drawer. Cutting board will replace existing drawer.

Double-tiered cutlery/cutting board

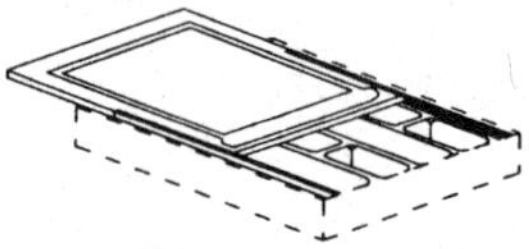

Includes cutting board and cutlery divider. Furnished with two hinges and necessary screws for installation. White cutting board is made of non-skid, non-absorbent polystyrene and is removable. Dishwasher safe. Side flanges may be trimmed.

Interior drawer		
Min. height	Width	Min. depth
3 1/2"	18 1/4 to 20 1/4"	17 1/4"
3 1/2"	12 1/4 to 14 1/4"	17 1/4"

Figure 1-8 (continued)

Base accessories

Figure 1-9

Metal bread box

Fits into
deep drawer.

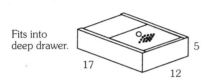

17   12   5

Vegetable bin kit

White metal rack.

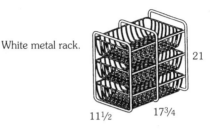

21

$11^{1}/_{2}$ $17^{3}/_{4}$

Door shelf kit

$1/4$" plywood.
Middle shelf is
adjustable.
$3/4$" depth.

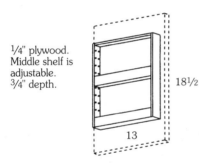

$18^{1}/_{2}$

13

Vegetable bin kit

White polystyrene
plastic bins
in a white metal rack.

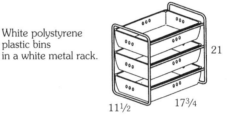

21

$11^{1}/_{2}$ $17^{3}/_{4}$

Under sink basket

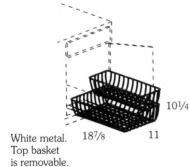

$10^{1}/_{4}$

White metal.
Top basket
is removable. $18^{7}/_{8}$ 11

A la carte

White metal.
Includes 3 baskets
for mounting in
base cabinets.
Center basket is
smaller to allow
for taller products
to be conveniently stored.   18

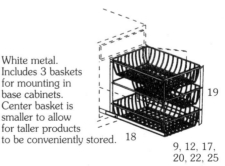

19

9, 12, 17,
20, 22, 25

*Base-cabinet accessories, including vegetable bins, wastebaskets, cutting
boards, ironing boards, and more.* Wellborn Cabinet, Inc.

Figure 1-9 (continues)

Figure 1-9

Base acessories

Pull-out towel box

3 slide-out prongs
for towels.
Mounts in all base
cabinets.
White metal.

16

Ironing board

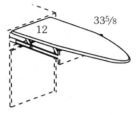

Built-in ironing board
fits into drawer cavity
and conveniently
pulls out and unfolds.

12   33⅝

Single wastebasket

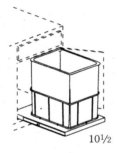

10½

White wastebasket has
30 quarts of storage.
Guides have epoxy-coated
sides. Full extension.
Includes mounts and screws.

Double wastebasket

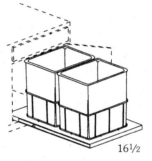

16½

White wastebasket have
60 quarts of storage.
Guides have epoxy-coated
sides. Full extension.
Includes mounts and screws.

3-bin recycle center

3-25 quart plastic bins. 1-18 quart cloth bin.
Equipped to separate recyclable materials:
plastic, glass, paper, and metals.
Full extension. Includes mounts and screws.

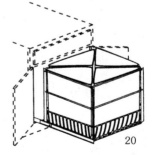

20

Figure 1-9 (continued)

Base cabinets

Figure 1-10

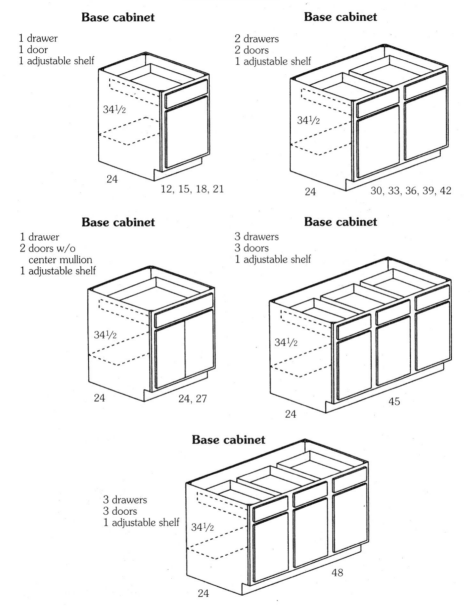

Base cabinet

1 drawer
1 door
1 adjustable shelf

34½

24

12, 15, 18, 21

Base cabinet

2 drawers
2 doors
1 adjustable shelf

34½

24

30, 33, 36, 39, 42

Base cabinet

1 drawer
2 doors w/o
  center mullion
1 adjustable shelf

34½

24

24, 27

Base cabinet

3 drawers
3 doors
1 adjustable shelf

34½

24

45

Base cabinet

3 drawers
3 doors
1 adjustable shelf

34½

24

48

Base cabinets with doors and drawers, including slide-out shelves and sink and range base cabinets. Wellborn Cabinet, Inc.

Figure 1-10 (continues)

Figure 1-10

Base cabinets

Base cabinet w/pull-out shelves

2 drawers
2 doors w/o center mullion
2 adjustable pull-out shelves

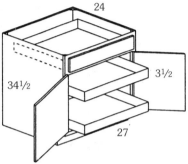

24

$34^{1}/_{2}$

$3^{1}/_{2}$

27

Can be used to house cooktop by converting drawer to drawer blank. Measurement from the top of the cabinet to the top of the drawer is $1^{1}/_{2}$". Shelves adjustable by moving brackets. Shelves are $^{3}/_{4}$" solid wood and bottom is $^{1}/_{2}$" plywood.

Base cabinet w/pull-out shelves

2 drawers
2 doors w/o center mullion
2 adjustable pull-out shelves

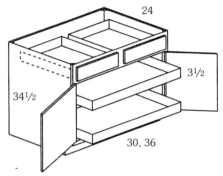

24

$34^{1}/_{2}$

$3^{1}/_{2}$

30, 36

Can be used to house cooktop by converting drawer to drawer blank. Measurement from the top of the cabinet to the top of the drawer is $1^{1}/_{2}$". Shelves adjustable by moving brackets. Shelves are $^{3}/_{4}$" solid wood and bottom is $^{1}/_{2}$" plywood.

Drawer base cabinets

Drawer base

4 drawers

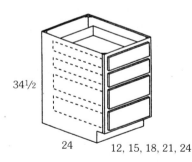

$34^{1}/_{2}$

24   12, 15, 18, 21, 24

Drawer base

5 drawers

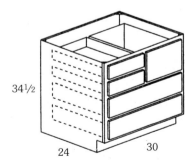

$34^{1}/_{2}$

24   30

Figure 1-10 (continued)

Sink and range base cabinets

Figure 1-11

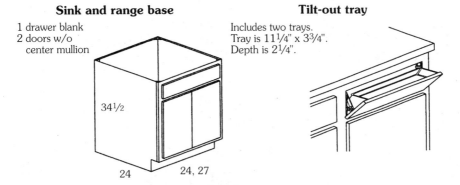

Sink and range base

1 drawer blank
2 doors w/o
   center mullion

$34^{1}/_{2}$

24   24, 27

Tilt-out tray

Includes two trays.
Tray is $11^{1}/_{4}$" x $3^{3}/_{4}$".
Depth is $2^{1}/_{4}$".

Sink and range fronts

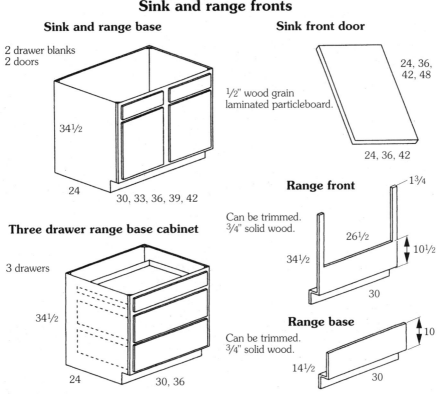

Sink and range base

2 drawer blanks
2 doors

$34^{1}/_{2}$

24   30, 33, 36, 39, 42

Sink front door

$1/2$" wood grain
laminated particleboard.

24, 36,
42, 48

24, 36, 42

Three drawer range base cabinet

3 drawers

$34^{1}/_{2}$

24   30, 36

Range front

Can be trimmed.
$3/4$" solid wood.

$1^{3}/_{4}$

$26^{1}/_{2}$

$10^{1}/_{2}$

$34^{1}/_{2}$

30

Range base

Can be trimmed.
$3/4$" solid wood.

10

$14^{1}/_{2}$ 30

Sink and range fronts. Wellborn Cabinet, Inc.

Figure 1-11 (continues)

Figure 1-11

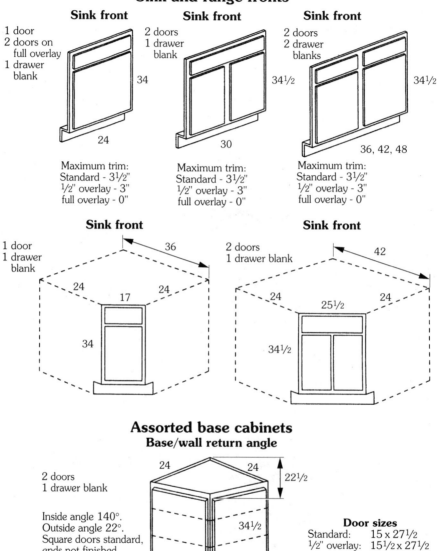

Sink and range fronts

Sink front

1 door
2 doors on full overlay
1 drawer blank

34
24

Maximum trim:
Standard - 3¹/₂"
¹/₂" overlay - 3"
full overlay - 0"

Sink front

2 doors
1 drawer blank

34¹/₂
30

Maximum trim:
Standard - 3¹/₂"
¹/₂" overlay - 3"
full overlay - 0"

Sink front

2 doors
2 drawer blanks

34¹/₂
36, 42, 48

Maximum trim:
Standard - 3¹/₂"
¹/₂" overlay - 3"
full overlay - 0"

Sink front

1 door
1 drawer blank

36
24   17   24
34

Sink front

2 doors
1 drawer blank

42
24   25¹/₂   24
34¹/₂

Assorted base cabinets
Base/wall return angle

24   24
22¹/₂

2 doors
1 drawer blank

Inside angle 140°.
Outside angle 22°.
Square doors standard, ends not finished.

34¹/₂

18   18

Door sizes
Standard: 15 x 27¹/₂
¹/₂" overlay: 15¹/₂ x 27¹/₂
Full overlay: 17⁵/₈ x 29⁵/₈

Figure 1-11 (continued)

Wall cabinets

Figure 1-12

30" high
1 door
2 adjustable shelves

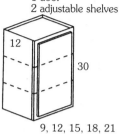

9, 12, 15, 18, 21

24" high
2 doors w/o center mullion
1 fixed shelf

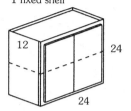

30" high
2 doors w/o center mullion
2 adjustable shelves

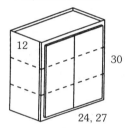

24, 27

30" high
2 doors
2 fixed shelves

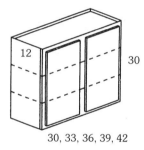

30, 33, 36, 39, 42

30" high
3 doors
2 fixed shelves

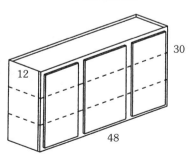

48

Cabinet specifications for wall cabinets, corner wall cabinets, and diagonal corner wall cabinets. Wellborn Cabinet, Inc.

Figure 1-12 (continues)

Figure 1-12

Wall cabinets

24" high
2 doors
1 fixed shelf

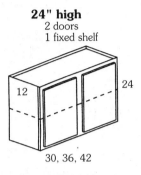

12 24

30, 36, 42

18" high
2 doors

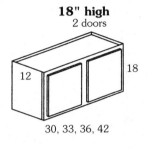

12 18

30, 33, 36, 42

18" high
1 door

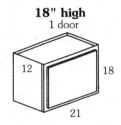

12 18

21

15" high
2 doors

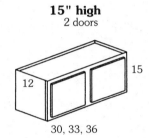

12 15

30, 33, 36

18" high
2 doors w/o center mullion

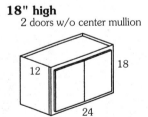

12 18

24

12" high
2 doors

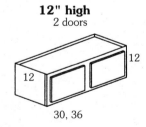

12 12

30, 36

Figure 1-12 (continued)

Corner wall cabinets

Figure 1-12

30" high corner
2 doors
2 fixed shelves

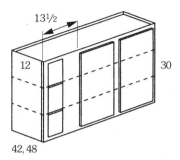

13½

12

30

42, 48

Corner wall cabinets

30" high corner
1 door
2 fixed shelves

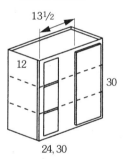

13½

12

30

24, 30

30" high corner
2 doors w/o center mullion
2 fixed shelves

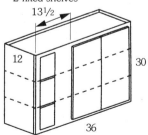

13½

12

30

36

Diagonal corner wall cabinets

30" high diagonal corner
1 door
2 adjustable shelves

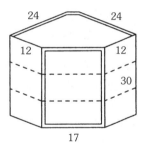

24   24

12   12

30

17

18" rotating shelves

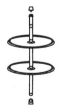

Figure 1-12 (continued)

27

Figure 1-13

Extended stiles

**84" oven cabinet
with 6" right stile**

**84"utility cabinet
with 3" left stile**

6" stile

3" stile

**30" wall cabinet
with 3" left stile**

**27" base cabinet
with 6" right stile**

**30" wall cabinet
with 3" left and right stile**

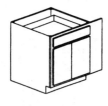

12" - 30" high walls, bases, vanities
36" high walls
42" high walls
84", 90" and 96" high utility, oven
3" per side
6" per side

Face cabinet in specifying left or right

Increased-depth wall cabinet

**30" wall cabinet
with 18" depth**

**30" wall cabinet
with 24" depth**

18" depth

Up to 24" deep.

24" depth

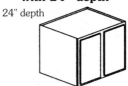

*Examples of customized stock cabinet specifications that allow for
extended stiles, increased depth, and other options.* Wellborn Cabinet, Inc.

Figure 1-13 (continues)

Cabinet depth reduction

Figure 1-13

**84" utility cabinet
with 8" depth**

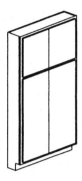

Wall cabinet: minimum depth of 8"
Base cabinet: minimum depth of 12"
  Please note: by reducing cabinet depth,
  the following drawer features will
  be eliminated:
    1. Self closing feature
    2. Tighness of front frame
    3. Drawers will need to be realigned
        when installed
Utility cabinet: minimum depth of 8"

**Base cabinet
with 16" depth**

**Wall cabinet
with 8" depth**

Peninsula cabinets

Peninsula wall cabinet

Peninsula base cabinet

**Refrigerator
cabinets**

Full-height doors

**Base cabinet
with full-height doors**

**Base cabinet
with full-height doors**

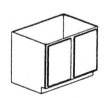

Mullion doors

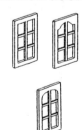

Figure 1-13 (continued)

Figure 1-14

Corner sink base cabinets

Adjustable shelf
2 shelves

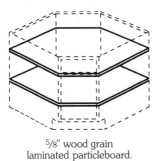

⁵⁄₈" wood grain
laminated particleboard.

28" Round spin tray

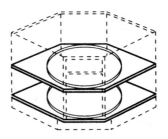

Wooden rotary shelf kit is ¹⁄₂" fiberboard
with ¹⁄₈" x 1¹⁄₂" plywood edgebanding.

Rotary kidney

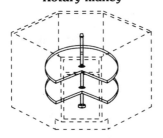

Shelves have height adjustability. 28"
diameter. Shelves are made of plastic.

Base lazy susan
Double doors attached to
rotary shelves

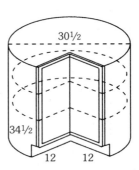

28" diameter.

28" Rotary shelves

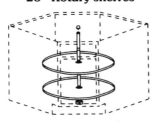

Shelves have height adjustability. 28"
diameter. Shelves are made of plastic.

*Cabinet specifications for corner sink bases, corner base cabinets,
and rotating shelves with a double-door cabinet.* Wellborn Cabinet, Inc.

Figure 1-14 (continues)

Corner base cabinets

Figure 1-14

Corner base cabinet installation instructions (reversible)

Drawer track comes installed on door side only. To reverse corner cabinet move drawer track to other side.

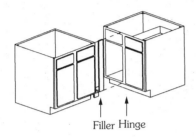

Filler Hinge

Left blind corner base cabinet is shown. Hinge is on blank side of cabinet.

	Standard	½" overlay	Full overlay
maximum pull	40¾	40¾	40¾
minimum pull w/hardware	37	37¼	40
minimum pull w/o hardware	36	36¼	37
maximum pull	43¾	43¾	43¾
minimum pull w/hardware	40	40¼	43
minimum pull w/o hardware	39	39¼	40
maximum pull	46¾	46¾	46¾
minimum pull w/hardware	43	43¼	46
minimum pull w/o hardware	42	42¼	43
maximum pull	49¾	49¾	49¾
minimum pull w/hardware	46	46¼	49
minimum pull w/o hardware	45	45¼	46

On all full overlay door styles use at least 1" base filler.

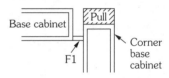

Base cabinet

Pull

F1

Corner base cabinet

36" Corner base cabinet
1 drawer
1 door
1 adjustable shelf

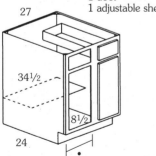

27
34½
8½
24

• Standard door = 16½
  ½ overlay = 16¼
  Full overlay = 15³⁄₁₆

39" Corner base cabinet
1 drawer
1 door
1 adjustable shelf

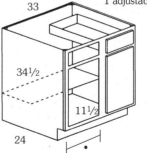

33
34½
11½
24

• Standard door = 19½
  ½ overlay = 19¼
  Full overlay = 18³⁄₁₆

Figure 1-14 (continued)

Figure 1-15

Assorted base cabinets

Desk file drawer cabinet

1 drawer
1 file drawer

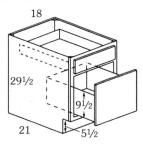

This file drawer will accommodate a Pendaflex file system. Specify Square or Cathedral door when ordering. File drawer is ½" solid wood. File drawer is 18½" deep and 13½" wide.

Corner sink base

Double doors
on piano hinge

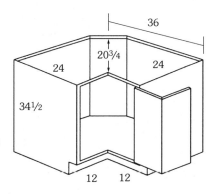

NOTE: Install shelves before countertop installation.

Wastebasket cabinet

1 full height door

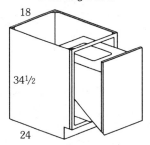

11 gallon capacity. Slides out 22¼". Trash bin holder is ½" plywood.

Adjustable shelf

2 shelves

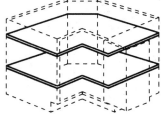

⅝" wood grain laminated particleboard.

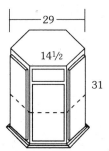

Island base

6 doors
1 drawer
1 shelf

Base molding 1½" high.
Cut countertop moldings at 30°.

Base cabinets that offer special features, such as file drawers, wastebasket bins, and recycling centers. Wellborn Cabinet, Inc.

Figure 1-15 (continues)

Corner sink
base cabinets

Figure 1-15

Rotary kidney

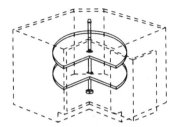

Shelves have height adjustability. 28"
diameter. Shelves are made of plastic.

Corner recycle center

14³/8

21

3–32 quart
white plastic bins.

Super lazy susan kit

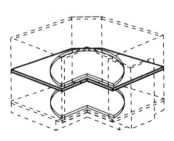

Wooden rotary shelf kit is ¹/2" fiberboard
with ¹/8" x 1¹/2" plywood edgebanding.

Diagonal corner sink base
1 door
1 drawer blank

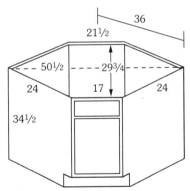

36

21¹/2

50¹/2 --- 29³/4

24   17   24

34¹/2

NOTE: Install shelves before
countertop installation.

Figure 1-15 (continued)

33

Figure 1-16

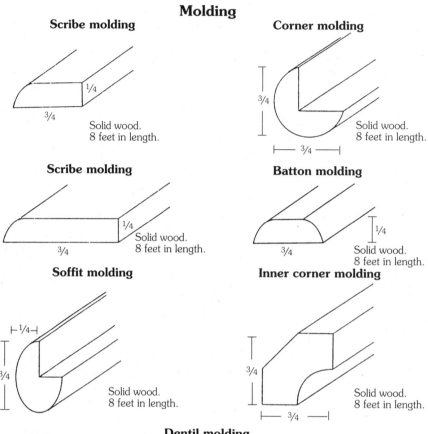

Molding

Scribe molding

$^1/_4$

$^3/_4$

Solid wood.
8 feet in length.

Corner molding

$^3/_4$

$^3/_4$

Solid wood.
8 feet in length.

Scribe molding

$^1/_4$

$^3/_4$

Solid wood.
8 feet in length.

Batton molding

$^1/_4$

$^3/_4$

Solid wood.
8 feet in length.

Soffit molding

$^1/_4$

$^3/_4$

Solid wood.
8 feet in length.

Inner corner molding

$^3/_4$

$^3/_4$

Solid wood.
8 feet in length.

Dentil molding

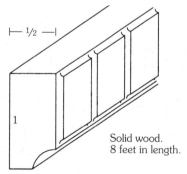

$^1/_2$

1

Solid wood.
8 feet in length.

Cabinet moldings that include dentil, inner corner, soffit, corner, scribe, and batten molding. Wellborn Cabinet, Inc.

Utility storage cabinets

Figure 1-17

Pantry storage kit

24 x 84 utility storage cabinet

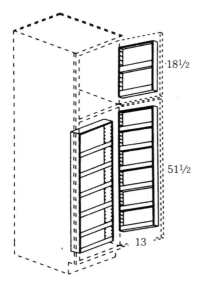

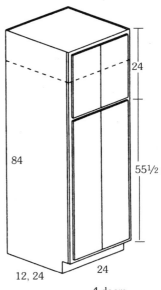

Allow 6" on both sides of pantry cabinet for door opening. ¾" plywood kit with ½" plywood adjustable shelves.

4 doors
1 adjustable shelf
(full depth)

Top view

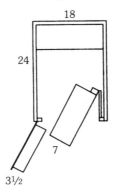

Pantry and utility storage cabinets, including one unit with pull-out shelves. Wellborn Cabinet, Inc.

Figure 1-17 (continues)

Figure 1-17

Utility storage cabinets

24 x 90 utility storage cabinet

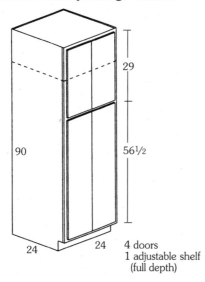

4 doors
1 adjustable shelf
(full depth)

Utility sliding-shelf kit

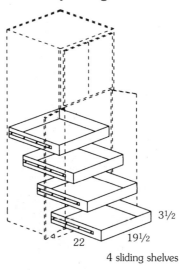

4 sliding shelves

24 x 96 utility storage cabinet

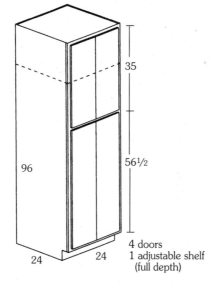

4 doors
1 adjustable shelf
(full depth)

36 x 84 utility storage cabinet

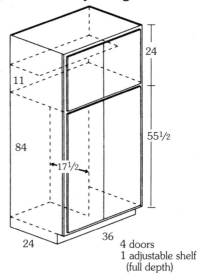

4 doors
1 adjustable shelf
(full depth)

Figure 1-17 (continued)

Utility storage cabinets

Figure 1-18

36 x 90 utility storage cabinets

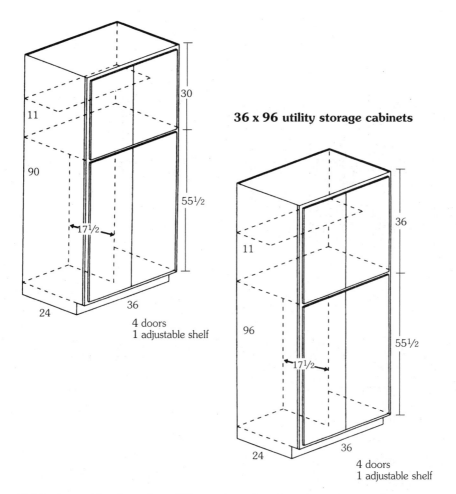

36 x 96 utility storage cabinets

Cabinet specifications for utility and pantry storage systems. Wellborn Cabinet, Inc.

Figure 1-18 (continues)

Figure 1-18

Utility storage cabinets

Pantry storage kit

$18\frac{1}{2}$

$51\frac{1}{2}$

13

6 adjustable shelves
($10\frac{5}{16}$ x $16\frac{5}{16}$)
included. Back shelves
also adjustable.

Universal utility cabinet

24

11

84

$55\frac{1}{2}$

36

24

Cabinet can house
4 sliding shelves or
can be used as a
broom closet.

Top view

36

24

7

$3\frac{3}{4}$

Sliding shelf kit

2 shelves and hardware

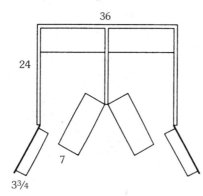

22

$31\frac{5}{8}$

$\frac{5}{8}$" oak sides, front and back.
$\frac{3}{16}$"plywood bottom.
$3\frac{1}{2}$" deep drawer. Adjustable
wooden mounting brackets.

Figure 1-18 (continued)

Base accessories

Figure 1-19

Cutting board

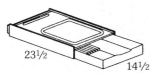

23½   14½

Includes cutting board, knife divider and drawer. Cutting board will replace existing drawer. Use existing drawer front with two hinges that are supplied. Nesessary harware is included also. Cutting board kit is made of oak wood.

Double tiered cutlery/cutting board

Includes cutting board and cutlery divider. Furnished with two hinges and necessary screws for installation. White cutting board is made of nonskid, nonabsorbant polystyrene and is removable. Dishwasher safe. Side flanges may be trimmed.

Interior drawer		
Min. height	Width	Min. depth
3½"	18¼" to 20¾"	17¼"
3½"	12¼" to 14¾"	17¼"

Drawer spice rack

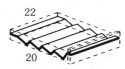

22

20

White high-density polyethylene. May be trimmed.

Silverware tray

Double-tiered white tray.
Guides have expoxy-coated sides.

Top drawer integrates with bottom drawer by sliding back to reveal bottom drawer. Side flanges may be trimmed. Back of drawer must be removed for tray to be functional.

Interior drawer		
Min. height	Width	Min. depth
3½"	12¼" to 14¾"	17¼"

Ironing board

12   33⅝

Built-in ironing board fits into drawer cavity and conveniently pulls out and unfolds.

A variety of accessories for base cabinets. Wellborn Cabinet, Inc.

Figure 1-19 (continues)

Figure 1-19

Base accessories

Vegetable bin kit

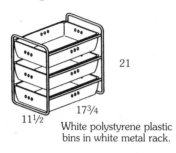

21

11½   17¾

White polystyrene plastic
bins in white metal rack.

Vegetable bin kit

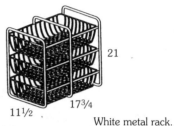

21

11½   17¾

White metal rack.

Double wastebasket

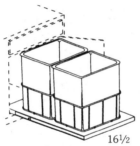

16½

White wastebaskets have 60 quarts of storage.
Guides have epoxy-coated sides.
Full extension. Includes mounts and screws.

3-bin recycle center

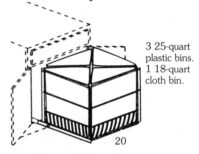

3 25-quart
plastic bins.
1 18-quart
cloth bin.

20

Equipped to separate the four most common
recyclable materials: plastic, glass, paper and
metals. Full extension. Includes mounts and
screws.

Single wastebasket

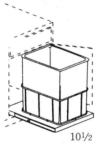

10½

White wastebasket has 30 quarts of storage.
Guides have epoxy-coated sides.
Full extension. Includes mounts and screws.

Under-sink basket

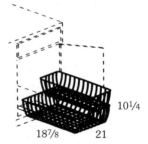

10¼

18⅞   21

White metal. Top basket is removable.

Figure 1-19 (continued)

Base accessories

Figure 1-20

Fluted base pilasters

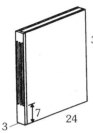

34½

3   7   24

Finished ends.
Pilasters use ¾"
solid wood for
front, back, top
and bottom.
Sides are ½"
plywood.

Pull-out towel bar

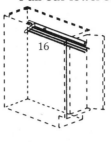

16

3 slide-out prongs
for towels.
Mounts in all base
cabinets.
White metal.

Matching base end panel

34½

¾" thick solid oak,
cherry, hickory,
or maple.

24

Full overlay base end panels are ¾" wider
than the standard and ½" overlay base
end panels. Continental door style is ⅝"
melamine. Standard and ½" overlays are
notched for face frame and full overlay have
spacers to compensate for the face frame.

A la carte

19

9, 12, 17
20, 22, 25
White metal.

18

Includes 3 baskets for mounting in base
cabinets. Center basket is smaller to
allow for taller products to be conveniently
stored.

Base cabinet step

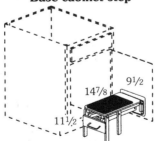

9½

14⅞

11½

Folds up to 3⅜" thickness. Base cabinet
step is made of ¾" solid wood with ¼"
poplar hardwood top.

*Examples of base cabinet accessories, utility cabinets, and a base cabinet
step.* Wellborn Cabinet, Inc.

Figure 1-20 (continues)

Figure 1-20

Utility storage cabinets

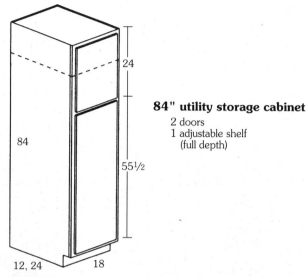

84" utility storage cabinet
2 doors
1 adjustable shelf
(full depth)

24

84

55½

12, 24   18

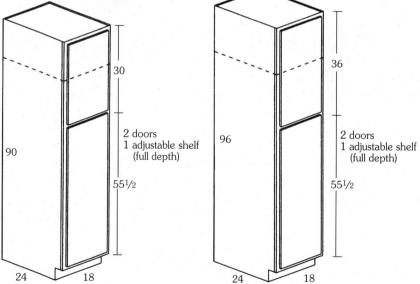

90" utility storage cabinet

30

90

2 doors
1 adjustable shelf
(full depth)

55½

24   18

96" utility storage cabinet

36

96

2 doors
1 adjustable shelf
(full depth)

55½

24   18

Figure 1-20 (continued)

Base accessories

Figure 1-21

Silverware tray
1/4" oak.

17   9,12

Sliding shelf kit
5/8" oak sides,
front and back.
3/16" hardwood bottom.
Adjustable wooden
mounting brackets.

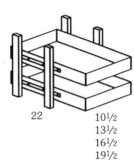

22   10½
            13½
            16½
            19½

Silverware divider
1/4" oak.
Can be trimmed
to 15".

17   18

Single roll-out shelf
One shelf and guides
for installation.
1/2" wood grain
laminated
particleboard sides.
5/8" oak front.
Bottom is 1/8"
hardboard.

22
            10½
            13½
            16½
            19½

*Whatnot shelves for base cabinets, bread boxes, door shelves,
and other base cabinet accessories.* Wellborn Cabinet, Inc.

Figure 1-21 (continues)

Figure 1-21

Base accessories

Utensil drawer kit

Sides are $3/8$" oak.
Bottom is $3/16$" plywood.
Kit includes 2 shelves and
guides for installation.

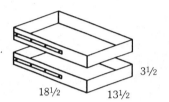

Metal bread box

Fits into deep drawer.

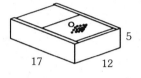

Door shelf kit

$1/2$" plywood.
Middle shelf is adjustable.
$3^1/2$" depth.

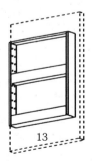

Bread box cover

Fits in drawer base 12"–24".
Can be trimmed.
Overall size is $17^1/8$" x $21^1/4$".
Mounts to drawer sides.

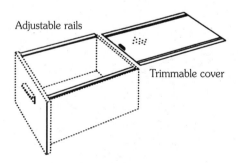

Figure 1-21 (continued)

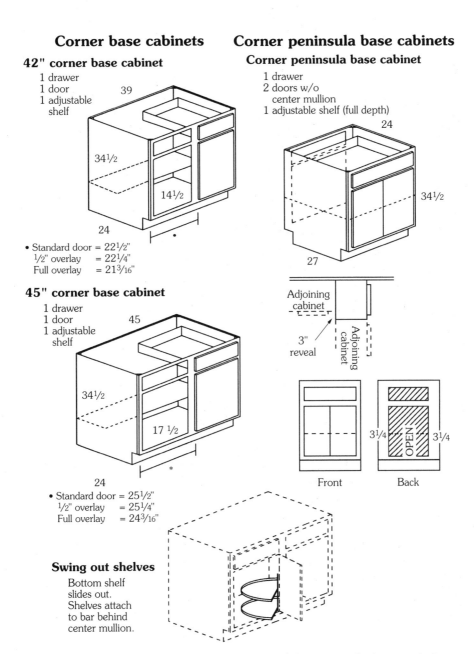

Corner base cabinets

42" corner base cabinet

1 drawer
1 door
1 adjustable
  shelf

39

34½

14½

24

• Standard door = 22½"
  ½" overlay   = 22¼"
  Full overlay = 21³/₁₆"

45" corner base cabinet

1 drawer
1 door
1 adjustable
  shelf

45

34½

17 ½

24

• Standard door = 25½"
  ½" overlay   = 25¼"
  Full overlay = 24³/₁₆"

Swing out shelves

Bottom shelf
slides out.
Shelves attach
to bar behind
center mullion.

Corner peninsula base cabinets

Corner peninsula base cabinet

1 drawer
2 doors w/o
  center mullion
1 adjustable shelf (full depth)

24

34½

27

Adjoining
cabinet

3"
reveal

Adjoining
cabinet

Front   Back

3¼   OPEN   3¼

Figure 1-22

Corner base cabinets, corner peninsula base cabinets, and whatnot shelves.
Wellborn Cabinet, Inc.

Figure 1-22 (continues)

Figure 1-22

Base whatnots

Peninsula base whatnot

12" depth
4½" matching toe kick
¾" solid wood shelves

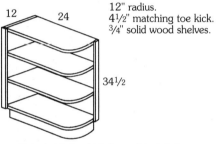

24

34½

Detachable toe kick
for wall installation.

Base end shelf

12" radius.
4½" matching toe kick.
¾" solid wood shelves.

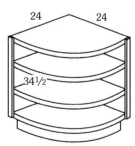

12   24

34½

Detachable toe kick for wall installation
and L or R reversibility.

L-Shaped corner base shelf

24" depth
4½" matching toe kick
¾" solid wood shelves

24   24

34½

Detachable toe kick for wall installation.

Peninsula base cabinets

Peninsula base cabinet

1 drawer
1 drawer blanks
2 doors on both sides
  w/o center mullion
1 adjustable
  shelf (full depth)

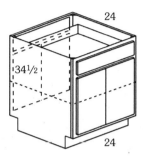

24

34½

24

Peninsula base cabinet

2 drawers
2 drawer blanks
2 doors on both sides
1 adjustable
  shelf (full depth)

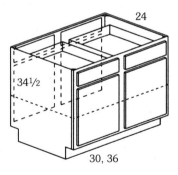

24

34½

30, 36

Figure 1-22 (continued)

Figure 1-23

A beautiful kitchen accented with an unusual kitchen window, an indoor grill surrounded on two sides by counter space, and a wood hood where light is cast on the grill. Wellborn Cabinet, Inc.

Figure 1-24

The hickory finish on these cabinets is striking and unusual. The use of a desk area in kitchens is growing in popularity, as are glass-front cabinets. Schrock Handcrafted Cabinetry, Arthur, Ill.

Kitchen designs

Chapter 2

THERE are a multitude of ways for you to come up with custom designs. Looking through books of house plans is a fast and easy way to get ideas. If your local building supplier has a certified kitchen designer on staff, you can look though plans with your supplier. It's not unusual for suppliers to offer design and drafting services. This source of ideas is often overlooked. Magazines that cater to kitchen remodeling are another good place to look for creative concepts in kitchen designs.

Most of your customers will want large kitchens that join other living space without a barrier, but the remaining details can be quite varied. It's possible to mix and match kitchen accessories, designs, and decorations (Fig. 2-1) to create a unique look. For example, a colonial kitchen could boast a flintlock rifle over the mantle of a fireplace. A pioneer kitchen would look equally good with the rifle. However, it would look strange to have a replica or antique flintlock hanging on a wall of a contemporary kitchen.

Figure 2-1

Tile is the main accent in this kitchen. Combining simple porcelain pulls on plain cabinets with the tile creates an earthy look that many customers find appealing. Wood-Mode, Inc.

It has been my experience that few homeowners are trying to capture the realism to exact details of any particular era when they have their kitchens converted. Most people go with what they want and don't worry about keeping every detail in step with the kitchen's theme. You don't have to be a rigid historian to come up with believable kitchens. What you do have to do is stimulate your customers with creative suggestions. Get them thinking. Be prepared for a lot of changes in plans before a final plan is adopted. This is a normal part of most remodeling jobs.

Once you have become familiar with several styles of kitchens, you can propose the pros and cons of the various types to your customers. When you look through the many photographs (Fig. 2-2) in this book, you will get a feel for how many options are available to your customers. Study the options and learn as much as you can about the types of kitchen jobs you plan to sell. The more you know about kitchens, the more successful you should be in the field.

Figure 2-2

The open shelves in this kitchen hint at a bygone era. The rustic cabinets and tile counter combine for a comfortable kitchen. Pottery, which was so popular during the Colonial era, adds to the overall effect of this kitchen. Rowe Pottery Works, Inc., Cambridge, Wisc.

The colonial kitchen

The colonial kitchen is a good model on which to style your own kitchen designs. This type of kitchen is filled with wood and has a homespun flair. If you get a chance, you should visit Williamsburg, Virginia. Colonial Williamsburg is a living history lesson in which you can see people blowing glass, making pottery, hammering out hot iron, and doing all sorts of authentic colonial activities. Not only this, but you can inspect some reproduced colonial homes and their kitchens. Seeing this type of authentic recreation firsthand will give you a much better understanding of the design styles for a colonial kitchen. This knowledge will allow you to talk more intelligently with your customers about their kitchen dreams.

The makings of a colonial kitchen should start with either a wood or tile floor (Fig. 2-3). If you use tile, it should be an earthy, quarry tile. Cabinets should be kept simple in a colonial kitchen. In fact,

Figure 2-3

This dining area is in keeping with the simple kitchen look. Notice the wide plank flooring. Rowe Pottery Works, Inc., Cambridge, Wisc.

simplicity is the key to a colonial kitchen. The kitchen should appear as if it has been made from materials that were derived directly from the land (Fig. 2-4).

Figure 2-4

Wallpaper and tile have been used to make this kitchen desirable. The installation of multiple windows adds light and a feeling of space.
Wood-Mode, Inc.

One thing to keep in mind with any type of primitive kitchen is that you will want to break away from the appearance of any modern conveniences, such as running water and electricity. Your customers will obviously want all the comforts of a modern kitchen, but you can disguise some of the more commercial aspects of present-day life. It's not necessary to install a stainless-steel sink and a shiny, single-handle faucet or track lighting. There are many ways to get the conveniences of a modern kitchen without spoiling the feel of a period kitchen (Fig. 2-5).

It is still possible to buy very deep sinks that sit below the kitchen cabinet. If you don't want a sink that is available commercially, you can

Figure 2-5

White is bright, and bright is good in kitchen and dining areas. Color-coordinated appliances add to the clean, bright look. Wood floors present the finishing touch.
KitchenAid Major Appliances

make your own sinks with some shower-pan liner, a shower drain, and some tile. Or, you could have a slate sink made for your customers. As for the faucet, you can install an older, wall-mount faucet, or you can even have just two simple spigots stick out over the sink.

There are many light fixtures available that are styled after old designs. For example, candle holders are available with electric candles that light up. With enough research into specialty catalogs (which can be located throughout the numerous magazines about decorating kitchens), you can transform kitchens into beautiful re-creations of the past.

Whether you decide to accent your kitchens in colonial motifs (Fig. 2-6) or along some other theme, you will have to work out the basic floor plan. Ideally, a kitchen should be as open as possible, with the room

Figure 2-6

Here is a kitchen that takes advantage of white cabinets and brass pulls to set itself apart. Stenciling and tile designs add to the effect. Notice the front edge of the main counter and how the island is done in a contrasting material. KitchenAid Major Appliances

flowing into a dining area (Fig. 2-7). This, however, isn't always possible. Matching the needs and desires of your customers with your remodeling and building skills can require a significant amount of time and thought. One of the best ways to come up with fantastic kitchen layouts is to study successful designs that are already in use.

The replica kitchen

If your customers enjoy the look of antiques and the convenience of modern appliances and fixtures, a replica kitchen should be just right for them. This type of kitchen will look old, but will work with

Figure 2-7

Wood floors, bright colors, track lighting, and wallpaper combine to make this island kitchen a pleasing place to work.
KitchenAid Major Appliances

high-tech equipment. For example, the stove may give the impression of an old-fashioned wood-burning cook stove when, in reality, the appliance is a modern gas or electric range.

When I was growing up, wood-burning cook stoves were not uncommon. I even rented a house once that was equipped with such a stove. It had a copper hot-water tank, a bread warmer, an oven, and the cook eyes. This stove was fantastic in the winter, but it tended to overheat the house in the summer. Plus, carrying wood into the house and building a fire before every meal is a bit more work than most of today's busy people want to bother with. Even though these stoves are rare, I worked in a house earlier this year that was still using a wood cook stove, so I guess in some rural parts of the country they are still in fashion.

I wouldn't want to have to prepare my meals with a cook stove under my present living conditions, but I do like the way they look. If I were designing a kitchen for myself, I'm sure I'd buy a replica stove (Fig. 2-8). These stoves provide all the benefits of modern technology while retaining the charm of another era. Old-time wall ovens are also available (Figs. 2-9 and 2-10).

Figure 2-8

Some customers enjoy recreating the past in their kitchens. You can help them do this with replica appliances like this cook stove. The House of Webster, Rogers, Ark.

Do you remember when kitchens housed ice boxes instead of refrigerators? I can't say that I've ever seen an ice box serving active duty, but they certainly were an integral part of the kitchen of the past. You may want to consider finding a supplier who can provide modern refrigerators that resemble old ice boxes (Fig. 2-11); this could be the selling point that wins you your next bid. You could even build

Figure 2-9

Here is a replica of an old-time wall oven with the convenience of modern microwave.
The House of Webster, Rogers, Ark.

a false shell to fit around a new refrigerator that would make it look like an antique; this may very well make your customers sign your contract on the spot. If you do tackle this project, however, be sure to allow adequate ventilation for the refrigeration to work properly.

Some manufactured cabinets are patterned after models from years ago. If these commercial cabinets don't suit your customer's needs, you can have cabinets custom-built to your customer's specifications. This gives you a free hand to make your customer's dreams come true. Also, many specialty stores can provide you with all sorts of antique-looking hardware (Figs. 2-12 through 2-17).

Old kitchen sinks were usually big, deep, and heavy. They were made from slate or other hard materials. The sinks were normally installed

Figure 2-10

You can see here that replica appliances look good, even in modern-style kitchens. Heartland Appliances, Inc.

so that the top of the sink touched the bottom of the kitchen counter. There was often a backsplash that ran high up on the wall behind the sink. Very old kitchens had pitcher pumps mounted on the counter, next to the sink. This type of arrangement can still be made from modern materials.

I recently installed such a sink in an old farmhouse. The original sink was made of slate. The homeowners hired my company to handle the remodeling work, and they wanted to maintain the same basic look they had with the old sink. The new sink I installed was white. It fit in the same space as the old slate sink and it looked just as natural. I updated the plumbing under the sink, added a dishwasher and a new

Figure 2-11

Replicas of an old-time wall oven, cook stove, and ice box have been used, in conjunction with fancy cabinets fronts and stenciling, to build a country kitchen. Heartland Appliances, Inc.

faucet. My customers were planning to upgrade a little at a time, so I'm not sure what the next phase will entail. However, their goal is to maintain the look of the original kitchen and use replicas for modern convenience (Fig. 2-18).

When you enter the realm of replicas, the possibilities are nearly endless. I looked through a number of magazines as I prepared to write this book, and I was amazed at the number of ideas that jumped out at me. There are companies that sell just about anything you can imagine. You can buy old-fashioned nails, paint that will appear aged, cabinet pulls, hardware, stoves, refrigerators, and a host of other things that will look as though you have just brought them down from

Figure 2-12

Replica hardware for cabinets. Horton Brasses Inc., Nooks Hill Rd., Comwell, CT 06416, (203) 635-4400

Figure 2-13

Replica cabinet pulls. Horton Brasses Inc., Nooks Hill Rd., Comwell, CT 06416, (203) 635-4400

Figure 2-14

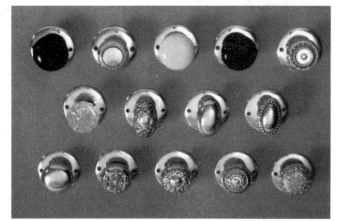

Antique-style cabinet pulls. Antique Hardware, 1-800-422-9982

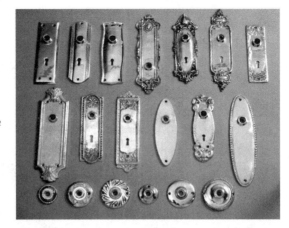

Figure 2-15

Old-style brass cabinet hardware. Antique Hardware, 1-800-422-9982

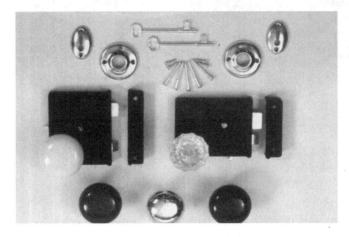

Figure 2-16

Replica hardware for passage doors.
Antique Hardware, 1-800-422-9982

Figure 2-17

Antique-style replica hinge. Antique Hardware, 1-800-422-9982

Figure 2-18

Notice how spacious this replica kitchen is. There is plenty of safe space where children can play in while parents work at the kitchen desk or do kitchen chores. Heartland Appliances, Inc.

Granny's attic. Every newsstand I went to had a variety of these magazines, and most of the magazines were filled with sources of unusual items (Fig. 2-19). It will definitely pay for you to flip through some of these publications before you tackle your next remodeling job.

Look over the pictures in this book and in magazines (Fig. 2-20). Enjoy yourself and make some notes as you go along. You're sure to see many items that will put your customers on the edges of their seats (Fig. 2-21).

Figure 2-19

This small kitchen is made more user-friendly with sidelighting from a window. Antique Hardware, 1-800-422-9982

Figure 2-20

This family-style kitchen has been designed to take advantage of replica appliances, simple cabinets, rustic trim, and wide floor planking. Heartland Appliances, Inc.

Figure 2-21

This kitchen is likely to be too dark unless it has natural light available from multiple windows and, perhaps, skylights. The glass-front wall cabinets are good, but the finish used on the cabinets to capture an old look is probably too dark for most kitchens. Heartland Appliances, Inc.

The pioneer kitchen

If your customers like rustic surroundings, a pioneer kitchen could be just the ticket. This type of kitchen won't fit in with every house style. However, if a home lends itself to a primitive look, the pioneer approach can be a lot of fun. The kitchens of old were rough-hewn and filled with atmosphere. You can re-create this aura of the wilderness without a lot of expense for your customers.

What might you expect to find in a pioneer kitchen? Well, if you daydream your way back in time, you can see the kitchen. One wall is filled with a massive, stone-faced fireplace. The inner stones are black from countless meals that were over the open flames of the fire that not only cooked the food, but warmed the cabin. There's a hook holding a large, black pot over the embers that radiate at an even cooking temperature. The aroma of wood smoke and wilderness stew blend to create a sense of security and peacefulness.

Breaking away from the trance created by the fireplace, your attention is diverted to the wide beams (Fig. 2-22) that hold up the plank ceiling. The marks made by a broad axe and a drawing knife are evident in the beams. Light and shadow play a game of tag as the soft rays of sunlight wrap around the beams. You are taken in by the handiwork of crafts and dried arrangements that adorn the beams and walls (Fig. 2-23).

Figure 2-22

This rustic pioneer-style kitchen has so many nice features that you have to study it for awhile to take everything in. Some of the key points are the ceiling beams, ceiling fan, wood flooring, extended soffit with recessed lighting, and the angled counter, which provides a better traffic pattern. Wood-Mode, Inc.

Figure 2-23

A family can sit down to a quick meal at the counter in this kitchen and enjoy the warmth of wood cabinets and natural lighting. This kitchen is simple, yet effective. Wood-Mode, Inc.

A board squeaks as you turn, drawing your attention to the wide-plank floor (Fig. 2-24) beneath your boots. The cracks between the boards are filled with years of history. Surrounding you are the rough-cut edges of wooden walls. The kitchen is dark, but you feel right at home. There is a sense of privacy and contentment.

Sitting on a handmade counter is a pitcher pump with its spout directed into a huge, sunken stone sink. Furniture is sparse but sturdy (Fig. 2-25). Wooden pegs protrude from the walls, supporting a vast array of spices, utensils, and other everyday needs.

Figure 2-24

Here is an example of a combination hutch and work area placed in a rustic kitchen with plank flooring and doors. Schrock Handcrafted Cabinetry, Arthur, Ill.

Figure 2-25

The owners of this kitchen mixed tile and rough wood to create a country look.
Rutt Custom Kitchens and Lis King

You open your eyes and resume planning the perfect design for a pioneer kitchen. Having drifted away in your daydream, you have conjured all sorts of ideas for your customer's kitchen. Of course, they won't be cooking many meals over an open fire, but installing an indoor grill would give a similar sense of satisfaction. While your customer may not want a floor filled with cracks, a tongue-and-groove plank floor does sound enticing. Weathered barn boards might make just the right statement on the new walls of the kitchen, and a pitcher pump, even though it may not be functional, would make a dandy conversation piece. The process continues as you ponder your new kitchen design of yesteryear.

As you can see, a little imagination can go a long way in creating a custom kitchen. As I wrote these words, I got a clear picture of how I would feel in moccasins and buckskins as I threw another log on the fire. The idea of being a mountain man in my hillside cabin was a great escape. If I were designing my own rustic kitchen, perhaps I could escape into this fantasy each time I took on kitchen duty. You, too, can create a room with the power to indulge your customer's fantasy.

If you are going to describe a pioneer kitchen in just one word, the word is rustic. This style of kitchen will have a plank floor, wood or stucco walls, exposed beams, a fireplace, and plain cabinets (Fig. 2-26). There will be nothing fancy about the room. Of course, you can compromise and mix in some wallpaper or tile, according to your customers' wishes.

In a pioneer-style kitchen, the cabinets should be either plain or painted wood (Fig. 2-27). If you want to go for realism, the wall cabinets will be nothing more than open shelves. The doors on base cabinets will be curtains that hang just below the counter. There will probably be hooks in the walls that hold pans, cups, and similar items. You might use black iron racks to suspend pots and pans from one of the exposed beams. A dry sink would be fitting, and bricks could be used on the floor if the idea of planks doesn't suit your customer's fancy. Interior doorways might be covered

Figure 2-26

Massive beams are the key to this kitchen. Wide plank flooring, beams, basic cabinets and wall-mounted racks are used here to create a pioneer look. Wood-Mode, Inc.

with curtains or fitted with plank doors and old-looking hardware. Of course, not all customers will want to maintain such a rigid sense of realism. Compromises will probably be made.

The decorations in a kitchen have a lot to do with the theme that is created. A few trips to antique stores can produce a wealth of ideas, not to mention a lot of stuff to hang on the walls. You might find an old branding iron or a pair of spurs. Even some coarse rope coiled and hung on the wall will get your kitchens going in a unique western way.

Figure 2-27

Large quarry tile creates a durable, easy-to-clean floor in this kitchen and presents an image unmatched by vinyl flooring. Small beams and a tile counter add to the customized look of this kitchen. Wood-Mode, Inc.

Antique stores are not the only place to look for decorative kitchen accessories. Many specialty stores sell reproductions of stoves, hardware, and other kitchen goodies. A replica black-powder rifle with a bag and a powder horn could be hung in a pioneer kitchen. You could also take a different turn and decorate the room with pioneer farming tools. Spend some time looking at the photographs in this book—they should spark some great ideas.

The contemporary kitchen

Not everyone wants a kitchen that looks like it came out of an old photo album. For these folks, a contemporary kitchen is a good choice to consider. In this type of kitchen, you can have a kitchen faucet the extends upward to accommodate a large pot and a first-class dishwasher that is not concealed by a barn-board front. A garden-style window is a typical sight, and there is no guilt in installing a garbage disposer. A triple-bay sink is okay. It is acceptable to have under-cabinet lighting and shiny surfaces.

Now I'll admit, unconcealed, modern conveniences can make a kitchen a lot more enjoyable to use. You see, the style of the kitchen should be patterned around the people who will use it. No, old kitchens never had microwave ovens hanging under their wall cabinets, but so what? If your customers want microwaves, let them have what they want.

When you mix kitchen styles, you are unlimited in your design and decorating options (Fig. 2-28). You might have woven baskets hanging on one side of an exposed beam and track lighting on the other side. These decisions will be up to you and your customers. In

Figure 2-28

The island in this kitchen makes for a narrow but productive space. The strip wood flooring helps to create a comfortable flow visually, and the kitchen design is very effective, right down to the dining room adjacent to the kitchen. KitchenAid Major Appliances

the past, kitchens didn't have the types of cabinets that are available today, but there is nothing wrong with installing turntable base cabinets in a kitchen.

Fancy wall cabinets with leaded and stained glass can be absolutely beautiful. Stacking baskets, dried arrangements, and similar adornments (Fig. 2-29) on top of the cabinets may add a touch of a country look. It is perfectly acceptable to mix and match to suit individual tastes.

Figure 2-29

The under-counter microwave oven is a space-saver in this kitchen, and the tile backsplash is both decorative and functional. KitchenAid Major Appliances

When you sit down to design a contemporary kitchen, you must spend some time thinking about what you can offer your customers that will be considered a very special layout. If you are working with contemporary kitchens, there are few restrictions on how you should put your kitchens together. This makes the design process fun.

Can you have a microwave mounted under a wall cabinet with a replica of an old icebox just a few feet away? You can if it's all right with your customers. After all, it is the homeowner who has the final say. Your customer might want a kitchen that shares a floor plan with an older style of kitchen but that does not compete in the furnishings (Fig. 2-30). Chrome, black metal, and a lot of glass may set the stage for furnishings. It's also not unusual to find a kitchen with skylights.

Figure 2-30

Notice the ceiling in this kitchen and dining area. It has been wallpapered, which is unusual but attractive. KitchenAid Major Appliances

As much as a deep, slate sink will resemble those found in old farmhouses, there is nothing wrong with having a stainless-steel corner sink in the counter and another vegetable sink in an island cabinet (Fig. 2-31). The same goes for an island-mounted indoor

Figure 2-31

This kitchen takes advantage of an open concept. Pay attention to the tile backsplash, the wood floor with accents, and the wallpaper. KitchenAid Major Appliances

grill. All of these contemporary fixtures and features can be blended into any kitchen plan (Fig. 2-32).

The elements that made up a kitchen in the 1800s don't have to be duplicated in order to have a pleasant kitchen atmosphere. Modern kitchens take on many shapes and sizes (Fig. 2-33 and 2-34). Some are small galley-style kitchens. L-shaped kitchens have been popular. Many people have U-shaped kitchens. And, of course, there are a significant number of traditional kitchens. Does this mean that homeowners can't enjoy a spacious style of kitchen while taking advantage of all the most current modern conveniences?

Figure 2-32

Here is a different angle of the kitchen shown in Fig. 2-31. From this angle, you can see how cabinet fronts have been applied to the refrigerator and how the island base cabinets are accessible from either side. KitchenAid Major Appliances

There is absolutely nothing wrong with wanting a user-friendly area to cook in. If the cooking area expands into a dining area (Fig. 2-35) and maybe even a play area for kids, so be it. Good kitchens, in my opinion, have one key goal associated with them. I believe they are meant to be cozy and comfortable. By cozy, I don't mean small. In this instance, I use the word cozy to indicate an environment that is pleasant to be in.

As times and trends change, old ideas are improved upon. Maybe it is time to redefine what a good kitchen is. From a remodeling contractor's point of view, a great kitchen design is one that makes a customer happy. Keep this in mind. If you go around with a

Figure 2-33

The large floor tiles in this kitchen are enough to attract anyone's attention. The wine rack adds to the versatility of a base cabinet, and the glass-front cabinets are a nice touch. Stenciling and trim complement the upper sections of the kitchen walls. Wood-Mode, Inc.

preconceived notion of what a kitchen has to be to meet your criteria, you will probably lose out on several jobs that could have been awarded to you if you had been a little more open-minded.

Since people often say that a picture is worth a thousand words, let's see if it's true. Throughout this book, I'm going to show you thought-provoking photographs. I believe the pictures will tell the story better than I can. As you look at them, you will see how contemporary measures can be mixed in with older styles (Fig. 2-36). The mix is sometimes subtle and sometimes blatant. But in all cases,

Figure 2-34

The designer of this kitchen took full advantage of the water view with a glorious window. The beam ceiling with a wood finish presents a chalet-type image, but the tile floor, tile walls, and range hood can alter the mood. This kitchen offers a lot of possibilities. Wood-Mode, Inc.

if the mixture makes your customers happy, it is the right recipe for a kitchen plan.

The family-style kitchen

The family-style kitchen is one of my favorites. As an individual, I prefer something along the lines of a pioneer kitchen. However, as a husband and father, I favor the benefits of a family-oriented kitchen and dining area. Recently I built a new house for myself, and it has a

Figure 2-35

If bright is better, this kitchen must be one of the best. Look at how bright the room is. There is even extensive ceiling lighting to make up for dull days. Also, check out the dining table. Wood-Mode, Inc.

family-style kitchen in it. The house design is that of a modified contemporary. The kitchen is equipped with modern fixtures and appliances, but it has a antique appeal to it.

My wife and I have two children. Our daughter is nearly eight and our son is nearly two years old. Keeping an eye on the kids, especially our son, requires good visibility. With our kitchen layout, it's easy to let the kids play while we cook since their playroom is visible from the kitchen. If we open a sliding pocket door, we can see the entire living room. But guests who are seated in the living room can't see into the kitchen if the sliding door is closed.

Figure 2-36

This kitchen gives me a feeling of cramped space. There are, however, some nice features, such as the large cabinets and work surface. Wood-Mode, Inc.

We have a formal dining room, but most of our meals are eaten in the dining area that is part of the expansive kitchen. The work area is divided from the dining area by cabinets and a counter. But we can look between the countertop and the overhead cabinets to keep an eye on our son as he's eating. There's adequate space in the kitchen and dining area for the kids to be close to us without being in danger of a hot stove or accidental spills. It's possible for us to fill the dishwasher while talking to the children. The work area provides plenty of space and still maintains an efficient work triangle.

Many family-style kitchens adjoin a family room. The open concept behind a family kitchen (Fig. 2-37) makes such a plan ideal for couples who have small children. The kids can be playing in the

Figure 2-37

The cabinets and countertops in this kitchen are superb. The tile floor is nice, but it's too dark for my taste. Wood-Mode, Inc.

family room while the parents work in the kitchen. The supervision of children is easy and doesn't interfere with preparing meals, putting away groceries, and cleaning.

I remember my grandmother's kitchen vividly. It was of a galley design. One wall accommodated the wall-hung kitchen sink and range. The other wall consisted of some makeshift counter area and cabinet space. When the oven door was open, it was impossible to walk through the kitchen. I suspect the total distance for a traffic pattern between the obstacles was no more than 3 feet. My grandmother prepared countless meals in the confined space. But if she was cooking, a traffic cop was needed to help anyone get to the refrigerator or bathroom that was farther down the hall.

I have fond memories of my grandmother's kitchen, but it was one of the worst kitchen designs I have ever seen. There was no dishwasher. After a big meal, there was hardly enough room for one person to wash dishes while another person dried them. Also, getting the dishes put away in the pantry was a feat best handled by acrobats. To say that the kitchen was cramped would be an understatement.

Family-style kitchens should be large (Fig. 2-38). There are times when my wife and I are both working in our kitchen at the same time. If both kids come in with a question or in need of some help, we have enough room to make the gathering comfortable. Even so, our space is not large enough for me to feel good about calling it a family-style kitchen.

Figure 2-38

This is a huge, family-style kitchen that uses a lot of tile. The cabinets and counter space in this room are fantastic. Wellborn Cabinet, Inc.

A true family kitchen is both wide and long. It can act as a gathering place even when relatives are visiting for the holidays. Many existing homes simply don't have adequate space for a remodeler to create a family-style kitchen unless an addition is built onto the home. And this is exactly how most remodelers overcome the problems of tiny kitchens.

Expanding an existing kitchen can be easy. Since designers tend to place kitchens so that there is an outside wall to accommodate a sink and a window, it is usually not very difficult to expand the kitchen outward. If a house is positioned tightly on a small building lot, there might not be room to build an addition. Zoning requirements and setbacks might not allow the extension of new living space. However, many homes do have potential for major remodeling that includes the addition of new space.

When there is enough real estate to work with and an outside wall making up part of a kitchen, gaining extra space is relatively easy. The existing outside wall can be opened up and new kitchen area can be added using routine building procedures. But what can you do if a kitchen can't be opened up and extended beyond the existing foundation?

Most houses are built with kitchens where at least one of the walls is an outside wall (Fig. 2-39). When this isn't the case, some creative planning is required. An energetic remodeler can almost always find a way to make more space in a home. You might extend the kitchen into some existing room, such as a formal dining room or family room. The removal of an interior partition may be all it takes to add substantial square footage to a kitchen.

Suppose you extend an existing kitchen into an existing dining room to get a large, family-style kitchen (Fig. 2-40). However, your customer wants to replace the formal dining room that was consumed to make more kitchen space, what can you do? Perhaps you can build an addition that will house a new dining room. With the exception of

Figure 2-39

Here is a family-style kitchen with more-than-ample cabinet space. Not only are the cabinets abundant, features such as the glass doors are charismatic. Wellborn Cabinet, Inc.

homes on small building lots, there is almost always some way of building an addition that can replace the interior room that was sacrificed to make a larger kitchen.

Size and a comfortable traffic pattern are the two key elements of a family-style kitchen. Something as simple as using a cantilever to create dining space in a bay window can make a huge difference in both the appearance and functional use of a kitchen and dining area. It all comes down to creative ideas (Fig. 2-41). If you have enough of them, you are sure to find a way to make the most demanding customers appreciate your skills.

Figure 2-40

Breakfast for two is possible at the counter in this kitchen. The wood floors and cabinets complement each other nicely. Wellborn Cabinet, Inc.

Now that we've touched on a few types of specialized kitchens (Figs. 2-42 and 2-44), let's move onto the steps needed to create custom kitchens in an efficient and profitable way. We'll start with some business topics and then move into hands-on remodeling. When you combine the skills you are about to learn, you should be ready to make some serious money as a kitchen specialist.

Figure 2-41

This kitchen has some nice touches, like the spice shelf on the range hood, but I feel it has been done in colors that are too dark. Wood-Mode, Inc.

Figure 2-42

Glass-front cabinets and tile are the key features of this kitchen. Wood-Mode, Inc.

Figure 2-43

Notice how this kitchen uses two windows. Few contractors grasp this type of opportunity. Wood-Mode, Inc.

Figure 2-44

The wallpaper in this kitchen certainly makes a statement. For my taste, the pattern is too busy, which is something that you have to watch out for when you are advising customers on material selections. Wellborn Cabinet, Inc.

Cost estimates

Chapter 3

ESTIMATING the costs of a remodeling job is not an easy task. Many professional contractors have a lot of trouble accurately projecting the costs of labor and materials. Anyone who takes the importance of cost estimating for granted is sure to be in for an unpleasant surprise.

Assuming that you have not been a professional contractor for an extensive period, your responsibility in building viable cost estimates might seem overwhelming sometimes. You might not have the knowledge, skills, and experience needed to make accurate estimates. Don't panic; this chapter is going to help you develop some reliable cost estimates.

My experience covers a broad spectrum, but much of my work has involved custom remodeling. As you may know, remodeling is a field of construction that calls for specialized talent. A carpenter or plumber who can perform very well with new construction can be at a total loss when it comes to remodeling. The only real way to learn professional remodeling thoroughly is through on-the-job experience. However, I'm going to attempt to teach you how to manage kitchen remodeling with minimal financial risks.

Cost estimates are prepared in many ways. Some methods are better than others. Although estimates can be a formidable task, most people are capable of completing them successfully with a little help. You can get the help you need from this book.

Chapter 1 instructed you on planning your work, and Chapter 2 gave you ideas for kitchen styles you may encounter in your career. Now, it is time to put price tags on the work and materials that will be required in remodeling. You should make notes as you go along. Every kitchen job is different, so you need to customize your estimating procedure in a way similar to customizing your kitchen. Get a note pad and pencil before you read any further.

The importance of cost estimates

Cost estimates are of paramount importance to successful remodeling jobs. If your cost figures are off, your whole job and bank account could suffer. Contractors who fail to make accurate cost estimates don't stay in business very long. Mistakes in planning the costs of jobs can put you in very bad, even professionally fatal, situations. In extreme cases, a contractor can lose everything when one large job goes awry.

Can you imagine that after installing new kitchen cabinets you didn't have enough money to install a kitchen sink? How are you going to feel when you are nearing the finish line and find out that you can't afford the new appliances you and your customer had planned for the kitchen? I don't want to make you overly fearful, but I've seen these horrible scenarios over and over again.

The crucial elements of solid estimates

The development of solid estimates has several crucial elements. The figures derived during the estimating process will fail to be useful if any of these elements are not accounted for. Let's explore these key aspects of good estimates on a one-by-one basis.

Detailed plans

Professionally drawn blueprints are not required for all types of remodeling work; however, detailed plans are essential. In the case of minor kitchen remodeling, simple line drawings (drawn to scale) are suitable. If your project calls for structural changes, physical additions to a home, or other extensive work, more complex drawings are in order.

Detailed plans are instrumental in the estimating process. They are used to develop material take-offs. Code enforcement officers depend on the plans during the approval process for construction permits. Material suppliers may use the drawings to determine your material needs. Having plans that are drawn to scale also helps you to make sure your remodeling design is feasible. Let me tell you a quick story about one of my experiences with plans that were not drawn to scale.

I recall an occasion when a husband and wife called my company to bid a major kitchen job. The remodeling was going to be very extensive. It would involve tearing out the existing kitchen, adding a dining addition, and making both areas flow together in a harmonious floorplan. The mental plan the homeowners had for their kitchen was beautiful. However, the plan they put on paper was a nightmare.

This couple had drawn a line sketch of the layout for their new kitchen and dining area. They had been meticulous in keeping all of the lines straight and neat. The numbers used to represent various sizes on the drawing appeared to have been drawn with a stencil. Just looking at the drawing, one would think the plan was ideal. There was, however, a glitch in the works.

When the couple had drawn their new plan, they failed to draw it to any type of scale. The refrigerator was represented by a lovely rectangle, but the size was not to scale. Oh, they had written the width of the refrigerator in the box, but that was the extent of their measurements. Other appliances were drawn in similar fashion. The plan also included an island work space, complete with a sink. In the drawing, the island was centered perfectly between the cabinets, and the size of the island cabinet was marked in the box. All of the objects were included on the drawing, and each of them had sizes written in or near them. The problem was, the symbols and shapes were not to scale, and there was not enough floor space in the kitchen and dining areas to accommodate all of the proposed appliances, cabinets, and accessories.

The people who had drawn the plan were disappointed to find that their plans were going to have to be altered. They were, however, happy that their error was discovered before they committed to the financial responsibilities involved in the proposed remodeling. If I had not discovered the discrepancies in the drawing, those homeowners would have been very upset once the job was in progress. Please let this little lesson serve as evidence for your need to create scaled, detailed plans.

Specifications

Clear specifications are needed for all remodeling jobs, large and small alike. As a contractor, I've experienced the use of specifications from both sides of the table. When I act as a general contractor, I deal with the specifications given to me by my customers and create specifications for the subcontractors with whom I arrange to work. I've got to tell you, I've seen plenty of specification sheets that left a lot to the imagination. Without details, specifications are useless. Let me give you a quick example of the wrong way to specify a job.

Assume that as a part of your kitchen remodeling job you want the plumber to replace a kitchen sink and faucet. Here is the wrong way to write the specs:

> Plumber is to replace existing kitchen sink with a stainless-steel, double-bowl sink. A new, single-handle faucet with spray attachment is to be installed. New cut-offs, supply tubes, and drainage tubing shall be supplied and installed by the plumber.

> Allow me to explain what's wrong with the specs you just read. The specifications call for a stainless-steel, double-bowl sink. However, they don't mention a brand name, a model number, a size, or a weight. Not all stainless-steel sinks are created equal. A cheap sink could be purchased for about $30. A good sink will cost between $50 and $100. A great sink could cost well over $100. Based on the specifications in the example, a plumber could bid the job with a $30 sink when you thought that you would be getting a $100 sink. Since the weight and/or gauge of the sink is not mentioned, the plumber bidding the job can opt for a cheap version of the sink that will be pulled down by the weight of a garbage disposer. The gauge of a stainless-steel sink is very important in terms of quality.

> The single-handle faucet mentioned is very vague. The cost for such a faucet could be less than $40 or upwards of $150. Which version is being supplied? It's anybody's guess. Will the spray attachment be attached on the faucet spout, deck-mounted in the base of the faucet, or mounted in a spare hole in the sink? If these details matter to you, you need to specify them.

The little blurb about cut-offs and drainage fittings is far too ambiguous. Who is supplying the basket strainers needed for the sink? What type of cut-offs are being used? Will the drainage fittings be metal or plastic? If these details are not mentioned in the specs, frustration and aggravation will arise in the course of the remodeling job.

Include as much data as possible when creating specifications for your job. Cover items such as colors, brand names, model numbers, sizes, weights, dimensions, material types, and any other details that are pertinent to the work. Leave nothing to the imagination of the bidder. Most importantly, never allow a clause that gives a subcontractor an option to substitute some other material for the item you specified. If you see a clause in an estimate that reads "or equal," the subcontractor has just set you up for a substitution that you don't want.

A complete scope

A complete scope of all work and materials involved with your project should be included in an estimating package. Many times parts of a job are overlooked. Sometimes the missed phases of work are minimal, but these oversights can add up to substantial sums of money. For example, how will you get rid of all the debris created from ripping out an old kitchen? If you have to pay someone to haul away the rubble, the cost could run into hundreds of dollars. Take time to thoroughly review all aspects of your job in your head. Make written notes as you go along. Try to avoid omitting any possible expenses during the planning stage.

Written checklists

Written checklists are one of the best ways to avoid forgotten elements of a job when creating cost estimates. It is impossible for someone to create a generic checklist that will work for every remodeling job. Too many possibilities for variations exist. The best checklists are those that you have created through your own experience.

Written commitments

When you get estimates from suppliers and subcontractors, get them in writing. Written commitments serve more than one purpose. Estimates on paper are easy to file and refer to. These commitments also force subcontractors and suppliers to take their estimating work a little more seriously. If a subcontractor is going to commit to a price in writing, he or she will not pull the price out of thin air. Best of all, written commitments are enforceable. Verbal commitments are almost impossible to prove.

Hard costs

When you begin gathering prices for a job, you may hear about hard costs. Hard costs are the expenses that are incurred for items such as cabinets, flooring, and lumber. These expenses are not usually overlooked during the estimating process.

Soft costs

Soft costs are expenses that are sometimes hidden during the development of cost estimates. Examples of soft costs include building permits, blueprints drawings, and bank fees for loans to pay for the work. Soft costs must not be overlooked; they can add up to a substantial sum of money.

Availability

The unavailability of materials and subcontractors can have disastrous affects on cost estimates once a job gets underway. If you get a quote for custom cabinets, you might assume that the cabinets will be available when you need them. Don't count on it. In fact, insist on a written commitment of availability. If items such as cabinets, sinks, or skylights are not available when you need them, you may be forced to buy more expensive or unwanted substitutes in order to get your customer's kitchen put back together. At best, this change in plans will disappoint and discourage you. At worst, you will have to spend a lot more time and money than you estimated in order to complete the job in the manner you intended.

Subcontractors, like materials, are not always available when you want or need them. Suppose you found a great deal on the carpentry work you will need. The carpenter has given you a price that is a few thousand dollars lower than the other bids. Therefore, you put all of your eggs into that one basket and planned your cost estimates around the carpenter with the low price. What are you going to do if that carpenter is not available when you are ready to have the job done? Chances are, you will have to pay one of the more expensive carpenters to complete the work, and your budget will be destroyed.

A margin of error

Always build a margin of error into a cost estimate. Professional estimators wouldn't think of bidding a job without padding the price a little. If you are not an experienced remodeler, it is especially important for you to beef up the cost estimates in order to allow for unforeseen problems. Material prices could go up. Prices in material estimates might not include everything you will need. There are dozens of other possible situations that prove you need a float figure built into your estimate.

Back-up plans

Always create back-up plans when you prepare an estimate. I don't think that I've ever had a remodeling job in which everything went as planned. Therefore, I normally estimate jobs with three separate approaches; the best case, the probable case, and the worst case. In doing this, I'm prepared for almost anything.

If you will be hiring subcontractors to perform parts of the job for you, don't base your cost estimates on the numbers from any single contractor. Collect several bids and review them to arrive at average, reasonable numbers. Organize your contractors in order of preference.

If your first choice is not available, you can move down your list to your second choice.

Estimating guides

You can get a feel for what your remodeling job is going to cost by using estimating guides. These books, available at most bookstores, are designed to help estimators put prices on goods and services. Estimating guides are very useful, but I would not recommend relying solely on them. I use the guides to compare their numbers with the figures I have compiled on my own. It has been my experience that there can be drastic differences between the estimated costs printed in books and the actual cost of goods and services on a local level. While the guides are a valuable part of a combination approach to estimating, they should not be used as the only source of cost data.

Shopping

Shopping for prices can be very time-consuming. Whether you are trying to find the best deal on a ceiling fan or a plumber, the process can wear you down. Shopping is, however, one of the most effective ways to determine what your real costs are likely to be. The legwork and phone time will be extensive for big jobs, but it is time well spent.

Quotes

Depending on subcontractor bids can be dangerous. I've already explained the risk associated with the availability of contractors, but there is more to talk about. Many subcontractors provide written estimates that inexperienced general contractors believe are solid prices. For the price to be firm, you need a quote, not an estimate. There is a huge difference in the meaning of *estimate* and *quote*. When you bid your job out, insist on written quotes, not estimates. Also, pay attention to any language that may put a time limit on how long the price is good. Some quotes are only good for a few days. This is just one more way that your original cost estimates can come up short.

Piece-by-piece method

The piece-by-piece method of estimating is one of the best cost-estimating techniques. In this process, you build out each phase of your job on a worksheet and account for its individual cost. This type of estimating takes longer than some of the other ways, but the accuracy of piece-by-piece estimates is unmatched.

In order to explain what a piece-by-piece estimate is, we'll look at carpentry work involved in a kitchen remodeling job. If you are looking for a fast way to estimate the job, you could simply lump all carpentry work into one category. However, if you want a clear picture of how your costs will run, you should break the category of carpentry down into phases. The subcategories might include rip-out work, framing, siding, roofing, subflooring, trim work, setting cabinets. When you take the time to break the job down into little pieces, it is easier to target your costs and to keep on budget.

Multiple methods

Combining multiple methods of estimating is another great way to avoid going over your budget. This is the method I use. I recommend that you refer to estimating guides, request bids from subcontractors and suppliers, and break the job down into specific phases. If you follow this method, you will hedge your bets in the best way I know to avoid cost overruns.

Your best deal

Cutting your best deal doesn't always mean paying the lowest price. There are many times when the lowest bid isn't the best bid. However, if your plans and specifications are precise and you verify the credentials of your potential subcontractors, the lowest price can be a safe bet. It all depends on how you handle the bidding and selection process.

Getting the best price on materials is much easier than determining your best value on labor. If you want a particular sink, it is easy to spec the sink and solicit prices. Since the sink will be the same regardless of which supplier provides it, you can take the low bid. This, of course, is assuming that all the suppliers included all costs for the bid, such as shipping costs and sales tax.

When it comes time to choose the best deal on an electrician or plumber, the selection process becomes a bit more complicated. While you may be reviewing quotes from three licensed electricians, you do not have a tangible way of determining which of the three electricians will give you the best service for the best price. The low bidder might not show up for work when scheduled. You might find that the price is low because the electrician overbooks, only working for a few hours at a time on one job before jumping over to another job. This type of behavior could greatly increase the time spent on your project.

Since selecting the best contractors is a key element in the successful completion of your project, you must look at more than the bottom line. You should check work and bank references (to make sure the contractor will still be in business to finish your job), visit the contractor's active job sites, and obtain all agreements in writing. The information obtained from your study of the contractor will help keep you from being blinded by the lowest price.

So much is involved in the process of cost estimating and control that I could easily write a complete book on the subject. However, space for this topic is limited, so we must move on to other aspects of the remodeling profession. Just remember, getting accurate cost estimates in the beginning will save you a lot of grief in the end.

Subcontractors' bids

Chapter 4

MOST remodelers rely on subcontractors to perform some aspects of their remodeling jobs. This means that remodelers acting as general contractors need to obtain prices from their subcontractors and suppliers before a job can be priced accurately. Putting your jobs out to bid is an important part of making a profit. Getting the right prices from dependable subcontractors and suppliers is often crucial to the success of a job. Not all general contractors are good at requesting clear and concise bids that contain no ambiguities about the proposed job. Since this aspect of general contracting is troublesome to some professionals, let's discuss the method to get accurate and reasonable prices on specific jobs and materials.

Remodeling requires both labor and materials. These two factors account for most of the costs incurred in a remodeling project. To stay on budget, you have to control both labor and material costs. The most effective way to control job costs is by using written quotes. Your goal is to expedite accurate quotes from several subcontractors and suppliers that you will compare to establish the best value for your dollar. Collecting quotes from different sources allows you to establish conclusive budget figures and finalize your plans and specifications. This is not a complicated process, but it requires an eye for details.

It is easy to overlook the smaller aspects of a remodeling job. These oversights can be expensive. Trash removal, permit fees, and clean-up costs are good examples of frequently missed expenditures. By using a cost estimate form, you may come across some of these smaller aspects that you want to have included in the quotes you obtain. The categories on the estimate form provide you with the information necessary for testing the integrity of labor and material quotes from subcontractors. For example, does the contractor's quote include rip-out, clean-up of rubble, and removal of all debris? A quote including these services should have them stated clearly.

Soliciting bids for labor and materials is a very important step in starting a project. The success of your job hinges on solid quotes. When remodeling costs get out of hand, the job suffers and corners must be cut to save money. Careful planning eliminates compromises and allows jobs to run smoothly. Estimates give you a monetary range in which to work, but quotes are needed in the final budgeting phase. Don't confuse an estimate with a quote.

Estimates and quotes

The difference between an estimate and a quote can mean thousands of dollars to you. An estimate is like a hypothesis—it is an educated guess. Prices listed on an estimate can fluctuate greatly from real costs. Therefore, some contractors use low estimates as a sales tactic. They use inaccurate estimates to win jobs. Then they add to their prices with extras. In these situations, work you thought was included in the original price becomes an additional expense. This procedure allows a subcontractor initially to be the low bidder and ultimately to leave your job with more money than the competitors would have.

These tricky contractors can get away with this scheme based on the fact that estimates only include a vague description of the work to be done, leaving much room for interpretation and problems. I once took my truck in to be serviced. I was careful to ask for an estimate of the repair cost and found that the price was reasonable. The final bill included additional parts, extra labor, and freight charges! "The first price was only an estimate," replied the manager. "Once we got into it, we found more problems." This is an example of why it is risky to allow anyone to work with only an estimated cost projection.

Estimates might contain a lot of words, which, when combined have little meaning. Consider a painting proposal with only a few details included: the room to be painted, the color of the paint, and the method of application. Details in the estimate are reserved for the payment schedule. The job requires a deposit on acceptance of the estimate. The second payment is due when the material is delivered to the job. The final payment is due upon completion of the project.

Does this appear to be an acceptable estimate? After all, the location of the job and the color and type of paint have been clearly specified. You should consider other details that need to be included in a painting proposal. If you visualize the painting process, you will discover the omissions. Interior painting involves moving furniture and possible spillage of paint. Will protection from spillage be provided by you or the painting contractor? You can bet an estimate will not address these matters.

There are many other considerations. Does the estimate say how long the job will take? Will primer or sealant be used before the paint is applied? During what hours of the day will the work be done? Maybe the contractor has a full-time job and only paints in the evening. When an estimate says the contractor will paint the walls and ceiling of a kitchen, what is actually included? Are they going to paint the baseboards and window and door trim as well? Are the holes and dings in the wall going to be patched before the walls are painted? Most estimates will not answer these questions either.

Another unanswered question involves the type of paint. Will it be flat or semi-gloss? The contractor agreed orally to allow your choice of paint, but paint prices vary with quality and type. What will you do when the contractor charges extra for the paint you selected? What happens if he or she tells you, after the fact, that the price was for a builder-grade paint, and your selection was a more expensive custom color? Do you have to pay the additional cost? The contractor will say yes, and you will say no. However, ultimately it might be up to a judge to decide. The bottom line is that an estimate cannot be compared to, or considered, a quote. You will have a difficult time suing someone based on his guess at a price, but a quote is an absolute commitment.

Make sure the quote addresses all of the pertinent aspects of a job. A painting proposal might say that the painting contractor will supply plastic for the floors, but who's responsibility is it to put it down? There may be no mention of protecting lights, outlet covers, and doors from over-spray. Do not rely on the contractor's assurance that he or she will protect these areas. Verbal agreements can't be proven in court.

Language

The description of the work might state that the walls, ceilings, and trim will be sprayed to allow proper coverage. How many coats are required, and what is proper coverage? Similar language mentions timely completion in a workmanlike manner. Who is to say what is timely or workmanlike? When you receive a quote, it is necessary to analyze the information and look for discrepancies. What might at first appear to be a reasonable quote, might turn out to be a nebulous, one-sided proposal.

Time-and-materials billing

Some general contractors are influenced by a contractor's low hourly labor rate and accept a proposal to do the project on a time-and-materials basis. Don't fall for this line. I've experimented with a few time-and-materials contractors. Very few of them have turned out to be a bargain. Whenever possible, avoid time-and-materials agreements. Costs can skyrocket uncontrollably in these situations. If you agree to have the work done in this manner, you are responsible for paying whatever the final bill may be. Labor rates can be very deceiving, even when dealing with honest contractors.

Contractors work at different speeds and skill levels. The total charge for time-and-materials billing is subject to the speed of the contractor. If Mr. Carpenter only charges $35 per hour and does all the work alone, he can cost you more than Zippy Carpenters, which charges $65 per hour for a crew of men.

Material prices in this type of billing can also have wide variances from contractor to contractor. One contractor might only charge 15% above his cost, while another could charge 35% above cost. When you are not protected by a firm quote, these costs can add up quickly.

Crooked contractors love time-and-materials jobs. They can drag the job out and bleed the general contractor of considerable sums of money. These subcontractors are masters in the art of working without accomplishing anything. To the untrained eye, they appear to be working hard every hour of the day. In truth, they are going through the motions. They put on their best performances in order to impress you and to collect as much money from you as possible. These contractors often meticulously unpack and clean-up their tools and materials each day. They need to make numerous daily trips: first to purchase extra nails, then to get one more stud, and then to the hardware store. You will pay for all of this extra time.

Without a quoted price and a contract, a contractor can set you up before you know what happened. The job may start smoothly. However, the situation will quickly take a turn for the worse. At first, the extra charges will be minor. They bill you for the first phase of completed work according to your understanding with only a few small extra charges included. Then, the job suddenly develops unforeseen problems, as did my truck, and the next bill is laden with extra costs.

Many contractors try to convince you that a time-and-materials job will save you money. After all, you only pay for what you get. They claim that they can't hide exorbitant profits as a contract price can. Just remember, no one does remodeling work without financial reimbursement. There are very few jobs for which competent contractors cannot give you a firm price. Once work is started, a contractor has potential lien rights against your customer's property. You cannot compare time-and- materials estimates, and they do not give you any information to finalize your budget. Avoid potential problems by using only subcontractors with a firm contract and quoted price. Subcontractors aren't the only people who use low bids as a ploy. Materials suppliers can be guilty of similar tactics. Envision going to a building supplier to order kitchen cabinets. After looking at the displays and catalogs, your customers make their choice. You obtain a written estimate from the company. The price looks good, so you order the cabinets. The salesperson tells you the cabinets should be available for delivery in four to six weeks. You head over to the job and get your crew started on the demolition work.

There are already many potential problems in this example. You just ordered cabinets, and your crew is already working on the demolition of your customers' kitchen. A few weeks later, the old cabinets, countertop, and kitchen sink have been ripped out. Your customers are not worried, because you have told them that the new cabinets will be installed next week. A couple of days without kitchen facilities is tolerable to most customers; it gives the homeowners a good excuse to enjoy dining in restaurants. You are confident since the job has been successfully coordinated to this point.

The big day arrives. The new cabinets will come today. By tonight, your customers can do dishes again. By late morning, you are getting concerned. By mid-afternoon, you're getting angry. Where are those cabinets? The carpenters and the plumber are waiting for the delivery. Paying them to stand around is eating up your profits. You call the supplier, and a counterperson gets on the phone. When you ask about the status of your cabinet delivery, you are put on hold; the counterperson has to check with the shipping department. The longer you are on hold, the higher your blood pressure gets. When the counterperson finally comes back to the phone, you find out that the cabinets had to be back-ordered and won't be in for a few more weeks. That's the breaking point, and you lose your temper. You demand to speak to the manager, who is on a break and not available to take the call. You hang up and rush out of the house, leaving the plumber and carpenters waiting for your return. You race to the supplier with your estimate in hand and go straight to the administrative offices. The manager is on the phone. You wait. Your anger is now building to a dangerous level. Finally, she invites you into the office. You're so upset when you show her the estimate sheet that it is shaking in your hand. Trying to maintain composure, you explain what is happening to you.

The manager reviews the estimate. You notice a strange expression on her face. When you ask what she intends to do to remedy the problem, she explains that this estimate is all she has to work with. She continues by stating that the details in the estimate are not very good and tracking the order could be a problem. She goes on to apologize for the present problem and offers to do whatever she can to find your cabinets. In the meantime, you have carpenters and a plumber waiting on-site. The clock is running, and the subcontractors are expensive. When you ask what can be done about the cabinets, the answer is not what you want to hear.

The manager explains the problems with the estimates. The estimate is ambiguous. It doesn't state a delivery date. The design of the cabinets isn't detailed in the paperwork. It is unclear whether a countertop was included in the order. The hardware for the doors and drawers is not included with this brand of cabinets. The hardware is a separate order and will take another week or so to get. There is no reference to delivery in the estimate. Delivery is available, but there is an additional charge for the service. Freight charges are not included in the estimate, and they are extensive since the cabinets are coming from 1800 miles away.

At this point, the supplier turns your adversity into their advantage. The manager reviews the situation and offers you a deal on cabinets she has in stock. She wants to make amends for your inconvenience. The cabinets in stock retail for 45% more than the units you ordered. As compensation for your trouble, she offers you the more expensive cabinets at a discount, with free delivery today. The total cost will be only 30% more than the original estimate. Since you must incur additional expenses and time delays for the original cabinets, you will save money and time with this deal.

If you order cabinets from another supplier, you may have to wait for another month or longer. If you wait for your original order, the additional costs will push your losses over the price of the special of the day. You need to decide on the spot. You can't forget about the carpenters and plumber waiting for you and the cabinets. Also, you must consider what you will face from the homeowners if you don't get their kitchen back up and running quickly.

Believe it or not, some companies make their profits from scenarios such as this. If the building-supply manager is a good salesperson, you will probably take delivery of the higher-priced cabinets. This is a prime example of the pain that can result from working with loose estimates. Use detailed contracts with enforceable clauses that leave nothing to speculation. As my wife once said, "There is never a problem until there is a problem."

Now you know the problems with estimates. You must recognize the need for written quotes. If your agreement is in writing, you know what you are paying for and how much it will cost. This is a crucial aspect of any remodeling project. If you allotted $2300 for cabinets and they wind up costing more than $3000, your out-of-pocket expenses have increased by 30%. Where will the additional $700 come from? You will be forced to take short cuts and reduce the quality or quantity of the work. This difficult situation can be avoided with detailed quotes.

The document that will save you time, money, and frustration is called many things. Quote, bid, proposal, or contract; regardless of the term, this is the written instrument you're looking for. Quotes contain much more information than estimates. Contractors know a quote is a firm price, so they will be much more specific in their description of labor and materials. The intent of a quote is to guarantee a fixed price. The cost of the service or material cannot exceed the amount specified in the quote. When you are dealing with quotes, you can be sure of your costs.

Budget

Establish your budget based on the average bid price from several bidders. This will protect you from a low quote that can't be performed. For example, to establish the average price of five different bids, add the total of each proposal together and divide the grand total by the number of bids (in this case five). Quotes that are well below average should arouse suspicion. More than likely there is a reason why one price is so much lower than the others. Perhaps you will be unable to get the contractor to do the work when you need it, or the material may not be available during your time table. By using the average quoted price, you won't be placed in a financial bind.

Identical bid packages

When requesting quotes, give all bidders the same information. You cannot expect competitive proposals if the bidders are working with different information. You'd probably be surprised at how often general contractors fail to give subcontractors identical bid packages. Your bid request needs to include specific details. The complete plans and specifications for the job should accompany the bid request. You want to establish consistency so that you receive prices for exactly the same work.

Ask bidders to note, as an addendum to the bid, any item you might have omitted. A contractor who includes code requirements you overlooked will be more expensive than the contractor bidding strictly by your plans and specs. Regardless, you will have to pay for the code requirements. You need to take this into consideration when comparing the bids. You can also use additions made by the bidders to help locate superior contractors. Make a note of who mentioned your omission and who did not. The contractor who considers aspects and requirements you did not specify exhibits the extra effort and knowledge to give you a thorough job.

Preparing your bid requests deserves a lot of attention. The bidders are only obligated to provide costs for the work you specify. This is where all the time and effort you put into your plans and specifications can pay off. Following a few rules in the bidding process can increase your savings. Don't allow suppliers to substitute materials in their bid. Specifications lose their purpose when substitutions are made. If substitutions are mandatory, ask that the substitutions be placed on a separate bid addendum. Uniformity in bids is essential for comparing them.

Specify the exact grade of materials to be used. For example, studs come in several grades. You don't have to require the best, but you need to specify the grade to be used. There is a great deal of difference in the cost between lumber grades. The same is true for other items. If your specifications simply call for sheathing behind new siding, what kind of sheathing will your bids be based on? One contractor might bid plywood for sheathing, another might plan to use wafer board, the third might base his or her quote on fiberboard, and a fourth contractor might quote insulated foam sheathing. All the contractors included a price for sheathing, but the prices are all different. It will be easy to tell which bid is lower, but which one is the better value?

The result of detailed plans and specifications is a quality quote. If your specs are detailed, you can easily compare all the prices and know, without a doubt, what is included in each bid. Compare all bids on a step-by-step basis. If you use a form like a bid request form, this is an easy task. All the elements of the quotes are broken down on the bid request sheets. You can scan the page and see every expense to determine who has the best prices on which items. This is another area with strong potential for saving money.

Materials bids

Many contractors prefer to deal with one supplier. This is definitely the easiest way to buy, but it is not always the best. Putting your job out to bid can be done several ways. The most common method is to request a lump sum price. This method indicates who has the lowest overall price, but it doesn't show you the items that could be bought cheaper elsewhere. Using a detailed bid sheet will expose these savings. Some suppliers resist detailed bids, because they want to mask their prices in a bulk figure. However, if they want the sale badly enough, they will comply with your request. If they are unwilling to show you all of their prices, you should not deal with them. These contractors are all but telling you they are hiding something.

Hardware stores price their items individually—why should a building supplier be any different? Just because they deal in larger items and higher volumes, they do not have the right to hide their prices. Be firm on this point. Insist on knowing what all the components of your job will cost. It's very easy to hide excessive profits on volume sales. It is not feasible to price every screw, hinge, and nail, but you can price all the major items. Break the items down into bid phases. Phase breakdowns are bargaining chips and can hold hidden treasures for you.

Contractors' quotes can be challenged in much the same way. Request a breakdown of labor and material. Some contractors will not give this information, knowing it could expose excessive, hidden profits. If you are suspicious, demand a breakdown. This is the only way to verify quotes and control your costs.

A common trick of the trade is to camouflage material substitutions. Vague language in a quote might specify that your product or "an equal" will be used. Who is to determine what is equivalent to your product? Your satisfaction might not be met with these so-called equal products. Require that the bids be based on specific names, model numbers, colors, etc., and you will eliminate these sneaky substitutions.

When you get your prices back, lay the bid sheets beside each other and scan the categories. You are sure to find some interesting differences. The bottom line will show the overall low bidder. The phase prices will expose ways to increase your savings. For example, look at the framing lumber section. Who is the overall low bidder on the framing prices? How do the window and door prices compare with other suppliers? Does their insulation price beat the other bidders? What do their numbers look like for the roofing phase? By now, you will have found areas to investigate. The overall low bidder won't be the lowest in all phases. It would be very unusual if one supplier had the lowest prices for every aspect of the job.

Selective shopping saves money. You don't have to buy everything from one supplier, but it is best to buy each complete phase from the same company. Don't spend a lot of time buying a little here and little there. Concentrate on the phases and buy from the lowest bidder in each category. Use your bid sheets as negotiating tools. Show the other bids to the supplier you prefer. When you put their competitor's price in front of them, the preferred supplier might offer you a better price. Suppliers price their material in different levels and, usually, have room to offer additional discounts. You won't get a better price if you don't ask for it.

Laying your bid sheets on the counter proves you are serious. The supplier knows you can easily buy from its competitor. When you get to this stage, you will have their attention. Don't deal with a sales associate; ask to talk with the manager. Only the manager has the ability to give you the lowest price. When the prices are close, you will almost always win. The supplier has invested time and money in preparing your bid. The only way they can recover their money is by making a sale. You are the buyer. You have the power in this situation. Use your power to save on your material costs. The slower the economy, the better your chances of winning. Don't be intimidated. It's your money and your decision where to spend it.

Time needed for bids

Putting your work out to bids requires time. Allow several weeks for the process. Many contractors and suppliers will be slow in responding to your request for quotes. Some will refuse to bid the job under your terms and conditions. To get the most for your money, you might have to shop in other areas. In large cities or other states, you may find lower prices. For example, Maine's materials prices are high. I can buy the exact same products in Massachusetts for up to 35% less. You might find similar savings with your exploratory bid requests. Take the time to conduct the bid process properly.

Number of bidders

You need to formulate a plan to have as many bidders compete on the job as possible. Your chances for saving money increase in proportion to the number of quotes you receive. Solicit bids by mail and include a complete bid package with each request. To save on the copying and the postage costs of mass mailings, start the process by sending a letter to verify the bidder's interest in the job. When you get favorable replies, mail the complete package.

When you get into serious negotiations, watch your step. Don't be fooled by low prices based on substituted materials. Confirm, in writing, the delivery and completion dates. Beware of any bidder beating all the others by a large margin. All the bids should be within the same range. If one bid is substantially lower, you can be sure that something is wrong. Double-check your plans and specifications before requesting quotes. Once you receive the quotes, you can begin to eliminate contractors and suppliers. Then you will be ready to negotiate for the best possible deal.

Savings negotiations

Chapter 5

A T THE end of the last chapter, I looked at ways to save money by comparing bids. In this chapter, I expose secrets that you can use to obtain the lowest prices possible. You can save a lot of money simply by using the right techniques. These savings are especially evident on larger jobs. The more you are buying, or contracting for, the more you can save. Subcontractors and suppliers rarely give you their lowest price on their first bid. They are in business to make money, just the same as you. Getting to the lowest bottom-line price takes time and planning on your part. However, it is time well spent, and your efforts will be compensated with substantial savings.

If you are relatively new to the contracting business, you might have difficulty recognizing inflated prices. You have very few prior purchases with which to compare prices, and you know of only a limited number of sources. All of the printed sources are looking to make money through increased list prices. How will you know when you have reached your best deal? Getting to the lowest price is a matter of trial and error. You have to keep negotiating until you reach a standstill. Using the special negotiating tactics in this chapter, you can be more successful at obtaining lower prices for goods and services.

Discounts

Suppliers offer you the most opportunity for savings. They price materials in different levels. As a general contractor, you should be entitled to a discount. If you work with a supplier, you should save a minimum of 10% off the price that would be quoted to a homeowner. These savings can be much larger, due to the varying percentages of markups on different items.

Almost any expensive item will have a large profit built into the sales price. Wholesale prices vary as much as 30%, and average consumer markups run from 10% to 50%. This means there is a big spread in the prices you might pay for identical materials. Buying from the right place can reduce your costs by an average of 15%.

Light fixtures

The products with the highest markups are frequently light fixtures. Lights carry price increases of up to 100% above what the electrical contractor pays. Why do light fixtures support a 100% markup compared to plumbing fixtures at a 25% markup? Some light fixtures are low-dollar items, allowing for a larger retail markup. An excessive markup on an already costly whirlpool would reduce its market appeal. However, no one questions the $20 price on a light fixture that wholesales for $10.

As a contractor, I have compared the contractors' prices with the retail price tags on light fixtures. The retail tags frequently carry a 75%, or higher, markup. Obviously, an electrical supplier has a lot more room to negotiate a lower price than many other suppliers. Sometimes all you have to do is ask for a lower price, but on occasion you must be a tough negotiator.

Plumbing fixtures

Now we know that light fixtures carry a large markup and are a good target for price savings. The next phase of remodeling to consider is plumbing. Plumbing fixtures are a good category to scrutinize. In some areas only licensed plumbers can buy direct from wholesale dealers. In other locations, you can buy from wholesale dealers at retail prices. Try to get prices from both your plumber and a supplier for the same products. Unless you compare the prices side-by-side, you can not be certain that you are getting the best price.

Some plumbing contractors sell their fixtures considerably above the suggested list price. Others let you have the material at 10% above their cost in order to win the overall bid. These plumbers often make their profit from their standard, hourly labor rate. When bought from a contractor, plumbing items costing more than $200 have an average markup between 10% and 35%. On less expensive items, the percentage might be as high as 100%.

Plumbing fixtures purchased directly from a supplier carry average markups from 20% to 50% above wholesale. In this scenario, the brand and price range of the item are the determining factors in the markup. A toilet will have a markup of about 75%, and a standard bathtub will carry a profit percentage of about 45%. Inexpensive wall-hung lavatories can be marked up 65%, while well pumps can have profit margins of 100%. The kitchen faucet that costs you $95 will cost the plumber around $58. More expensive items, such as whirlpools, carry markups in the 25% range. Armed with this knowledge, you can whittle away at plumbing profit margins during the negotiation process.

Heating systems

Heating systems carry markups in the 40% range. It is important that you not overlook heating accessories while campaigning for a lower price on the main heating unit. HVAC accessories can be sold at profits as high as 100%. As a savvy remodeling contractor, work all the angles to achieve the lowest prices possible. Furnace and boiler prices are worth negotiating, but the big savings are in the accessories. The contractor may sell the main heating system at only 20% above his cost, but will undermine your budget with the parts that go with it. The thermostats, valves, and similar items may be marked up by 75% or more. Ask for a detailed breakdown of all labor and material. Granted, you probably won't be installing complete heating systems while remodeling a kitchen, but there may be times when a home-owner wants you to do some major improvements to other parts of a home while you are working on the kitchen.

Basic construction products

You will find that it is hardest to save on basic construction products. Items such as drywall, paint, and lumber offer markups in the 10% to 20% range. These percentages are lower than many other markups, but the volume of materials used justifies negotiating. Spend enough time shopping to be sure that you are getting the best deals available.

Saving 5% on all the lumber and drywall used over the course of a year can make a huge difference in the profits you make.

Floor coverings

You can save a lot of money on floor coverings. Carpet and vinyl floor coverings are marked up by as much as 75%. Ceramic tile floors give contractors a hefty markup on materials. All the subtle little extras such as stain resistance and no wax add to the price. There are several grades and types of flooring to choose from. You can beat the prices on most types of flooring at outlet centers and through negotiations.

Kitchen cabinets and countertops

Kitchen cabinets and countertops are another expense area to attack. The profit percentage here can easily exceed 60%. The markups on custom cabinets are certain to be even higher. Special kitchen items carry the largest markups. For example, garden-style windows have absurd profits built into the sale price. The same is true for unique sinks and faucets. You can save money on any of these items with thrifty shopping. Research your costs and compare them to the subcontractor's material quote. Remember to allow for delivery charges, if you supply the materials yourself. By investing your time in personal research on prices, your savings can mount up.

Insulation

Price negotiations on insulation are not very fruitful, since the markups on insulation are low and the savings are minimal. Hire subcontractors to supply and install the insulation. In some cases, you cannot buy the material for the price a contractor charges to supply and install it. Not to mention, many people experience skin irritations from insulation. Unless you enjoy working with insulation for minimal savings and getting very itchy, avoid doing your own insulation. I feel that it is just not worth the effort.

Windows and doors

Depending on which brand you choose, the markup on windows and doors can hit 65%. This amounts to a lot of money in an addition full of windows. Make the supplier sharpen its pencils on the window and door prices. If possible, beat the supplier to its lowest price and supply your own windows and doors. You'll be glad you did.

Trim lumber

Standard trim lumber does not offer much room for savings, but custom-milled trim material does. If you are going to use standard trim, have the subcontractor supply it. Most of the savings you pass up will be made up for in fewer headaches.

Wallpaper

Wallpaper can be an excellent source of savings. It carries a profit ranging from 45% to 100%. By now, you're getting the picture. There are certain areas in which to aim your efforts when seeking lower prices. Now that you know what to save on, you must learn how to achieve those savings.

The approach

Is there a golden rule for obtaining maximum savings? Every seller responds to a different approach. The direct approach works with some vendors; simply asking for a better price can produce good results. Many estimators build a "giveaway" factor into their quotes in the form of a cash discount or an offer of an upgraded product for the same price of a less expensive item. In either case, these aren't the real savings that you are seeking. Yes, they are a savings from the original quote, but there is still more money to be saved. The first "giveaway" is from an inflated price. You should never accept this as the best you can do. Continue your pursuit with relentless negotiations until you achieve the absolute best savings.

I have found the best approach with material suppliers is to put numbers in front of them. This method was mentioned in the last chapter. In order to get the lowest price, you need to have your facts together and be ready to make a commitment. After collecting several bids from suppliers, you're ready to play the game. This is like playing poker, but, because you already hold the winning hand, you show your cards to the other players. Use your bid request sheet, which breaks down the different phases of the job, to compare various suppliers' prices. Listing these prices side-by-side creates a strong graphic tool. When a supplier sees the competition's prices, the effect is hard-hitting.

Sit down with the manager of the building supply store and show him or her where the store's prices are too high. Stress your interest in buying all of your material from the company. Then ask the manager to reconsider the store's original quote. The odds are good that you will be offered reduced pricing. If you aren't offered a suitable deal, pack up your bid request sheet and visit the other suppliers. Don't be haughty or rude to any of the stores; you might have to deal with them later.

Out-of-town shopping

If you live in a small town, branch out with your savings effort. Call suppliers in larger cities. Pricing is often more competitive in an area with more competition. Cities provide higher populations and higher demand. They also support more building supply outlets. These factors produce lower prices. Many out-of-town suppliers will deliver to your job at no additional cost. Even though it requires extra time to investigate these options, the savings can be outstanding.

Aggressive shopping

Most contractors try to avoid giving itemized breakdowns of their prices. The first strategy they use might be to show you the actual invoice on the product. They will explain that they are only marking the unit up by 20%. The contractor will try to justify the need for this markup with overhead expenses. These expenses include delivery, paperwork, and insurance. This explanation may make sense and sound reasonable. However, this is merely an attempt by the contractor to justify the profit margins and to get you to agree that their markups are fair.

Once you see the actual invoice on a product, you are expected to admit the price is rational. While the markup on the main unit is fair, they can fleece you with little items. The majority of contractors will not be trying to take advantage of you. Only a few will resort to these unsavory sales tactics. They put your suspicions to rest with the big-ticket items and empty your pockets with the accessories. Most homeowners stop asking questions after seeing the actual invoice on the most expensive item. This is where they make their big mistake. Don't accept evidence of one or two items as proof. You must require a detailed breakdown of all labor and materials costs. This is the mark of a professional.

I have priced my material 20% below my competitors and still made more money than they did. This was possible because of aggressive shopping. A savings of 20% on materials amounts to major money. If you find a discount supplier, you could save 30% on the total cost of your job. On a $20,000 job, this is a savings of $6000.

If you find a contractor with inflated material prices, offer to supply the material yourself. Be prepared for a battle. Many contractors will tell you that they don't work with materials that they don't supply. Some of their reasons have merit. Frequently, general contractors make mistakes ordering materials for their specialized subcontractors. These mistakes can cost the subcontractor time and money. When a contractor sends a full crew to a job, they are expected to work. If you make a mistake with the material acquisition, the crews might not be able to complete their work. The same is true if the supplier delivers either incorrect or damaged material. These situations are disappointing to you and devastating to the subcontractor. This type of problem occurs often enough to make experienced contractors apprehensive.

When they hit you with this objection, alleviate their fears. Tell the contractor that you will pay extra for any time lost due to your failure to have the correct materials on the job. When you make this offer, be prepared to volley back and forth for control. You have just agreed to put a special clause in the contract for the protection of the subcontractor; don't make this agreement completely one-sided in favor of the contractor. The sub may request to be compensated at an hourly rate for all lost time. If so, this rate should be reasonable and have an established, maximum daily limit.

They might try to require a daily penalty for every mishap you make. While you can understand the subcontractors' need to protect their income from your inexperience with their trade, you must remain in control at all times. The contract provisions should not include excessive penalties or compensation on your part. After all, if the shoe was on the other foot, would the contractor agree to pay you for every day a material delivery was delayed? Do not create a situation in which a contractor looks for reasons why his crews cannot work. Keep the contractor motivated to complete the job, rather than giving him an opportunity to abuse your bank account.

You can protect yourself by scheduling material deliveries to arrive two days before they will be needed. Agree to pay the contractor a delay fee only if you are unable to give him or her 24 hours notice of a scheduling change. With this much time, the subcontractor can change his or her schedule and not lose money from lack of work the next day. You want to propose a fair agreement, but you must also be fair to yourself and your customer. If the contractor still balks at your offer, you have exposed a greedy contractor. This subcontractor is either trying to hide excessive profit in material prices or wants to milk penalty fees out of you. You might reach a standoff with no satisfactory solution. If the contractor refuses to price the job based on installing your materials, find another contractor.

When subcontractors are working on contract prices, they can't afford lost time. The quicker the job is finished, the more money they make. If you supply the material, they don't have control of their job production time. Your offer to compensate for any lost time removes the contractor's risk of loss. Any continued resistance from the contractor indicates trouble. No reputable contractor will refuse to use your materials under the proper conditions. Conversely, be suspicious of contractors who insist that you supply all the materials. These may be remodeling bandits, setting you up to steal your materials and disappear into another state. Stick to your guns and keep the contractor leveraged into the job. Never pay retail prices for materials, and be sure to cover all the bases.

Getting contractors to lower their prices is difficult. Contractors can be very independent and stubborn. If you try to supply your own materials, some contractors won't do your work. They want the extra profit from material markups. If the contractor you choose is a small operator, he or she might appreciate you supplying the material. The subcontractor will not have to tie up money in materials and won't have to worry about getting paid on time for the materials. Supplying your own material is a great way to cut costs, if you can coordinate punctual, accurate deliveries.

Labor rates

Negotiating for lower labor rates is the hardest part of the bidding process. Good people won't work cheap, because they don't need to. There is a shortage of quality contractors. Superior tradespeople know they are in demand. These contractors know they can maintain their prices and still stay busy. In most cases, it is possible to shave up to 7% off the labor quotes without sacrificing the best contractors. Most good remodelers factor in at least this much to allow for problems.

If this buffer amount is the pivotal point, the contractor may forfeit it to secure the job. If one contractor refuses to lower his or her prices, chances are, you have found a good contractor. These expert tradespeople rarely take a job with the intent of breaking even or losing money. Keep in mind, contractors have overhead expenses and need a fair wage to survive.

Labor is different from material. It doesn't carry the same kind of profit latitude. Material prices are easy to negotiate. A supplier buys a sink for a fixed price and sells it for a profit. Labor doesn't work that way. A contractor can never be absolutely sure of the labor cost to do a job. He or she can't look in a catalog and determine the exact cost. All he or she can do is draw on experience to estimate the total labor needed for the project. With remodeling, this guesswork is especially difficult. How can you calculate the exact time required to replace kitchen cabinets? Determining the amount of time needed to do many types of remodeling work is difficult, to say the least.

Also, there is no way to know what will be found when wall coverings are removed. Suppose floor joists are rotted? Will the existing conditions allow for a satisfactory finish, without unplanned, additional work? Warped walls or floor joists require additional preparation before the finished products can be applied. On one remodeling job, we opened the wall to do a simple sink installation and discovered a swarm of bees. Working in a bee-keeper's suit slows your work down quite a bit! A seasoned contractor will have some money loaded into the quote to allow for these unforeseen problems. You can extract this money from the bid and enjoy the savings. How can you coerce the contractor to eliminate this buffer zone and drop the extra money figured into the price? You can offer guarantees and make your contract contingent on certain circumstances. This technique can save you money and put the contractor at ease. When a reputable remodeler pads a bid, it is to protect against unknown conditions. You can act as an insurance company and play the odds. How often will kitchen floor joists be rotted? Normally, there will be evidence to suggest a problem with the floor structure. The floor will slope, the floor coverings will be curled up, or the baseboard trim will be discolored. As a professional contractor, you should know how to look for these warning signs.

In the remodeling game, the odds are in the favor of an informed general contractor. Learn as much as you can about all the various trades. This is a strategic, mental battle, like chess. When a subcontractor has given you his best price, make your first move. Ask the contractor what he or she can do to reduce the price. The contractor will probably claim that he or she cannot go any lower on the price. Ask if an allowance for unforeseen problems has been included. If the contractor says he or she doesn't allow extras for problems, find a new contractor. This one is either inexperienced or lying to you. When the contractor admits to an extra cushion in the bid, make your next move. Explain that you understand the need to allow for unexpected problems. Offer to remove this risk from the contract by inserting a clause regarding existing conditions. The clause will protect the subcontractor from the unexpected.

Removing these risks from the subcontractor entitles you to a lower price. There is jeopardy involved in an offer of this nature. You are responsible for all costs incurred to correct existing problems. Assess the situation carefully before offering such a proposition. Be aware of the potential costs you might be responsible for. Request a lower price to compensate you for assuming the risks. If the contractor only has to be responsible for known conditions, he or she can afford to do the job for less. Checkmate, you win. If you are lucky, you will save money. If problems occur, you can use your savings to solve them. Weigh your savings against your risks before approaching the contractor with this offer.

You can try to lower a subcontractor's price by comparing the price to other subcontractors. In slow economic times this may be an effective tool. In strong economic times, you lose this leverage against the remodelers. Even in a poor economy, good remodelers are in demand. Slow economic conditions force people to remodel because they can't afford to buy or sell. These factors make it tough to get a reduced price from remodelers; good remodeler's rates are usually firm. If you can get any discount, you've done a good job.

Concentrate your savings efforts on materials. When you are shopping for specific brands and model numbers, it is easy to recognize a good deal. If the two products are identical and delivery is available, the lowest bidder should win. You don't have to use judgment in evaluating the differences in identical materials—there aren't any. With contractors, you cannot be so sure of your decisions. Don't bargain yourself into a bad deal.

Your goal is to obtain prices that are competitive and realistic. This requires detective work, determination, and the ability to gain the upper hand. Once you sit down at the bargaining table, judge the circumstances and play all of your hole cards. Increased savings is your reward for mastering the challenging game of negotiations.

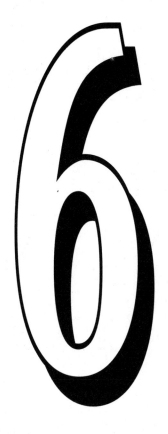

Quick decisions

Chapter 6

REMODELING involves working with unknown conditions. When you open up a wall, you never know what you will find. I have discovered old money, wild animals, snakes, termite damage, and a host of other surprises. Existing conditions can wreak havoc on the best remodeling plans. These unexpected complications dictate changes in strategy. Some of these problems will require on-the-spot decisions either to save time or rectify an emergency. Remodeling crews are expensive. You can't afford to pay them to stand around for very long.

General contractors are often responsible for on-the-spot decisions. There are, however, many occasions when customers should be consulted prior to making a quick decision. Having a problem with a material shipment is something that you, the general contractor, must deal with. However, if you find bats in the attic of a home as you attempt to install a skylight, your customer will have to make a decision on how to proceed. Working with your customers to resolve unexpected problems is usually the best course of action when these situations arise.

If your carpenters come to you with an unexpected problem, such as rotted floor joists under a kitchen floor, you should talk to your customer before making a decision. The joists will have to be replaced. Your chances of getting paid for such work depends on the contract you have and the basic personality of your customer. Many homeowners will pay extra to have a hidden, but legitimate problem, corrected. Some property owners may, however, stick to the letter of their contract and make you absorb the additional cost. This alone is cause for including provisions in your contract for hidden expenses.

This example is not unusual. Kitchens sinks sometimes leak. Such a leak can rot flooring and floor joists. This type of structural damage can go unnoticed for years. Typically, it is only the subfloor that has been heavily damaged. If this is the case, you should consider yourself lucky. The cost of replacing the subflooring is minimal compared to many problems that could arise in the course of a remodeling job.

Subcontractors may come to you with unanticipated complications involving their work. Depending upon your contractual arrangements, hidden trouble affecting subcontractors may have to be paid out of your profits. Maybe your customer will assume responsibility for the cost. Perhaps you have subcontractors who value your business and who are willing to invest a little extra time, at no cost to you, in order to keep you happy and continue working with you.

If a subcontractor comes to you with a dilemma that will result in additional costs, what should you do? The first thing you need is information. What are the details of the work needed? Can you determine on your own if the problem being pointed out to you is real? A crafty subcontractor could be trying to slip some extra work past you that doesn't need to be done. If a lot of money is involved and you are unable to assess the true need for the extra work, you should consider having another professional in the trade take a look at the problem. Even if you have to pay for a professional opinion, you may be better off in the long run.

Proper planning eliminates most on-the-spot decisions. Many of the problems that catch you off guard are a result of improper planning. Think your project through completely before starting the work. Ask the subcontractors what type of problems they might expect. Experienced remodelers have a good idea of what to expect from a job. They can be of great help to you in the planning stage. If you address potential problems before they happen, you will lower your stress level during the job. Even with the best planning, unexpected incidents occur. Knowing how to deal with these problems is important. Quick decisions can turn into mistakes and disappointments. There are very few problems that require an immediate answer. Avoid deciding on a solution without reflecting on the problem.

Subcontractors will often want you to decide quickly. They don't want to pay their workers to stand around waiting for your answer. Remember, these subcontractors are working for you. Maintain your power position, and don't let them tell you what to do. Allow the subcontractors to make suggestions, but don't automatically accept their recommendations. The decision to accept their ideas, without thought, can be very expensive. If you are paying for it, contractors will take the path of least resistance, regardless of cost. Don't hesitate to get additional opinions on decisions requiring major money. You could become a victim of a greedy subcontractor. Stay in control. It's your job and your money, and you should make your own informed decisions.

Common problems

You are likely to have to make many snap decisions about problems that you would not even have imagined could arise. However, we are going to concentrate on some frequent problems. If your job comes to completion without any unexpected problems, it would probably be the first job to do so. Plan to encounter some obstacles during the course of a job. The following problems are examples of some of the most common occurrences. They will give you an idea of what to expect.

Unkept promises

The most common problem in remodeling is unkept promises. These can be promises made by subcontractors or suppliers. Remodeling is a business that revolves around accurate scheduling. When your work can not be completed as scheduled, you have several problems. An unkept commitment affects everybody. What happens when your electrician doesn't show up to rough-in the electrical work? The first effect is that your electrical work will not be completed on time. Your need to reschedule all the other subcontractors is the ripple effect. You will have to notify the insulation contractor of the delay. The drywall contractor will have to be postponed, and the painter will have to be rescheduled. The list continues. One subcontractor can ruin your entire job schedule.

A strong contract helps alleviate this problem. The subcontractor might not show up for his or her scheduled work, but you will have recourse. If your contract is worded properly, you have the ability to penalize him or her financially. This threat will keep the job rolling. If it doesn't, exercise your contractual right to bring in a replacement subcontractor. Going over this information with each subcontractor before the job begins shows them the seriousness of your intentions. Let them know that time is crucial and that you can't afford downtime. Be cordial, but firm. Don't give in on this issue.

Suppliers are harder to control. They can be undependable and can bring your job to a dead stop. The hardest-working contractor can't operate without materials. Many times you will be promised delivery dates that come and go with no material. This is a constant problem. When your remodeling crews can't work, they will go to another job where they can. After all, they must work to make money to feed their families. You can't expect them to wait indefinitely for missing material. Once the contractors leave your job, you will have difficulty getting them back.

You have to retain control over suppliers the same way you do with contractors. When you place a material order, write the name of the individual taking the order in a material log. Record the date and time that you ordered the material and the delivery date you were promised. Be sure to call back the next day and ask the manager of the store to confirm your delivery date. Make written notes of this confirmation and get the manager's name. If delivery day comes and the material doesn't, go to see the manager. Go in person and take your log with you. Having notes of your conversations can be very impressive when you have to face a supplier regarding a delinquent order.

Supplier-related problems cause the most trouble during remodeling. A special order that wasn't requested properly could cost you six weeks in time. When completing your material order log, request order numbers. All special orders will have some type of order or reference number. These numbers are your proof that the order was placed.

It is important to have materials delivered before you need them. This cushion gives you time to check the order before it's required. If something is missing from the order, you have time to react before the job is interrupted. Plan ahead, and check all orders closely. Compare the material order to the delivery ticket and check for back orders. If items are in boxes or crates, inspect them for damage. You don't want to wait until the plumber is ready to install a new sink to find out it is defective.

Animals

On-the-job problems happen. Hidden, existing problems are likely to be present. Animals can cause some of the worst, and most unexpected, problems. Over the years, I've worked around animals many times. The pets of your customers are potential problems. You need to make arrangements to allow workers to come to and leave the job site freely. Do not ask subcontractors to take on the added responsibility of keeping a pet in the house. Have the homeowners provide any necessary protection to you and your workers from pets. A lovable canine companion that would never hurt a flea may become confused or frightened by strangers invading its home. I have seen placid puppies become raging balls of claws and teeth.

The presence of wild animals is always an unwelcome surprise. Right now, I'm working on a house inhabited by raccoons. These native inhabitants can create some interesting remodeling problems. Once, when I was working on a house in the mountains, strange events started happening. The job had progressed to the finished drywall stage. The drywall was hung and coated with the first coat of drywall compound. The next day, there were holes in the walls. The first hole was around the water supply pipe to the toilet. We thought the plumber had made a mistake and enlarged the hole to correct a problem. When confronted, the plumber denied knowing anything about the saucer-sized hole. We found the next hole in the ceiling of a closet. Later that day, I was downstairs with the painter when we heard a loud banging upstairs. Upon investigation, we were confronted by an angry Norway rat. It was the size of a rabbit. Our construction had disturbed the rat's domicile, and it was claiming homestead rights in the customer's house. This problem required a professional exterminator.

It isn't too unusual to find wild creatures living in, and around, rural homes. I've run into rattlesnakes, bats, and skunks. Is there anyway to prepare for these unwanted neighbors? You might find signs of wild animals when you inspect a property during the bidding phase. Bats are not difficult to detect, because they leave quite a mess. Animals that burrow under homes may be found during an inspection. I once came face-to-face with a skunk family while crawling under a house to check existing conditions. Some animals can be removed without harming them. However, others require more serious measures. You have to deal with each case independently.

Termites

Rotted lumber and termite damage are more common problems that might alter your remodeling plans fast. If you were planning to attach to existing wood and find it's rotted, you have to make new arrangements. In the course of replacing a window, you might discover decayed structural members. If the extent of this type of damage is beyond the work area of the window opening, a lot of additional expense might be incurred. These are very serious problems. You need time to decide what course of action to take.

When the insulating contractor comes out of your customers' attic with bad news, sit down. Insulators can be the first people to have been in the attic for years. They could come down with discouraging information about small piles of sawdust in the attic. These sawdust piles indicate wood-boring insects. These little creatures can do more damage to wood than a beaver can. The bugs are present in the wood when the house is built and become active under the right conditions. They eat through rafters and ceiling joists, weakening the roof structure. This situation calls for prompt, serious action.

The removal of these wood-infesting insects can be very expensive. If your customer is a victim of these brutal bugs, have the homeowner contact pest control companies. You should suggest that they call several companies and request a damage report and extermination estimate. These services are usually performed at no cost to your customer. Some wood-eaters can be stopped by treating the wood; others require a total fumigation of the house.

Taking your time

Quick decisions are dangerous. If you're busy selling prospects on a new job when one of your subcontractors calls with a problem, you aren't in the best position to make a good decision. If the situation has to be dealt with immediately, consider the following option. Get all the information from the subcontractor and agree to call back in 15 minutes. Fifteen minutes isn't a lot of time, but it will allow you the opportunity to think. Any remodeling problem can wait a few minutes for a solution. Take a coffee break and review the circumstances. Decide if you should go to the job and see the problem for yourself. Many modest problems can be solved on short notice over the telephone. Some, however, warrant a personal inspection and even a conference with the homeowner.

If, during a job, your plumber calls because the opening for the new dishwasher is too small, you can make a fairly quick decision. The opening will have to be enlarged. Determining the best way to make the hole larger may take more thought. More complex problems, however, take time to evaluate and determine the alternative solutions. There could be a rudimentary solution the subcontractor has overlooked. Use your own judgment but avoid immediate decisions whenever possible. When problems arise, don't panic. Allow enough time to calm down before making a decision.

If a problem is expensive or complicated and doesn't have to be resolved immediately, wait until the next day to make your decision. Sometimes the first reaction to a problem is one of anger. You will have to work through this anger before you can make a good decision. Sometimes you need a day or to get through these emotions. If the problem is big enough, allow yourself the necessary time to calm down.

Another common reaction to threatening problems is one of fear. These emotions normally arise due to the way a subcontractor presents the problem. Keep in mind that some subcontractors try to sell work using scare tactics. They hope you will decide immediately to correct the deficiency without shopping for prices. This approach is effective on many homeowners. However, a professional contractor should know better than to fall for this old trick. When someone feels there is impending danger, they will act quickly and poorly. This is the reason behind subcontractors' scare tactics. You need to take your time, assess each problem, and search for sensible solutions.

If you are presented with a problem involving possible danger, you need to act quickly by calling the local codes office to request an emergency inspection. Before you actually call the codes office, apprise the subcontractor of your plans to do so. The urgency of the repair may dissipate quickly. If the contractor is exaggerating, he will probably change his opinion when he learns that a code officer will be coming in response to his claim. If the contractor sticks to his story, you probably do have a real problem.

Wait for the code officer to arrive before making a decision. He or she will be able to advise you on the nature of the problem and the extent of repairs needed. Once you know what needs to be done, start getting some quotes on the work. You are not obligated to allow the existing contractor to do the work. Realistically, he or she should give you the best price, but he or she might try to take advantage of your working relationship. Get other bids before awarding an expensive, unplanned job to the existing subcontractor. This subcontractor won your original job with good prices and is already working on the job. Unless he or she is trying to take advantage of you, his or her prices should be competitive. If his or his price is competitive or just a little higher, let this subcontractor do the job. You already know something about the person and his or her work. This is an advantage over dealing with unknown contractors.

Common sense will get you through most on-the-spot decisions. The first rule is to try to avoid making rash decisions. The second rule requires that you be fully informed. The third rule is to shop for prices for an expensive decision. The fourth rule is to get everything in writing. If the existing contractor will be doing the work, use a change order. If a new contractor will be doing the work, complete a contract for the work. Follow these rules and most of your decisions will be good ones.

It is important that you don't leave your customers out of decisions that they are entitled to participate in. If you make a judgment call on your own, you're assuming all of the consequences. It's best to involve your customers in some of your decision-making process. Don't bring customers into situations that you, the general contractor, should control, but allow them to participate in any decision that is not a pure general-contractor call.

Rip-out of the existing kitchen

Chapter 7

RIPPING out the existing kitchen for a remodeling job can be as simple as removing wallpaper and cabinet fronts or as complicated as stripping the kitchen to bare studs and subflooring. The extent of the work required depends on the goal of the remodeling effort. Cosmetic makeovers don't require a lot of complicated rip-out work. Kitchen expansions and jobs where all kitchen components are replaced, however, are another story. Regardless of your intentions, this chapter shows you how to take an existing kitchen apart, piece by piece, so that it can be put back together again as a new kitchen.

Preparations

Preparing for a rip-out properly can make the work go faster and smoother. Very little has to be done before you can start demolition work in a kitchen. However, depending upon the extent to which you will be tearing into the space, some aspects of the job should be worked out beforehand. For example, what will your plan of attack be? How will you handle the debris? Is dust going to infiltrate the rest of your customer's home? If you answer these questions before they become a problem, you can enjoy the job more.

Plans

Planning your work ahead of time is always a good idea. If you start ripping out a kitchen in random fashion, you might have it dawn on you around suppertime that your customer no longer has a range or a kitchen sink. If you are doing a complete rip-out, you will, of course, have to remove appliances, cabinets, and sinks. You can, however, plan the removal of these items to minimize your customer's time without kitchen conveniences. Let me give you an example of what I'm talking about.

Let's say you decide to start demolition work on a Friday. You're doing the work yourself with the help of a new employee who is just learning the business. For the sake of this example, we will assume your customer lives in a nice neighborhood where the lawns are well kept and where they are required to keep the exterior of their home and grounds in an attractive manner. You and your helper are feverishly ripping out everything in sight on Friday. By the end of the day, you realize you have a huge pile of trash and debris outside the kitchen door. What will your customer say about having a pile of trash sitting around over the weekend? What will the neighbors say? You've just created quite a problem for yourself.

In any major rip-out, a lot of debris will have to be hauled off to the dump or recycling center. Even if you don't work in neighborhoods where you are prohibited from creating trash piles, you have to dispose of the debris at some point. Why complete this process twice? If you arrange for an on-site trash dispenser you can simply toss the old materials into the container and be done with them. A word of caution: You might need more than one disposal unit. With new landfill requirements, it might be necessary to have all wood in one container, all drywall in another container, and so on. A quick phone call to companies that provide temporary container services should answer your questions on cost and availability of these containers.

Now, let's look at what you and your helper ripped out. You took out the sink and the countertop. How is your customer going to cook supper and wash dishes? Maybe you should have started with the wall cabinets and other items that would not have left your customer with a dysfunctional kitchen so soon. Plan to take the room apart in a way that will keep it in working condition for as long as possible.

As you tore down the old drywall, you probably never thought about all the dust that was settling throughout the remainder of the home. The carpet in the rest of the house might look as though it has suffered from a light snow flurry. This problem can be avoided by hanging plastic over the openings that connect the work area with the rest of the house.

Now, let's consider the big question. After a hard day of work, you have the majority of the kitchen torn apart. When will new cabinets and counters be delivered? How long will your customer have to eat out at fast-food places? The delivery time on cabinets can run into months. Don't rip out an existing kitchen too soon. Line up replacement materials and have them available before you disable your customer's kitchen.

Are you starting to see how a little advance planning can make your life easier? Before you tear into a kitchen, spend some time drafting a production schedule. The schedule should cover new work needed to put the kitchen back into shape, as well as the rip-out work.

Ceilings

Assuming that all of your preparation work is complete, you can start a kitchen makeover with the ceiling. In many remodeling jobs the kitchen ceiling is not removed. Often the ceilings are cleaned, sealed, and painted or textured. There are, however, times when rustic beams are added, skylights are cut in, insulation is installed, or the old ceiling is simply torn out. Since a ceiling is not needed for kitchen duties, the ceiling is a good place to start your work.

If you are going to remove an existing ceiling that has attic space above it, you should check the attic before you start removing the ceiling. You might find that bees, bats, squirrels, or other critters have taken up residency in the attic. You don't want to drop a section of ceiling and have a swarm of bees or bats fly into your face.

Existing electrical wires are another consideration you must keep in mind when tearing out a ceiling. If you start cutting blindly with a saw, you might have a shocking experience. Whenever I have to open a wall or ceiling, I start with a hammer. By knocking a hole in the ceiling with a hammer, you won't zap yourself on a hot wire. Once the hole is open, you can inspect the area and cut out the remainder of the ceiling safely.

Eye protection should be worn for most phases of a rip-out. This is especially true when working on areas over your head, such as a ceiling. Safety glasses are cheap. Injuries to your eyes are a high price to pay. I know goggles fog up and safety glasses can be a bother, but you must protect your eyes at all times.

Cabinets and countertops

Once the ceiling is taken care of, you can concentrate on the cabinets. Start with the wall cabinets, since they will have the least impact on the functional use of your customer's kitchen. In addition to the screws that hold the cabinets to the wall, there are usually other screws that connect individual cabinets to each other. All of these screws can be removed with a screwdriver, but an electric screw gun makes the work both faster and easier.

Keep in mind that as you remove the screws the cabinets are going to become loose and could fall. If you have enough help to take the cabinets down in large sections, you should prop the cabinets up while the screws are being removed. The prop sticks (which can be scrap studs) will support the cabinets until you and your helpers are ready to remove them. If you are working alone or with just one helper, you should remove the screws that hold the cabinets together before you remove the screws that hold the cabinets to the wall. This will allow you to take the cabinets down one module at a time.

After the wall cabinets are down, you can turn your attention to the base cabinets and counters. Avoid disturbing the sink base until the last minute. Most sink-base cabinets are about 5 feet long. If you want to keep the kitchen up and running for as long as possible, cut the countertop on both sides of the sink base. This allows you to remove the counters and the base storage cabinets without disabling the kitchen sink.

Most countertops are held in place with screws. The screws can be accessed from the base cabinets. When you look inside the cabinets, you should see screws at the corners of the cabinets that protrude into the counter. Remember to wear eye protection when you remove these screws. Once you have removed the screws, the counter should simply lift off. You might, however, have to cut through some caulking before the counter can be removed. If the counter was caulked where its edge meets the wall, use a sharp knife to cut along the seam of caulking if necessary.

After you have removed the countertop, you can disassemble the base cabinets and remove them. Like the wall cabinets, the base cabinets will probably be attached to each other with screws. By now, you will really be making progress, and your customer will still have appliances and a sink to work with.

Trim

Trim work is very easy to remove. A pry bar and a hammer will remove any standard trim. As long as you are not planning to use the existing trim when you put the kitchen back together, it is quick and easy to rip it out. If you are trying to salvage the trim, you will have to work slowly, moving the pry bar a little at a time to prevent the trim from snapping as it is taken off.

Windows

Windows are often replaced during remodeling efforts. Although window units are easy to remove, you should be aware that there may be some damage to the exterior siding on the home. A lot of rookie remodelers overlook this exterior damage only to discover the problem after the units are removed. This exterior damage will not create any real problem if you are replacing the existing window with a larger unit. Since the larger window will require you to cut away some of the exterior siding to make a larger hole, the damage to the existing edges of the siding will not be a problem.

The first step in taking out a window unit is the removal of the window trim. Use a hammer and a pry bar for this part of the work. Once the trim is off, you will be able to see the framework of the window. There will be nails or screws that hold the window frame into the opening. These nails can be removed with a nail puller. Once the inside and outside trim is removed, you can lift the entire window unit out of the wall. If you are not ready to replace the window immediately, you can use a piece of plywood to block the window opening. However, it is wise to have a replacement window on the job before you remove an existing window unit.

Doors

If you have any doors to remove, the process will be similar to that used with windows. To expose the framework, you must remove the trim from both sides of the door. Then you can pull the nails from the framework and lift the door frame out of the opening.

Walls

When you are ready to work with walls, you have to assess your situation carefully. It is easy to seal and paint the existing walls. However, if you want to strip the room down to bare studs, use a hammer to open up wall cavities. Inspect for any electrical wiring, heat ducts, or plumbing that may be in the path of a saw, and then continue with your demolition work.

If your plans call for the removal of existing walls, you must make sure that the walls are not load-bearing. In many cases the walls will be simple partitions with no structural significance, but you don't want to yank out a wall and cause a roof cave in on you. With experience, a load-bearing wall is easy to spot. However, inexperienced remodelers must be very careful in deciding what walls to eliminate. If there is any chance that a wall is load-bearing, you must have adequate plans to maintain roof support during the wall removal and remodeling.

Plumbing

All modern kitchens have plumbing in them. If you're doing a full-scale remodeling job, some of the plumbing will have to be disconnected and replaced. You can bet that you will have to redo plumbing work for the kitchen sink. There might also be a garbage disposer, a dishwasher, or some other plumbing fixture or appliance.

Plumbing work intimidates a lot of people. The removal of a kitchen sink, dishwasher, or garbage disposer is work almost anyone with basic mechanical skills can handle. Chapter 8 is dedicated to the subject of plumbing. Therefore rather than risk redundancy, I'll let you refer to that chapter for your plumbing advice.

Electrical work

Electrical work can be very dangerous. If you don't know what you are doing with wiring, you can be seriously injured. I'm not a licensed electrician, and I don't proclaim to be an expert on electrical wiring. Nevertheless, I have done some electrical work both on new construction and remodeling. I should clarify that the work that I have done has been on properties that I owned. I would never attempt electrical work for customers, since I am not a licensed electrician. As a general contractor, it is my job to know enough about the electrical code and good working practices to make sure my subcontractors are doing a good job. Of course, after spending a long career in the field around electricians, I've picked up a lot of on-the-job experience. Just as plumbing concerns have their own chapter, so do electrical considerations. Refer to Chapter 9 for electrical questions.

Heating and air-conditioning

Typically, there isn't much heating and air-conditioning work involved in the remodeling of a kitchen. Unless you are adding space to the kitchen, you probably will not have to deal with the heating and air-conditioning (HVAC) equipment. There are, however, some times when the HVAC system requires alteration, and Chapter 10 addresses these issues.

Flooring

Flooring falls into two main categories, rough flooring and finish flooring. It is likely you will work with both types if you are doing a complete remodeling job. How you remove existing kitchen floors depends largely on the type of flooring you are working with.

Chapter 11 goes into great detail on how to handle new flooring, but I'll look at the removal of existing flooring right here.

Sheet vinyl

Sheet-vinyl flooring is very common in modern kitchens. This is flooring that comes in continuous rolls and is installed in large sections. In fact, it is not uncommon for the finished floor to be made from a single sheet of vinyl. This type of flooring can sometimes be left in place, and new flooring can be installed on top of it. It is usually better, however, to remove the existing vinyl before installing a new finish flooring. I should mention here that some types of older flooring contain asbestos, and the removal of these products can be harmful to your health. If you run across an asbestos-type flooring, you should contact competent professionals to perform the removal. Most jurisdictions require specialized training and licenses for contractors who work with asbestos.

Assuming that you are dealing with a non-asbestos floor, removal is usually pretty simple. Once the base cabinets are removed, you should have access to edges of the flooring. You will probably have to remove threshold strips at doorways in order to gain access to the edges of the flooring in those locations. If you're lucky, the flooring will be loose and will pull off of the subflooring without much effort. If, however, you find that the material is stuck to the subflooring, you may have to resort to heating it and removing it with a floor scraper.

If you must heat the floor to remove it, avoid putting an open flame or too much heat in close proximity to the flooring. Special heat guns are available that make the work easy and relatively safe. Heat guns can be rented from tool rental centers. If you use a torch with a flame spreader, be careful not to bring the heat into direct contact with the flooring. I recommend that you avoid the use of open flames during flooring work. Your goal is to warm the flooring, not to burn it.

Individual vinyl tiles

Individual vinyl tiles can be removed in a way similar to the method just described for sheet vinyl. However, individual tiles are not linked together, so they will not come out in one large piece. Each tile will have to be removed individually. A floor scraper and a heat gun make this job much easier. As you move the heat gun over the tiles, they will loosen to a point where the scraper can be used to lift them easily.

Ceramic tiles

Ceramic floor tiles can be removed quickly with a hammer. When the tiles are hit with the hammer, they will shatter and break. This method makes for a quick removal of ceramic tiles, but the procedure does create some safety hazards. Flying pieces of tile can embed in your skin or eyes. If you use this method, wear eye protection, gloves, long pants, and a shirt with long sleeves.

An alternative method of removing ceramic tiles is available, but the process takes much longer. You can remove the tiles one at a time with a pry bar and a hammer. By sliding the bar under the tiles and popping them up, you are only working with an individual section of the flooring at any one time. This reduces the risk of flying pieces, but you should still observe good safety procedures during the course of the job.

Wood floors

There is rarely a need to remove a wood floor from a kitchen. However, if you need to remove wood flooring, the job can be accomplished with just a few tools. A saw will be needed. Reciprocating or circular saws are preferable. In addition to the saw, you will need a pry bar, a nail puller, and a hammer.

Before you begin cutting out sections of a wood floor, check beneath the floor for any hidden wires. Electrical wiring shouldn't be located close enough to the flooring to cause any problem, but never take this for granted. Always check for plumbing, wiring, or heating systems that may be close enough to the floor to cause an injury to yourself or another contractor or damage to anything other than the flooring

Once you have established that a clear path exists for your saw, cut out sections of the flooring. Make sure you are cutting between and not through floor joists. As you make your cuts, the pry bar can be used to lift the sections of flooring out. Be aware, some sections may fall down on their own, so take the proper precautions if there is anything under the floor that you don't want sections to fall on.

Plumbing points
to ponder

Chapter 8

THIS chapter is going to give you all sorts of plumbing points to ponder. It starts with the disconnection and removal of existing plumbing and takes you all the way through the remodeling process to the point of installation of new plumbing. With a few tools, some basic skills, and some concentration, you will learn how to be your own plumber. I should mention, however, that the installation of new fixtures normally requires a plumbing permit. To obtain a plumbing permit, most jurisdictions require the permit holder to be either a master plumber or the owner-occupant of the property where work is being done.

Local code requirements vary. You should check with your local code enforcement office before attempting to install any new plumbing. Depending upon where you are working, you may be allowed to make simple installations without a permit, but don't just assume that you can. When plumbing permits are required, seek the services of a licensed plumber. In any event, this chapter provides you with a wealth of knowledge that can be used to perform plumbing tasks or to simply supervise the work being done by others.

The plumbing work involved with kitchen remodeling might not seem very extensive. There are only a few pipes with which you need to work. Therefore, unless you are relocating fixtures, the work appears to be simple. However, there are times when the job is anything but simple. Many times completing a little more than necessary will pay big dividends in the future. Let me expand on this for a moment.

The minimum plumbing requirements for the remodeling of a kitchen are not beyond the abilities of most people who possess some skill level in working with their hands. There are, however, some traps and pitfalls that force even licensed plumbers to wish they had followed a different path in their jobs. Take a moment to look over the case history that I'm about to share with you, and you will see what I mean.

When I was a young contractor, galvanized steel pipe was often used as kitchen drains. As galvanized pipe ages, it tends to rust on the inside. The rust develops rough edges that snag grease, bits of food, and other items as they go down the drain. After a number of years, it is not uncommon for the inside of a galvanized kitchen drain to become restricted to a point that water cannot flow through it. It is easy to diagnose the cause of a complete blockage, since drainage backs up into the sink. However, if the pipe is only partially blocked, the evidence is not so clear. Any blockage can cause problems during remodeling.

I remember one of my earliest kitchen remodeling jobs. The plumber on the job was to remove the existing plumbing and install new plumbing. This particular job had a galvanized drain. When we were removing the old plumbing, we had an opportunity to replace all of the galvanized pipe with modern plastic pipe. However, we didn't replace the pipes, because there was no obvious need to do so.

The old kitchen sink had worked properly. The new kitchen sink also worked well initially. But in less than a week after finishing the job, I got a call from the homeowner who said that the kitchen sink was stopped up. The plumber was sent back to the job to clear a stoppage in the kitchen drain. Then, a couple of weeks later, I got another phone call about the same problem. A pattern of stoppages developed, and the customer was unhappy.

When the plumber installed new fixtures, a garbage disposer was added to the system. The old sink had not been equipped with a food grinder. To make a long story short, the kitchen drain was partially blocked with rust and years of build-up. The remaining opening in the pipe was large enough to allow water to drain. However, the bits of food from the garbage disposer could not fit through the narrow opening in the pipe. Due to the old, short-turn, galvanized elbow fittings, it was impossible to scale the drain with a cutting head on an electric snake. A snake along with a spearhead could cut a hole through the stoppages, but in a few weeks the drain would plug up again. As a result, I had to cut into the customer's new wall in order to replace the old drainage pipe.

If I had asked the plumber to replace the galvanized pipe during the rough-in of the new plumbing, this problem would never have occurred. The cost of the replacement would have been minimal and there would have been no need to destroy a new wall. The customer would have been happy, and the plumbing company and I would not have lost nearly as much money on the job. By trying to save a few feet of pipe and less than an hour's worth of work, I caused a lot of trouble for everyone involved.

As we move through this chapter, I will give you my opinion on when you should go the extra mile during a plumbing job. It will be up to you to decide if you want to follow my recommendations on additional work, but the suggestions given will be the result of many years of mistakes and experience. Now, let's get down to business and discuss the removal of the old plumbing from a kitchen and installation of new plumbing and appliances.

Cutting off the water

Cutting off the water is usually the first step to be taken during the removal of existing plumbing. Most kitchen sinks have cut-off valves below them. These valves don't always work properly, so it pays to check them before you trust them. The valves can be turned off by rotating the handles in a clockwise motion. Turn the handles until you cannot turn them any further. When you have completed this step, turn on the kitchen faucet and see if there is any water pressure. If there isn't, the valves are working. When water flows out of the faucet with pressure, you can assume that the valves are defective and that you will have to find some other way of cutting off the water. Note that some water may come out of the faucet, without much pressure, as a result of the system draining. This type of water will stop flowing in a matter of minutes. If the water continues to flow, it is seeping past the valves.

The cut-off valves under a kitchen sink are convenient, but they may not be the answer to your remodeling needs. If you are planning to remove the base cabinet that holds the kitchen sink, you will most likely have to remove the valves in order to get the cabinet out. It is not uncommon, when the base cabinet is to be replaced, to cut the water pipes off and cap them. This requires cutting the water off at a more remote location such as the main water cut-off for the house.

If an existing kitchen is equipped with a dishwasher, you will also need to cut the water off to it. There are usually two ways to do this. An independent valve may be installed on the water line to the dishwasher, or a combination valve may be used to cut off the hot water to the kitchen sink and the dishwasher simultaneously. Trace the water pipe from the dishwasher to its valve and turn the handle clockwise until it stops. Turn the dishwasher on and demand water for it. If no water fills the appliance, the valve is working. Once you are sure that all of the water is turned off to the areas you will be working with, you can proceed with the rip-out.

Removing a kitchen sink

Removing a kitchen sink can be more difficult than it might appear. The difficulty is not so much a technical issue as it is a physical issue. Sometimes sinks are very stubborn, heavy, and awkward. As I give you directions for removing existing fixtures, I'm assuming that you will not be reusing them. If you are going to reuse your fixtures, read this complete section before taking any action. I will give advice on how to salvage the old plumbing later in this and other sections. The procedures for fast removal of fixtures are not always suitable for saving old fixtures.

Once you have the water cut off, you can begin to dismantle the plumbing system. Most kitchen sinks don't offer a lot of work space beneath them. In fact, I sometimes think that whoever designed the installation methods for plumbing must sit back and laugh at the thought of a plumber working on the system. Saying that the conditions are cramped is an understatement. To give yourself the best working conditions possible, you should remove the drainage fittings from the sink first. This will open up the cabinet space and give you a little more room to work.

When you look under a kitchen sink, you will see a piping arrangement that conveys waste water from the sink to the drainage system. This piping arrangement is normally made up of tubular sections, but it could be made with standard plumbing pipe. The drainage originates at the bottom of the basket strainer, or strainers, in the sink. If you look in this location, you should see a slip-nut connected to threads on the bottom of the basket strainer. Use a large pair of water-pump pliers to turn this nut in a counterclockwise motion. When the nut is loose, it will slip down onto the vertical section of the drain.

If the drainage system is connected with slip-nuts, take the system apart one nut at a time. When you're done, the only drainage left should be the trap. This drainage is where the trap connects to the pipe coming out of the wall or floor. The trap will contain a small quantity of water. If you are concerned about the water spilling, place a small pail or bucket under the trap while you are removing the plumbing.

If for some reason the piping under the sink is not put together with slip-nut connections, you can use a hack saw to cut the piping out. Some sinks are connected to solid copper drains. Others are drained through solid plastic pipe. Either of these materials can be cut with a hack saw. The basket strainers in the sink can be left alone. They will come out as part of the sink and be discarded.

The procedure for removing the trap depends on the type of trap in use. There may be a slip-nut connection that can be loosened to allow the trap to be pulled out. If not, you may have a trap ell that is threaded onto the drain pipe. Turning this type of trap counter-clockwise will remove it. If the trap is glued or soldered to the drain pipe, you can simply cut the pipe in order to remove the trap. Once the trap is removed, you will have better access to the water pipes.

To remove the water supplies from the sink, you must investigate the connections of the pipes to the cut-off valves. Some sinks are connected directly to the water pipes without the use of valves. In this case, you must either disconnect or cut. Cutting the pipes is often easier than disconnecting them, especially if you don't happen to have a basin wrench.Most supply tubes connect at the kitchen faucet and extend to a compression fitting on a cut-off valve. This is the easiest type of supply to remove. All you have to do (after you make sure the water is turned off) is turn the small compression nuts counterclockwise with an adjustable wrench. When the nuts are loose, the supply tubes can be pulled out of the valves, and the sink will be disconnected from the plumbing.

▲

Unless you are working in a very old house, the water supplies to the kitchen sink will be made of copper or polybutylene. Both of these materials are easy to cut. Copper is cut best with a specially designed roller-type cutter (Fig. 8-1), but it can be cut with a hack saw. Polybutylene (which is a gray, plastic-like pipe) can also be cut with a hack saw. Galvanized water pipes can be cut with a hacksaw, but the effort required will be much more than what is needed to cut copper. Remember that if you cut the pipe on the wrong side of the cut-off valve, you are going to create a flood (unless the main water supply to the house has been shut off).

Figure 8-1

Roller-type tubing cutter.

Disconnecting supply tubes where they enter cut-off valves or cutting water supplies is usually easier than trying to disconnect supply tubes from faucets. To loosen the nuts that connect supply tubes to faucets, you most definitely need a basin wrench. This wrench is designed specifically for the purpose of disconnecting faucets. It is possible, but difficult, to remove faucet nuts with an adjustable wrench. Fortunately, when a kitchen sink is going to be removed completely, there is no need to remove the faucet from the sink. The sink, faucet, and basket strainers can be removed as a single unit.

Removing a dishwasher

Removing a dishwasher does not require great skill, but, like a kitchen sink, the working conditions are not always the best. The drain from a dishwasher usually comes into the base cabinet where the kitchen sink is housed. At that point, the dishwasher drain will either connect to an airgap or directly to a part of the drainage system for the sink. The rubber hoses used to drain dishwashers can be cut with a knife or a hack saw. After you sever the drain hose, you can then disconnect the water supply.

To disconnect the water supply from a dishwasher, you must first remove the access panel from the front of the appliance. This panel is below the door of the dishwasher. You may need a nut driver to remove the screws that keep the panel in place.

Once you have the access panel out of the way, you should see the water line under the dishwasher. This line will be connected to a special type of elbow with either a compression nut or a flare nut. In either case, turn the nut counterclockwise to disengage the water line.

When all the plumbing connections are separated, open the door of the appliance. There will be a tab near the top on each side of the dishwasher. In these tabs, you should find screws that secure the dishwasher to the counter. After the removal of these screws, the dishwasher should simply pull out of its opening.

There are two main precautions that you should take when removing a dishwasher. First, the electrical connection for the appliance must be disconnected before the dishwasher can be removed completely. (You will learn about electrical work in the next chapter.) Second, if you are not planning to replace the existing kitchen floor, be careful not to cut or scratch it when you pull the appliance out. Dishwashers have a lot of sharp edges that can slice floors and fingers. Putting heavy cardboard on the floor as a protective covering is a good way to prevent damage to the flooring.

Removing a garbage disposer

Removing a garbage disposer requires the disconnection of both plumbing and electrical connections. You should refer to the next chapter for suggestions on the electrical work. To disconnect the plumbing from a disposer, you should first loosen the slip-nut that connects the disposer elbow to the drainage system.

Normally, in order to remove a disposer from the bottom of a sink, you need to turn the mounting ring counterclockwise. This can usually be done with your hands. However, if the ring is seized, you may have to tap it with a hammer. **WARNING:** When the ring is loose, the disposer will drop. Don't let it fall on you.

Putting it all back together

Now that you know how to take old plumbing out, let's see what's involved with putting it all back together again with new parts. I first discuss rough-in work that you may want to do during the remodeling stage. Then I get into the setting of fixtures and appliances.

Unless you are adding new plumbing fixtures or greatly relocating old fixtures, there is not much rough-in plumbing work required for a kitchen remodeling job. In most cases, the plumbing is capped off during the rip-out and left alone until new fixtures are installed. This makes the basic plumbing pretty easy to manage.

I told you earlier about my experience with galvanized kitchen drains. If a drain is made of steel pipe, I strongly suggest that you replace it with plastic pipe. When galvanized pipe is used as a kitchen drain, it usually only runs a short distance and terminates into a cast-iron drain. There should be no need to replace the cast-iron pipe.

The easiest method for replacing a galvanized drain involves cutting the pipe. This can be done with a metal-cutting blade in a reciprocating saw or a hack saw. Cut the pipe about 6 inches from where it enters the cast-iron drain. Use a pipe wrench to turn the short piece of pipe counterclockwise. The pipe should unscrew, leaving you with a female inlet where you will screw in a new, plastic adapter. If for some reason you can't get the old galvanized pipe to turn, you can convert to plastic with the use of a rubber coupling. The coupling slides over the galvanized pipe and is secured with a clamp. The new plastic drain enters the other end of the coupling and is held in place with a clamp. This is a fast, easy, inexpensive way to convert from steel pipe to plastic pipe.

Given the opportunity, you should also replace any old galvanized water pipes with some type of new piping. The old pipe will gradually rust and close to a point where, ultimately, little or no water will come through. It is also quite common for the threaded portions of galvanized pipe to rust away and leak where the screw joints are made. Converting from galvanized water pipes to modern piping materials is not difficult. However, you cannot use the rubber couplings described earlier with pressure pipes. Those couplings are intended for use on drain pipes, not water pipes.

When you are ready to replace galvanized water pipes, make sure the water is turned off. Trace the pipes to the point where they screw into a fitting. Cut the pipe, if necessary, and use a pipe wrench to turn the pipe counterclockwise. Once the steel pipe has been removed, you will have a female fitting that a male adapter, or some other type of pipe, will screw into. From that point, you can follow standard installation procedures for whichever type of modern material you choose.

Roughing-in drain pipes

Roughing-in drain pipes is not difficult. With today's plastic drainage pipes and fittings, plumbing is much easier than it was in the old days. There are two types of Schedule-40 plastic pipe that can be used, and either one of them will go together easily. Remember, most plumbing installations require a plumbing permit and the supervision of a master plumber.

ABS plastic pipe is black. PVC plastic pipe is white. When used for drainage and vent work, both should be rated as Schedule-40 pipe. Either of these pipes can be cut with a hack saw or a regular wood-cutting saw. After cutting the pipe, clean off any rough edges on the end of the pipe with a common pocket knife.

ABS and PVC pipe are put together with solvent-weld (glue) joints. It is important to use a glue that is specially designed for the type of pipe you are working with. In other words, don't use ABS glue on PVC pipe or PVC glue on ABS pipe. Before you make a joint, be sure that the surfaces that will receive glue are clean and dry. Dirty or wet pipes and fittings encourage leaks. Also, if you are using PVC pipe, you should use a cleaner and a primer on both the pipe and the fitting prior to applying any glue. The cleaner and primer are available where glue is sold and will be marked for use with PVC pipe.

Once the pipe and fittings are properly prepared, apply a liberal coating of glue. Insert the ends of the pipe into the fittings until they bottom out. When the ends of the pipe are seated, twist the pipe so that it turns about one-half of a full turn. This spreads the glue and allows for a more secure joint. If you see that you've made a mistake in a measurement or want the pipe out of the fitting for any reason, act quickly. The glue used with plastic pipe sets up fast, especially if you're using ABS pipe.

Roughing-in water pipes

When it comes to roughing-in water pipes, you have three common options for a piping material. You can use CPVC plastic pipe, copper tubing, or polybutylene tubing. Copper has long been the standard material for water pipes, but polybutylene is gaining ground quickly. CPVC never caught on with professional plumbers, but it is popular with homeowners who don't know how to solder. Since you have three options, let me explain a little about each type of material.

CPVC

CPVC pipe is often the first type of material amateur plumbers turn to for water pipes. The plastic pipe is easy to cut with any type of saw, glues together, is inexpensive, and appears to be easy to work with. These features give it an ideal appearance to inexperienced plumbers. However, CPVC is not as easy to work with as it seems.

The glue joints made with CPVC do not dry quickly. If a joint is made and moved before it has set up, the joint will leak. The procedure for putting CPVC together is about the same as I described earlier for PVC drainage pipe, but the slow-setting joints are a key difference. Professional plumbers cannot afford to wait between joints for the length of time required with CPVC. If you are willing to take your time between fitting joints together, CPVC is a suitable material choice. There is, however, one other major drawback to CPVC; it is very brittle. If CPVC is roughed-in and someone hits the stub-out with a cabinet or tool, the pipe is likely to snap right off. I avoid the use of CPVC whenever possible, but I also recognize its appeal to some do-it-yourselfers.

Copper tubing

Copper tubing and pipe is by far the most common water-pipe material in use today. It enjoys a long life, cuts well (with the proper cutters), and doesn't usually leak after being installed and tested. For amateurs, the only drawback to copper is the need for soldering skills. The thought of putting a torch inside a cabinet or trying to solder pipes that are holding residual water is more than a little intimidating for some people. While soldering is not an act easily accomplished with the first attempt, it is not a feat of magic. Learning to solder takes practice, but the skills can be mastered by almost anyone with patience and persistence.

Copper tubing and pipe can be cut with a hack saw, but a pair of roller-type copper cutters will do the job faster and produce a cleaner cut. The inside of all copper fittings should be cleaned with either a wire brush or sandpaper (Fig. 8-2) until the finish is shiny.

Figure 8-2

Cleaning copper pipe. Model: Andrew Wallace

Once you have cleaned your pipe and fitting, apply flux to the inside of the fitting and around the outside of the pipe end (Fig. 8-3). The flux will clean and aid the solder in running around the joint (Fig. 8-4). A word of caution: Flux is an eye irritant and if you get it in your eyes, mouth, or open cuts, it will produce a burning sensation.

Figure 8-3

Applying flux to copper pipe. Model: Andrew Wallace

The solder used for making joints for potable (drinking water) water pipes should be lead-free. There are many types of solder available, but plumbing code requirements restrict the amount of lead a solder

Figure 8-4

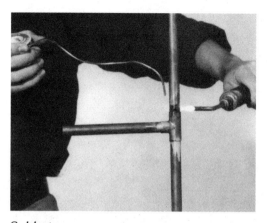

Soldering copper pipe. Model: Andrew Wallace

used with water pipes may contain. For years, 50/50 solder (50% lead) was used when installing water pipes, but it is no longer acceptable. Don't let some clerk in a store talk you into anything less than a lead-free solder.

When you are going to solder joints, you need a torch. A handheld propane torch, like those sold in hardware stores, costs very little and works fine for small jobs. If you only solder occasionally, you should not purchase a large, expensive soldering tool.

Before you begin to solder a joint, you should be sure that the pipes being worked with do not contain any residual water. If water is present, the solder cannot meld into a joint properly. The result will be a leak. If you are dealing with a vertical pipe that is holding water and don't have any lower place to drain the water, you can blow the water out with a drinking straw. Put the straw in the pipe, shut your eyes, and blow. This will remove enough water to allow you to solder. When a horizontal pipe is holding water, you can pack the pipe lightly with white bread without the crust. The bread will block the water while you solder, but when water pressure is turned on to the pipe, the bread will dissolve and flow out of a faucet. These two tricks of the trade can save you a lot of time and frustration.

Once your joints are properly prepared, you are ready to solder them (Fig. 8-5). It is wise to wear eye protection and long sleeves to protect you from dropping and splashing solder. Light the torch and hold the flame on the hub of the fitting. When you see the flux begin to bubble and drip, touch the end of the your solder to the gap between the pipe and the fitting hub. If the temperature is right, the solder will melt and run around the joint. If the joint is too cold, the solder won't melt. If the joint is too hot or too dirty, the solder will melt into little balls that will drop off the pipe.

Figure 8-5

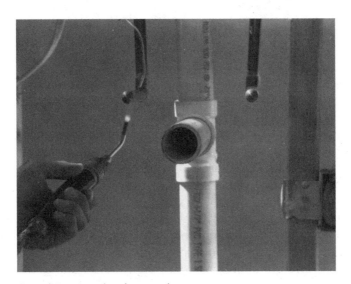

Roughing in a kitchen sink. Model: Andrew Wallace

Horizontal joints are easier to solder than vertical joints. Basically though, solder will follow the heat and the flux you are applying. If you are soldering a vertical joint, keep your heat near the back of the fitting hub. When the temperature is right, the solder will be sucked up into the joint. A joint that is too cold won't take at all. One that is too hot may take some of the solder without creating a solid joint, but this will usually be indicated by beads of solder falling off the work area. Learning to solder takes practice. Since you might not wish to invest the time and energy to learn how to solder, it might be best for you to use CPVC materials or polybutylene materials.

Polybutylene

Polybutylene (PB) pipe is, in my opinion, the water pipe of the future. It is a gray, plastic-like pipe that can be purchased in long coils or in shorter, straight lengths. Joints for PB pipe are made with either compression fittings or crimp fittings. Crimp fittings are the most dependable, but they require a special and expensive tool. The tool can, however, be rented from most rental centers.

Soldering is not necessary when working with PB pipe. When you compare PB to CPVC, you will find that PB offers all of the benefits provided by CPVC without any of the drawbacks. PB is not brittle, and its joints are made solid at the time of installation. There is no drying time. This piping is inexpensive, easy to work with, and an all-around great material.

Making joints with PB pipe, when using compression fittings, is as simple as sliding a nut and ferrule over the pipe, inserting the pipe into a fitting, and tightening the compression nut. If you choose the professional installation method, a crimp ring is placed over the pipe. Then the pipe is pushed onto a barbed fitting, and a crimping tool is used to compress the ring over the fitting. This is a very simple method of making joints, but you need the proper crimping tool. We don't have space in this book to discuss in great detail how plumbing goes together or the possible pitfalls you may encounter, but I would recommend that you consider polybutylene as a prime material choice in your remodeling project.

Setting fixtures

Setting plumbing fixtures can get tricky. However, if you use the right materials and methods, the job is easy. During my work as a contractor, I've learned some shortcuts to success in dealing with the plumbing aspect of kitchen remodeling. I'm going to share them with you now.

Sinks

The difficulty level of installing a sink depends largely on the type of sink being installed (Figs. 8-6 through 8-8). If you will be working with a stainless-steel sink, there shouldn't be anything that you can't do yourself. A cast-iron sink, on the other hand, is heavy enough to warrant help. Regardless of the weight of the sink, the plumbing aspects of installation are about the same.

Figure 8-6

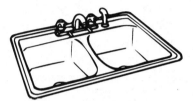

Standard double-bowl kitchen sink. Eljer Plumbingware

Figure 8-7

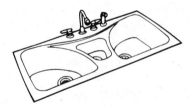

Triple-bowl sink, often used in conjunction with a garbage disposer. Eljer Plumbingware

Figure 8-8

Double-bowl sink. Eljer Plumbingware

Depending on where you are purchasing a counter and a sink, you may be able to have the supplier cut the hole in your counter for the sink. If this is not possible, the job will be up to you. A template will be supplied with a new sink. This is a line drawing that you can place on the counter to determine the size of the hole needed. If you are new at cutting holes for sink installation, you might want to cut the hole a little on the small side and enlarge it as necessary. It is much easier to make a hole larger than it is to make it smaller.

If, for some reason, the sink doesn't have a template, you can use the sink itself to mark your hole. Turn the sink upside down and place it on the counter where you want the finished product. Trace around the outside edges of the sink with a pencil. Make sure to use a pencil, not a pen, since pencil mark will wash off later. An ink mark might not come off so easily.

Once you have an outline of the sink, you have a starting point. Don't cut along the line you have just created, because the hole will wind up being too large. Measure the lip of your sink. Allow for this measurement as you draw a second line inside the outline. Cut along the inside line. If you are unsure about this procedure, start with a small hole and make it bigger as you go along. There must be enough counter left to hold the rim of the sink. It is normal for sinks to be secured with clamps that bite into the underside of a counter. This requires a certain amount of counter to extend under the lip of the sink.

Assuming that you are working with a standard counter material, the best way to cut the hole is with a drill and a jig saw. Start by drilling a hole within the outline. This allows you to put the blade of the jig saw into the hole and begin cutting. The key is to avoid cutting the hole too big.

Once you have a hole that your sink will sit in, you can get back to plumbing. This is when you will mount the kitchen faucet and basket strainers on the sink. This work is easier to accomplish before the sink is installed permanently. I'll give you details on these installations later in this chapter. For now, assume that you have already installed the basket strainers and faucet. You are now ready to mount the sink in the counter.

Apply a bead of caulking around the edge of your sink hole. Put the sink in place. If it is a cast-iron sink, this is the end of your installation procedure. Stainless-steel sinks, however, require that you secure them with the clamps that are supplied with the sink.

Clamping a stainless-steel sink in place doesn't require much skill, but it does demand some physical flexibility. Instructions packed with your sink will explain the proper installation, but let me give you a thumbnail sketch of what's involved. The head of the clamps slide into a channel that protrudes down from the sink. As you tighten these clamps with either a screwdriver or a hex-head driver, the clamps bite into the underside of the counter and hold the sink in place. Clamps should be spaced evenly on all four sides of the sink. The only difficult part of this job is that you must work in cramped conditions.

Kitchen faucets

Installing a kitchen faucet is easy. The job goes best, however, if you install the faucet prior to installing the sink. If you proceed in this order, you can have the sink out on the floor where you have more work space. If you wait to install the faucet until after the sink is installed, you will need a basin wrench to tighten the mounting nuts and supply nuts.

When you unpack your new faucet, you might find a rubber gasket that is designed to be set under the base of the faucet. This gasket keeps water that is spilled on the rim of the sink from running under the faucet and dripping into the base cabinet. Assuming that you have this type of gasket with your faucet, slide it over the supply outlets of the faucet prior to putting the faucet on the sink.

If you don't have a gasket packed with your faucet (not all faucets come with them), you need some plumber's putty to make your own seal (Fig. 8-9). Roll the putty in your hands until it is in a long, round shape. Lay the putty around the holes in the sink so that it encircles the holes completely. When you mount the faucet, the putty will compress and spread out to make a watertight seal.

Figure 8-9

Apply putty to kitchen faucet to eliminate leaks around base of faucet.

With the faucet sitting on the sink, install and tighten the mounting nuts over the supply outlets. If the sink has not yet been installed, you can use an adjustable wrench for this job. If the sink has been installed, you will need a basin wrench to tighten the nuts. Check the faucet to see that it is setting straight on the sink and tighten the mounting nuts until the base of the faucet will not move. You have now finished installing a faucet. There are many types of faucets available (Figs. 8-10 and 8-11), but most of them are easy to install.

If the faucet is set up to accept a spray attachment, you will have to connect the spray hose to the base of the faucet. Most faucets with spray attachments utilize a fourth hole in the sink. A few faucets have a spray hose that comes right through the faucet base. Your individual situation depends on the type of faucet and sink you have. If you have one of the common types of spray attachments, there will be a collar that you must install in the fourth hole of the sink. Put putty under the rim of the collar, push the threaded portion through the hole in the sink, and screw on the mounting nut from beneath the sink.

Figure 8-10

Kitchen faucet options. Gerber Plumbing Fixtures Corp.

Figure 8-11

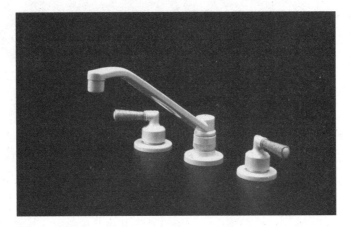

Kitchen faucet. Gerber Plumbing Fixtures Corp.

After the spray collar is installed on the sink, the spray hose can be fed through it and attached to the female threads provided on the base of the faucet. The male threads of the spray hose must be coated with a pipe-sealant compound or a sealant tape.

Installing basket strainers

Installing basket strainers in the drain openings of the sink is the next step in rebuilding the plumbing in a kitchen. Basket strainers are not normally provided with a new sink; they must be purchased separately. There are three common types of basket strainers.

The most difficult of these threes types of basket strainers to install is one that is held in place by a large nut that screws over the strainer threads. Trying to tighten this type of strainer often requires the effort of more than one person. You should avoid these basket strainers.

The other two common types of basket strainers can be installed by a single individual. One of these strainers has a large collar that slides up on the strainer from beneath the sink. The collar is held in place by a nut that can be tightened without assistance.

The last common type basket strainer is held in place with three-stud pressure plates. Since these are the easiest strainers to install, they are the most popular type of basket strainer. I will base the installation procedure on their use.

When you look at the basket strainer, you will find a rubber gasket. This gasket is installed on the underside of the sink. Prior to putting a basket strainer in a sink, you must make a seal for the rim of the strainer out of plumber's putty by spreading the putty all around the bottom of the strainer rim.

With the putty in place, insert the strainer through the drain hole and push it down to compress the putty. Position yourself under the sink and slide the rubber gasket over the protruding strainer. Follow the gasket with a metal ring and then the retaining clamp. Turn the retainer studs counterclockwise to allow the retaining clamp to thread onto the strainer. The retaining clamp will screw onto the threads of the strainer until you are left with exposed threads for the installation of a slip-nut. At this point, begin to tighten the retainer studs by turning them in a clockwise direction. Alternate this procedure among the three studs, turning each of them an equal amount. This procedure allows the clamp to tighten evenly. When the putty in the sink bowl spreads out and the strainer no longer shifts in the sink, the studs are tight enough.

Water supplies

Now you are ready to connect water supplies to the kitchen faucet. You need two supply tubes, which are special pieces of tubing available in various lengths and materials. One end of the supply tube will have a molded head, and the other end will be a flush-cut piece of $3/8$" tubing. Supply tubes are available in chrome-plated brass, polybutylene, flexible hose, and other materials. Polybutylene supplies are the easiest to work with. However, if they are not available to you, opt for a flexible hose style. Inexperienced hands often have trouble bending brass supplies without kinking them.

The head of each supply tube fits into an inlet opening on the faucet. Supply tubes are held in place with the supply nuts provided with faucets. If you wait to install supply tubes until after the sink is set in the counter, you need a basin wrench to tighten the nuts. It is best to install the supply tubes prior to installing the sink.

Supply tubes are connected to main water supplies at a valve. If your water pipes are roughed-in without valves, and they usually are, you will have to install the valves. To do this, you must cut off the main water supply. Then you cut the caps off the ends of the stubbed-out water supplies. There are several types of stop valves to choose from, but compression-type stop valves are the easiest to install.

To install a compression valve on copper tubing, all you have to do is slide the valve onto the pipe and tighten the compression nut. When this is done, you can insert the supply tube from the faucet into the valve and tighten the smaller compression nut. If a polybutylene supply tube is used, the compression ferrule that is used with it should be nonmetallic. A brass ferrule will cut into the polybutylene if the compression nut is tightened too much.

Drainage

The job of connecting the drainage system for a kitchen sink starts at the basket strainers. Flanged plastic or metal tailpieces are used to start the system. The plastic tubing is easier to cut and work with. To install a tailpiece, you place a tailpiece washer (it should be included with the basket strainer) on top of the tailpiece. You then slide a slip-nut up the tailpiece and screw the nut onto the bottom of the basket strainer.

Assuming that you are installing a double-bowl sink, you need what is known as a continuous waste. This is a collection of tubular parts that connect the drainage of the two bowls together, allowing them to drain into a single trap. If you are installing a single-bowl sink, you do not need a continuous waste; the tailpiece from the basket strainer connects directly to the trap.

When you buy a continuous waste, you have the option of an end-outlet waste or a center-outlet waste. Which one you purchase is determined by the location of your drain and trap. If the trap is in the middle of the sink, you should use a center-outlet waste. When the drain is offset to one side of the sink, an end-outlet waste is appropriate.

The tubular pieces of a continuous waste are put together with slip-nuts and slip-nut washers. A slip-nut is placed over a tubular section, and then a washer is put on the tubular section. The end of the drainage tube is placed in a fitting or trap, and the washer is pushed up to the point of connection. When the slip-nut is tightened, the washer compresses and seals the joint. Once the continuous waste has been installed, you only need to connect the waste to the trap with another slip-nut and washer.

Garbage disposer

If you will be installing a garbage disposer, you install the disposer in place of the basket strainer. The drain collar that is included with the disposer is installed in the drain hole of a kitchen sink. You must apply putty under the rim before the collar is installed in the sink.

Not all disposers are installed in the same manner, but I can give you a good idea of what to expect. Once the drain collar is in place, you use some type of flange to tighten the seal of the drain collar. The flange will probably resemble the three-stud basket strainer I described earlier. After securing the drain collar, you will most likely install a metal ring by snapping it into place on the shank of the collar. This ring holds part of the mounting assembly in place.

When you are ready to mount the garbage disposer, you should hold it up against the collar and push upwards. There should be a large ring on the mounting hardware that, when turned, will lock onto the flange of the disposer and hold it in place. If you will be connecting the drain hose of a dishwasher to the special drain port on the disposer, you must knock out the plug that is in the port before you mount the disposer. This can be accomplished with a screwdriver and a hammer by putting the end of the screwdriver into the drain port and tapping the handle with a hammer. A thin piece of metal will be knocked out and will fall into the disposer. You must invert the appliance and shake the metal plug out.

Once the garbage disposer is hung in place, you can connect the drain. You will find a plastic elbow, a rubber gasket, a metal ring, and a screw needed for this procedure. The gasket goes inside the drain outlet. Then fit the plastic elbow up against the gasket so that the elbow's flange is touching the gasket. Slide the metal ring over the elbow. Insert the screw through the metal ring and into the housing of the disposer. Tighten the screw to compress the gasket and seal the opening. The remaining end of the elbow will act as a tailpiece and fit into a standard tubular drainage fitting or trap.

Dishwasher

When hooking up a dishwasher, you must make some additional provisions under the sink. The first of these provisions is for a hot water supply to the dishwasher. Instead of using a standard stop valve on the hot water supply, install a combination stop valve that has two outlets. One of these outlets is for the kitchen faucet supply, and the other one is for the dishwasher. A saddle valve (Fig. 8-12) can be used to create this type of water supply.

Soft copper tubing or polybutylene tubing can be used to extend a water supply to the dishwasher. One end of the tubing will be connected to the stop valve. The other end will terminate at a special

Figure 8-12

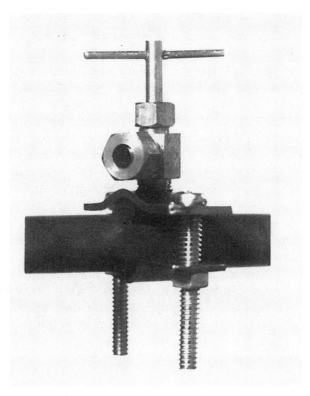

Self-piercing saddle valve, used for the ice-maker connections.

fitting that is known as a dishwasher ell. The dishwasher ell will screw into the water supply inlet of the dishwasher. You must remove the access panel on the front of the dishwasher to gain access to the water inlet and drain outlet. This panel is usually made up of two pieces, each of which is held in place with two screws. The other end of the ell will be fitted with a compression fitting. This is where the tubing is connected to the ell. Before screwing the ell into the dishwasher, you must put a thread sealant on the male threads.

Now you are ready to connect the drainage hose between the dishwasher and the drainage system. A new dishwasher is usually supplied with a drain hose and clamps. Place one clamp over the end of the drain hose. Slide the hose onto the drain outlet of the dishwasher, and clamp the hose into place. Feed the hose under the appliance and into the base cabinet of the kitchen sink.

Once the drain hose is under the kitchen sink, the hose must be elevated to prevent backflow into the dishwasher. This is usually accomplished in one of two ways. The simple way is to run the hose up the side of the cabinet until it is even with the bottom of the kitchen counter. Use a pipe clamp to hold the hose in place. Then the hose is looped downward to the drainage system. While this practice is simple, it might not be in compliance with the local plumbing code. Most codes require dishwashers to drain through an airgap.

An airgap is a simple device that is usually installed in an extra hole in the rim of a kitchen sink. Airgaps are also installed in holes drilled in kitchen counters. An airgap has a wye-shaped configuration with two ribbed barbs and one leg larger in diameter than the other. To install an airgap, you must first pull off its top cover. You then will see a threaded section and a mounting nut. Remove the nut and place the airgap through the mounting hole in the sink or counter by pushing the device through the hole from below. Once the threaded section is through the hole, screw on the mounting nut. Now you can replace the top cover.

From under the sink, you will see the two legs of the airgap sticking down. The drain from the dishwasher attaches to the smaller of the two legs and is held in place with a clamp. You will have to buy a section of drain hose with a $\frac{7}{8}$-inch diameter for the larger leg. Clamp one end of the larger hose to the airgap and attach the other end to the drainage system.

You can connect the large drain hose to the drain port of a garbage disposer. If you don't have a garbage disposer, you will need a special tailpiece called a dishwasher wye or tailpiece. This tailpiece will be installed on the bottom of a basket strainer in place of the standard tailpiece. You will notice that the wye in the dishwasher tailpiece protrudes to accept the drain hose. Slide the drain hose over the wye and clamp it in place. This will complete the plumbing aspects of a dishwasher hookup.

Following instructions

When you are installing plumbing fixtures and appliances, it is important to read and follow the instructions provided by the product manufacturer. If you fail to follow the instructions carefully, you may void any warranty that is offered on the product. It is also possible that you may damage the product if you do not follow the manufacturer's suggestions in a step-by-step manner. This advice extends beyond plumbing and includes all aspects of your remodeling job.

This concludes the look at plumbing. We are now ready to move onto the electrical phase of your job. Turn this page and prepare to learn about electrical wiring, fixtures, and devices.

9

Electrical considerations

Chapter 9

THE ELECTRICAL aspects of a remodeling job cannot be taken lightly. The responsibility involved when working with electricity is great. In plumbing, a mistake will do little more than get you wet. However, the wrong move with electrical work could kill you. This chapter is going to cover a lot of ground on the subject of electrical wiring, fixtures, and devices, but you must decide for yourself if you are competent to perform this work safely. If you do not have electrical experience, this is one phase of the job for which you should contract a licensed professional to do the work. If you are experienced in this field, you may still need to contract a licensed technician who can obtain the necessary permits.

Removing existing electrical fixtures

Removing existing electrical fixtures and devices can be done safely by almost anyone who is reasonably handy. The key to safe removal of fixtures is that the power is turned off and cannot be turned on inadvertently while the electrical work is being done. Modern homes are equipped with circuit breakers (Fig. 9-1), and older homes have fuses. In either case, if you plan to work with the electrical components of a home, you will have to locate the service panel that contains the fuses or circuit breakers. Then you must identify which circuit breaker or fuse controls the electrical components with which you plan to work. For the remainder of the chapter, I refer only to circuit breakers, since they are more common than fuses. If a procedure is affected by having fuses rather than circuit breakers, I make you aware of it.

When you open the door to a service panel, you will probably see a chart that lists the numbers of the circuit breakers and identifies what the various breakers control. **WARNING:** Don't trust this information! I have had many occasions when the charts in service panels were not labeled correctly. Always test whatever item you are about to work with to make sure that the fixture is not receiving electricity.

▲

Figure 9-1

Circuit breakers.

Pinpointing which circuit breakers control the electrical work in a kitchen is easier if you have someone else working with you. If you do have a helper, that person should remain in the kitchen to observe what happens as you go through a trial-and-error search. Start your search using the information on the chart next to the circuit breakers, but don't depend on the descriptions to be accurate. I know I'm being repetitive on this issue, but I don't want you to make a deadly mistake.

Have your helper turn on the kitchen lights. You should then begin cutting off circuit breakers until the lights go off. The lights going off is a prime indication that you have found the proper breaker. However, to be sure, turn the breaker back on and check to see that the lights come back on. If they do, you know you've found the right breaker. This may seem overly cautious, but it is conceivable that a light bulb could burn out during your test and fool you. As you progress through your search, mark each identified breaker that will be used during the remodeling for easy relocation.

When you are ready to test the kitchen outlets, plug a lamp or a small appliance, like a radio, into each outlet as you test for the proper circuit breaker. You should test both sections of each outlet, since many kitchens have split circuits. In a split circuit, the top section could be off while the bottom section is still hot.

If you will be removing a garbage disposer, dishwasher, or some other hard-wired equipment, turn the equipment on while you test the circuit breakers. When the equipment stops running, turn the breaker back on in order to confirm that it is in fact controlling the appliance. You will lose a little time taking these extra safety precautions, but they are well worth the time.

Once you are positive that the electrical fixtures, devices, and equipment you will be working with are no longer receiving electricity, you can begin to remove them. This part of the job is simple. In most cases you will need only a screwdriver in order to complete the job.

Ceiling lights

Most ceiling lights have a globe over the light bulb. The first step in removing a ceiling light fixture is to remove the globe. This is usually done by turning a knurled retaining nut with your hand. In some cases the globe might be held in place by several nuts. These nuts must be removed in order to take off the globe. After removing the globe, you will most likely be looking at a metal plate that is held in place by either screws or nuts. Remove the screws or nuts that hold the cover plate in place to reveal the wiring. These wires are attached to the light fixture and connected to the house wiring with wire nuts. Wire nuts are little plastic covers that connect and protect the bare ends of electrical wires.

The next step in the removal of a ceiling light is to remove the wire nuts by turning them counterclockwise. This procedure can normally be completed by hand, but you may need a pair of pliers. Once the wire nuts are off, you will see exposed electrical wires. Don't touch these wires. Don't allow the two sets of wires to touch each other, and don't let them come into contact with any metal. Even though the power is supposed to be off, you should test them with an electrical meter to be sure they are not hot. The meter used for this test doesn't have to be an elaborate, expensive professional model. A simple tester that has two test prongs and a light is good enough.

Before you test your exposed wires, test your meter. Take the meter to an electrical outlet that is being supplied with electricity. Plug the prongs of the tester into the outlet to confirm that the meter is working. If the meter is in service, test the bare wires at the fixture. If you don't get any reading, you can be fairly certain that the wires are safe to touch. As an extra precaution, you can hold the wires at the point where they are insulated and touch the bare ends together. If your meter was incorrect, this procedure will cause some sparks and the circuit breaker should throw itself into the off position in order to protect you from serious harm. Unwind the bare wires and place wire nuts over the ends of the house wiring. As an extra precaution, you might want to tape the wire nuts in place.

Outlets

The first step in the removal of an existing electrical outlet is to remove the cover by taking out the screw in the middle of the cover plate. When this is completed, there will be two screws that attach the outlet to the electrical box. Remove these screws, and the outlet will pull out of the box. There will not be any wire nuts for these electrical devices. The bare ends of the house wiring will either be attached to the sides of the outlet, held in place by screws, or pushed into the backs of the outlets. For safety's sake, go through the same test procedures with all electrical wires as described in the previous section on ceiling lights.

If the house wiring is stabbed into the back of an outlet, you can simply snip the wire at a point close to the back of the outlet. You might be able to simply pull the bare ends of the wiring out of the outlet, but as long as you have enough spare wire in the box, cutting the wire is quicker and easier. When the wiring is attached under screws, you can loosen the screws and free the wires or simply cut the wires. Always cover the bare ends of house wiring with wire nuts, even if the power is to remain off.

Removing electrical equipment

When you are ready to disconnect electrical equipment or appliances, such as garbage disposers and dishwashers, you have to gain access to their wiring. This is usually accomplished by removing the screw or two that hold the cover plate in place. With the cover removed, you will see an arrangement of wires similar to that described for electrical fixtures. This arrangement includes both equipment wires and the house wires. Follow the same basic procedures given for fixtures to remove this type of wiring. There will, however, be a stress clamp on the equipment that you have to deal with. This clamp tightens against the wiring in order to keep it in place. You must loosen the two screws on the clamp to free the stress collar and allow the wiring to be pulled free.

The removal of electrical wiring is not at all difficult. However, as a precaution against someone turning on the controlling breaker, it is a good idea to place heavy tape, like duct tape or a written message over the breaker. Now that you have discovered how easy it is to rip out electrical work, let's see what's involved in putting it back together again.

Roughing-in new wiring

Have you ever watched electricians who were roughing-in new wiring? If you have, you would probably agree that they make it look simple. They drill a few holes, nail an electrical box into place, pull a piece of wire into the box, and move on to their next task. Professionals, regardless of their trade, tend to make work look much easier than it really is. This is because they have preformed these duties every day over an extended period. For someone who is not familiar with a particular type of work, the same task may seem insurmountable.

When it comes to roughing-in electrical wiring, you must be either knowledgeable of both electrical work and the electrical code, or you must be willing to invest considerable time to learn both areas. The electrical code is very thorough. For example, there are code requirements that dictate how far apart electrical outlets can be and where ground-fault-interceptors must be installed. In addition to a complete knowledge of the code requirements, you need competent electrical skills and the required permits. If you are not the owner-occupant of a house or a licensed electrician, it is doubtful that you will be able to perform new installations without contracting a licensed electrician.

Local code requirements vary, since every enforcement jurisdiction has the power to amend state and national codes in order to suit its particular needs. For this reason, it is necessary for you to talk with you local code enforcement officer to determine the requirements in your area. There are, however, some common requirements and practices that I can share with you. Let's take a little time to discuss some basic wiring concepts that you may find helpful. However, remember that you should never attempt to work with electricity unless you completely understand the task you are undertaking.

Service panels

A service panel is where circuit breakers are located. If you will be adding new circuits to a kitchen, it is necessary to work inside the service panel. This procedure can be very dangerous, so proceed only under safe conditions.

When you open the door of a service panel, you see circuit breakers and a metal plate. Once the metal plate is removed, bare wires are exposed. These wires are the inner workings of the panel box. Some of the wires come into the box from the weatherhead outside. These wires provide current ranging, typically, from 100 to 200 amps and attach to what is known as a bus bar. Beyond the main bus bar, there is a main breaker. If this breaker is turned off, all of the electricity to the house if shut off. **WARNING:** The bus bar remains energized; never touch it. Power is completely off in a house only after the utility company has pulled the electric meter.

The main circuit breaker separates the incoming bus bar from the panel bus bar. The panel bus bar is where all of the individual circuit breakers are connected. Large breakers (typically 240-volt breakers) are known as double-pole breakers. Smaller breakers, like those used for light fixtures and outlets, are called single-pole breakers. You connect these breakers to the panel bus bar by clipping them into place. The type of panel box that I'm describing has the power feed from outside coming into the top of the box. Some boxes, however, have their power source coming in from the bottom. At the bottom of a panel that receives its incoming power from above will be a ground bar, also called a neutral bus bar. This neutral bus bar will have a large neutral (or ground) wire that extends to a grounding rod. This neutral bus bar is where the ground wires for all circuits attach.

To add new circuits in a home, you must install new circuit breakers in the service panel. You need to run new wiring from the panel bus bar to the new electrical locations in the home, snap in new breakers, and attach new ground wires from the new circuits. While this work is not too dangerous when the main breaker is turned off, you can never afford to be careless when working in a panel box or with any electricity.

The circuit breakers used for kitchen ranges, water heaters, clothes dryers, and other such appliances are typically double-pole, 240-volt breakers. Breakers for lights and outlets are usually single-pole breakers with amperage ratings of between 15 and 20 amps. Never install a breaker that is rated for more amps that what is recommended for the service being provided. If the breaker is rated higher than the electrical devices being used on it, there is a risk of fire.

To determine the number of amps that will be needed on a circuit, you can use a simple mathematic formula. The number of amps produced can be found by dividing the wattage rating of an appliance by the average effective voltage of the electrical service. Let me give you an example of this procedure.

Assume that you are going to run a blender, a can opener, a coffee maker, and a food processor off the same circuit. Check the wattage rating listed on the plate of each appliance. For the sake of this example, I will provide sample ratings. Let's say that the blender has a wattage rating of 300; the can opener has a rating of 100; the coffee maker has a rating of 1000; and the food processor has a rating of 300. Also assume that these appliances are running at 120 volts. First, add up the total wattage ratings and get the sum of 1700 watts. Divide the wattage (1700) by the volts (120) to arrive at an amperage of 14.17. This indicates a need for at least a 15-amp breaker (a 20-amp breaker might be a better choice).

If you are working in an old house, the existing service panel might not be large enough to accept a substantial load from new circuits. If this is the case, the old service panel will have to be replaced with one which has a larger capacity. If your breaker box is too small to handle the total amp needs for existing and new circuits, call an experienced, licensed, insured electrician to do the replacement work for you.

Outlets

One consideration during a remodeling project is the number of electrical outlets that should be present when the job is complete. If you're working in a fairly modern home, you may have no need to increase the number of outlets. Older homes, however, are often deficient in the number of outlets they possess. When remodeling, you have an excellent opportunity to upgrade the number of outlets in a kitchen. This is also the time to add ground-fault-interceptor circuits or outlets.

Ask your customers if they find themselves using adapters that allow the use of multiple plugs into a single outlet. Are there times when an extension cord is needed for some appliance in their kitchen? If they answer yes to either of these questions, you should install additional outlets during the course of your remodeling. Also, don't overlook the future needs of your customers. It may be that at a later time they will be increasing the number of electrical devices used in their kitchens. Plan for this possibility when evaluating a need for additional outlets.

The minimum spacing of outlets is controlled by the local electrical code. These requirements vary, so you will have to confirm them with your local code officer. Typically, outlets should be spaced no more than 4 feet apart in a kitchen. This rule is pretty common. There is another rule that may surprise you; many codes require outlets for every countertop. This code is logical and reasonable, but it can catch you off guard. Suppose you are installing an island cabinet and countertop in a kitchen. Would you think to provide outlets for it? A lot of people, including builders, sometimes neglect this part of the job. If your local code requires an outlet for every countertop, you will have to provide at least one for the island. This is not a hardship if you rough-in the outlet before your job is finished. However, if you find out that an outlet is required after the job is complete, you will have a lot more difficulty remedying the situation.

Wires

The type and size of the wire used to rough-in electrical systems is very important. An improper choice of wire size can result in fire. When you select electrical wire, you may be given a choice between aluminum and copper. Aluminum wire is cheaper than copper wire. However, a large number of electrically related house fires have been blamed on aluminum wire. Some of the reasons why aluminum wire does not perform as well as copper are easy to understand. Aluminum wire is not as good a conductor as copper wire. Heat resistance can cause the aluminum to loosen. Also, aluminum has been known to be attacked by corrosion and oxidation. The list goes on, but it is enough for you to know that the benefits of copper wire make copper wire well worth the additional expense.

Choosing the right wire size can get complicated, but for most kitchen remodeling jobs there are some rule-of-thumb factors that can be used. It was common for a long time to use a 14-gauge wire when running circuits for lights and outlets. However, 12-gauge wire (the smaller the gauge, the bigger the wire) has become accepted as the standard for circuits serving lights and outlets, especially in kitchens. A 12-gauge wire normally runs with a 20-amp circuit breaker. If it is used at all, 14-gauge wire should not be used with more than a 15-amp breaker.

Choosing a wire that is too small can result in overloaded wiring, tripped circuit breakers, and even fire. For example, two kitchen appliances can be enough to overload a circuit that is made with 14-gauge wire. You also need to consider the distance that the wire will be run and the number of amps that will be pulling on the circuit. For example, a circuit run with 12-gauge wire and a 20-amp circuit breaker can run for over 100 feet if the amperage pull is only 5 amps. If the amp load is increased to 15 amps, the same wire can run less than 50 feet. Your local code officer or licensed electrician can help you determine maximum runs and wire sizes.

▲

Electrical boxes

Electrical boxes come in different sizes and shapes. Each type of box has its own special use and benefits. The type of box you select depends on the type of fixture or device the box will house, how many wires will be held in the box, and where the box will be mounted. Ceiling lights require boxes that are either circular or rectangular. Junction boxes tend to be square or octagonal, and the boxes for switches and outlets (Figs. 9-2 and 9-3) are rectangular. The depth of these various boxes will be determined by the number of connections made within the box. For example, an octagonal box with a depth of 1½" can accommodate up to six 12-gauge wire connections. If the depth of the box is extended to 2½", the number of permissible connections jumps to nine.

Figure 9-2

Single-gang plastic electrical box.

The shape and size of electrical boxes are only two differences to be found in the boxes. For each style of box, there are different designs to allow a multitude of mounting possibilities. For example, plastic, rectangular boxes (Fig. 9-4) are available with nails already in place.

Figure 9-3

Plastic four-gang electrical box.

Figure 9-4

Plastic two-gang electrical box.

When using these boxes, an installer can merely place the box against a wall stud and hammer in the nails. These boxes are used mostly in new construction and remodeling jobs where open stud bays are accessible. Other rectangular boxes are made with special mounting provisions that are used to overcome the difficulties of working in old homes where the walls are not completely opened up. Bars and boxes that allow ceiling boxes to be mounted in the center of open space between ceiling joists (Fig. 9-5) are also available. Your electrical supplier should be glad to help you select the right boxes for your needs.

Figure 9-5

Metal octagonal ceiling box.

New circuits

If you are fortunate enough to be working with a kitchen that is located over a basement or crawlspace, the task of running new circuits is pretty easy. However, if your kitchen sits above other finished living space, the snaking of wires requires thought, patience, and persistence. Working wires through finished living space without disturbing the walls and ceilings is not an easy chore. However, it can be accomplished with fish tape. A fish tape is a thin metal strip that is rolled into a coil. A hook on the end of the fish tape allows wire to be pulled. These devices are not particularly expensive, and they are available at most hardware stores.

If you are gutting a kitchen down to the bare studs and the kitchen sits over unfinished space, your job as an electrician will be much more comfortable. You simply drill holes in the sole plates of your kitchen walls, stick the end of a roll of wire through the hole, go under the kitchen and pull the wire to the service panel, and connect the wire. In the case of a crawlspace, you will probably have to go to the service panel and drill holes down into the crawlspace in order to bring the wires up to the panel. If the house has a basement, the job will be easier since the panel is probably in the basement. **Caution**: Never connect new wiring to the service panel until all of the connections are made at the other ends of the wiring. Also, protect any wires that might be hit by a nail or a screw with special protective plates (Fig. 9-6).

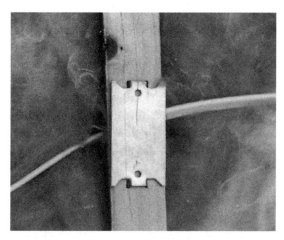

Figure 9-6

*Protective plate used by both electricians
and plumbers to prevent nails and screws
from hitting vulnerable materials.*

Running wires through concealed walls is much more difficult than
dropping them through sole plates. If you have a need to fish a wire
through a closed wall, you will need a fish tape. Most electricians tape
over the electrical wire where it connects to the fish tape. This gives
the combination a smoother profile and makes pulling the wire easier.

Trying to use a fish tape in an insulated wall is not feasible; it is just
too difficult to get the wire through the wall cavity. Avoid outside
walls as chaseways for your wiring. In a case where you must fish a
wire up or down multiple levels of a home, you will find it highly
advantageous to have a helper and two fish tapes available. Put one
fish tape into the wall cavity from the upper level and insert the
second tape from the lower level. You and your helper can work the
tapes around in the wall until the hooks on the fish tapes connect.
When this happens, you can pull one of the fish tapes all the way
through the wall and attach a wire that is to be pulled back.

Sometimes it simply isn't possible to hide a new wire in a wall. If
this is the case, you can cover the wire with molding that is made
specifically for electrical wires. Some electricians refer to this molding
as a metal raceway. This material has a hollow channel that installs
over exposed wiring to conceal and protect it.

Making electrical connections

Making electrical connections is a job that requires nimble fingers and caution. As long as you are sure there is no electrical power to the wiring with which you are working, making connections is not very difficult. There are, however, some general color codes that you should observe. Black and red wires are normally considered hot wires. White wires are generally neutral wires. However, some jobs require white wires to be used as hot wires, so never trust any wire to be safe without testing it with a meter. Bare wires and wires with green insulation are ground wires.

Black wires should connect to brass screws in an electrical connection. Red wires will normally connect to either a brass or chrome screw. White wires being used as neutral wires will be connected to chrome screws. The ground wire will connect to a green connector. It is best to secure electrical connections with a screw. Many new outlets are made to accept wires placed under screws, in the conventional way, or to accept them in a push-in method. The push-in method allows an installer to strip the wires and jab them into the back of the outlet. While this procedure is less time-consuming than wrapping the wire under a screw, it is not as secure or dependable. The push-in procedure should never be used with aluminum wire. When you crook the end of a wire that is to be placed under a screw, the hook should turn clockwise. This allows the wire to tighten under the screw as the screw is turned.

Many electrical connections depend on the use of wire nuts. The wire nuts must be the proper size for the size of the wire that will be connected. Wire nuts have a plastic exterior and a metal spring contained on the interior. To use a wire nut, you should first twist together the bare ends of the wires being connected. When the wires are wrapped together, slip the wire nut over them and turn it clockwise. When properly in place, the wire nut should be tight and difficult to turn.

When you bring a wire into an electrical box (Fig. 9-7), it is important to secure it with a stress clamp of some sort. There may be a built-in clamp in the electrical box, or you may have to install an individual

Figure 9-7

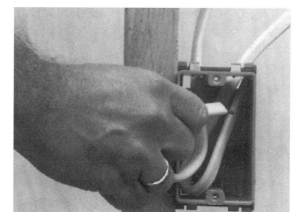

Roughing in new electrical wire.

clamp. Either way, you must make sure the wire is secured. In the case of most plastic boxes, wires are stapled to a stud within 6 inches of the box to provide a secure wire (Fig. 9-8). You must also be sure to attach the ground wire to the appropriate ground screw or clamp.

Figure 9-8

New electrical wires roughed-in.

Electrical connections can be simple or complicated. For example, if you want an outlet to be on a split circuit, you must work with the circuit a little differently. Take a standard outlet and look at the screws on the side of it. You will see a small electrical link that connects the two screws. If the outlet is to be used under normal conditions, this link should stay intact. When a split circuit is desired, the link should be removed with a screwdriver and a pair of pliers. By removing the link, you enable the top and bottom of the outlet to work independently.

A typical outlet will have one wire bringing in the power source. If the circuit will continue to another outlet, there will be a separate wire running between the two outlets. To make the connection, you combine the red wires with a wire nut. Under this same wire nut, you include a hot wire going to the second outlet. This same procedure holds true for the black wire. All of the ground wires connect to the outlet box. When running multiple outlets, it is often necessary to use white wires as traveler wires. In this situation, the white wires are hot wires, and it is a good idea to wrap a piece of black electrical tape around the white wires to indicate that they are carrying power.

If you are planning to get into extensive electrical work, you should either purchase a book that deals only with electrical work or consult local professionals. I've given you the basics on how home wiring is done, but you must make sure your work is safe and meets local electrical codes. Electrical work can be a complicated and difficult job. Please be careful in your electrical endeavors and consult the necessary resources to make your job proceed in the manner you wish.

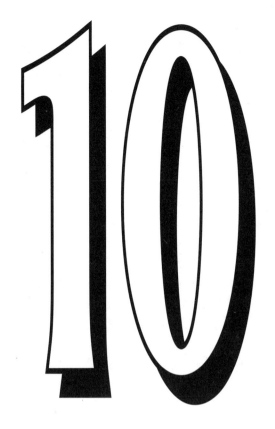

HVAC aspects of the job

Chapter 10

THE HEATING, ventilation, and air-conditioning (HVAC) aspects of your job may be minimal or extensive. The determining factor will be the amount of change you are making in the layout of a kitchen. Heating and air conditioning changes are often a very minor portion of a kitchen remodeling job, but they can create considerable problems. For example, you may have to move or discontinue the use of an old radiator that sits in a place where your customer wants a breakfast counter. If the present kitchen is always a bit on the cold side, you may want to install a kick-space heater under the cabinets. Perhaps the existing duct outlets are going to be covered with new cabinets. You must decide how to counteract these problems. This chapter will give you a good lesson in dealing with HVAC systems.

When we open the subject of heating systems, we open a large can of worms. There are electric baseboard heaters, forced hot-air heaters, hot-water baseboard heaters, radiators, in-floor heating systems, heat-pump systems, etc. With so many possible systems, you must be judicious in any approach to altering an existing heating or air-conditioning system.

Electric heaters

There are two basic types of electric heaters that are often installed permanently in homes. One type is mounted in a wall and is equipped with a fan to blow heat out of the heating unit. This type of heater is found most often in bathrooms, but it can be found in other parts of a home. The second, and much more common, type of electric heater is a baseboard design. These heating units are installed where the walls meet floors. The length of baseboard heaters varies.

Since it is highly unlikely that you will discover a wall-mounted heater in a kitchen, we will concentrate on baseboard heaters. Most kitchens are surrounded by cabinets. This leaves little room for the installation of baseboard-style heat. Therefore, you may find no existing heating elements in the kitchen you are remodeling. If, however, there are electric baseboard heaters that must be removed or relocated, you must first be sure to turn off the circuit breaker that controls the heater. A lot of electricity is provided for baseboard heating units, and you don't want to risk electrocution.

Once the power source for an electric baseboard heater is off, removing the heating unit is simple. First, the front cover of the heating unit is removed to reveal the mounting screws. Once these screws are removed, you can easily move the heating unit. If you are relocating the electric heater, you must disconnect the electrical wiring also. This can be completed by unhooking the wiring or by simply cutting the supply wire. If you are eliminating the heat altogether, you should find the end of the supply wire and disconnect it. A temporary disconnection can be protected with the use of wire nuts.

To reinstall a piece of electric baseboard heat, you just reverse the removal process. You simply connect the supply wiring and screw the heating unit to a wall. Ideally, the screws should be attached to wall studs. If this isn't possible, plastic anchors that expand when a screw is installed can be used to secure the heater to a hollow wall section.

Radiators

For an inexperienced contractor, radiators are one of the worst types of heat with which to work. Radiators are heavy, full of dirty water, temperamental, and easily broken. Not to mention that it is difficult to locate replacements for them. If your customer gets heat from radiators, go to all reasonable lengths to avoid moving them. Disturbing old radiators can cause a lot of trouble.

There are times when it is absolutely necessary to move an old radiator. Such a situation might arise if the floor under the radiator has rotted and needs to be replaced. When this is the case, you should call in a professional who is experienced with radiators. This person will often be a plumber. However, not all plumbers have experience working with radiators. Since radiators have not been the norm in construction for decades, it may take a little searching to find a plumber or heating mechanic who is qualified to work with radiators.

Let me give you an overview of what is involved with moving a radiator and some examples of what can go wrong. The basic concept of disconnecting a radiator is simple. In theory, you cut off the steam or water supply at the boiler, drain the heating system to a point below the radiator, and loosen the connection nuts on each end of the radiator. This sounds simple, but it can be a horror show.

Old radiators tend to develop problems once the existing seals are broken. In fact, they never seem to want to seal again. The connecting nuts on the ends of radiators are sometimes seized to a point where a 24-inch pipe wrench and a 24-inch cheater bar is needed to break them loose. Once a radiator is loose, it often empties ugly black water all over the place. If you've never tried moving a good-sized radiator, plan on having at least two strong people on hand to help. Did I forget to mention that the heating supply and return pipes often break off at the threads when radiators are disconnected? Well, they do. The solution to this problems requires tracing the pipes back to the next joint in order to replace them. This could mean the unplanned tearing out of walls and ceilings. I've worked with a lot of radiators, and I despise them because of these problems.

Now let's talk about putting old radiators back into service. Removing a radiator is bad enough, but putting one back in service can be much worse. Often, leaks develop that you just can't seem to stop, and the entire heating system gets air-locked and refuses to heat properly. If I'm scaring you, I'm doing you a favor. When dealing with radiators, call in reliable professionals to get the job done right without making yourself responsible for the leaks and other nasty possibilities that exist with radiators.

In-floor heating systems

In-floor heating systems often work very well, but they aren't found in many homes. If, however, an in-floor heating system is in use, your only concern during the remodeling will be to avoid damaging the heating system. In other words, don't saw through it or drive nails

▲

into it. Since in-floor heating systems provide uniform heating from beneath the floor, there is no need to alter the system when remodeling.

Forced hot-air and heat-pump systems

Forced hot-air systems and heat-pump systems are the most common types of HVAC systems. Both of these systems depend on duct work to deliver conditioned air, whether it is warm or cool, to the living space. Working with duct work is not very difficult, but you do risk getting cut on sharp sheet metal. However, almost any handy worker can accomplish this job.

The supply outlets for most duct-work systems are installed either in a floor or on a wall. Systems that supply only air conditioning may be installed with ceiling outlets or registers high up on walls, but heating systems and combined HVAC systems are installed at low points along outside walls. There will probably not be any need to alter these systems if you are remodeling without expanding.

When you look at an outlet of an HVAC duct, you will see a grill or register. This cover can usually be removed without any tools. You simply lift it out of the duct opening. The piece of duct work that houses the register is called a boot. Attached to the boot is a supply duct that runs to a main supply duct or plenum. Most ducts are made of sheet metal, but many are made of a flexible coil-type material. Some are even made from insulated rigid board. The edges of sheet metal can be extremely sharp and harmful, so wear heavy gloves and exercise caution when working with ducts.

If you only need to install a new floor covering over an HVAC outlet, you can just remove the register, lay your flooring, and cut out a hole in the flooring that will allow the register to be reinstalled. This is very simple. On occasions when you must relocate or add supply outlets, the work is a bit more complicated. However, the job is still within the realm of a typical contractor's capabilities.

Extending an existing duct doesn't require much effort. Take the duct apart at the most convenient joint and begin extending it with new duct work. Most individual supplies are round ducts that are the least complicated ducts to install. Bring the new duct to the area where you want it and connect it to a new boot fitting. The boot will have a rectangular section that will attach to the sub-flooring with either nails or screws. The fitting is designed to make a 90-degree bend so that it allows an installer to connect a supply duct with the boot and a main duct with minimal problems.

If you will be adding new duct outlets in remodeled space, you can connect them to a main trunkline or a plenum without much trouble. However, the trunkline (main duct) or plenum might not be sized to provide ideal results through new ducts. Duct systems rely heavily on their sizing for efficiency. If the sizing is not right, the quality of heating and cooling suffers.

To add a new duct, you need a take-off fitting. This is a fitting that can be mated to a main duct or plenum. You must cut a hole in the main duct or plenum, insert the take-off fitting, and bend over the metal tabs that hold it in place. When this is completed, you can connect a supply duct to the fitting and run it to your boot fitting. None of this work is complicated, but you must be careful when working with sharp sheet metal. When you cut in a take-off fitting, you can start the hole with a screwdriver and a hammer. Hammer the bit of the screwdriver into the sheet metal to get a starter hole. From there, you can use aviation snips to cut out a hole that will accept your take-off fitting.

Hot-water baseboard heat

Hot-water baseboard heat is common in parts of the country where the winter temperatures are typically extreme. As I mentioned earlier, there is very little room for any type of baseboard heat in an average kitchen. There are, however, heating elements known as toe-space or kick-space heaters. You may come across these heaters as you remodel, since they are designed for installation beneath kitchen cabinets.

During the remodeling of a kitchen, it is sometimes necessary to remove existing heating elements until the major portions of remodeling are complete. The same units are often reinstalled. In the case of hot-water baseboard heat, the job involves soldering skills and a bit of knowledge about boilers. If you can solder joints, you can manage this work. If you can't solder joints, you should call in professional help, typically a plumber.

In order to disconnect hot-water heat, you must first shut down the water supply to the boiler and drain the heating system to a point below the sections of heater you will be working with. To accomplish this task, you simply cut off a valve at the boiler's intake pipe and open a drain valve at the boiler location. Once the pipes have drained, you can cut the feed and return lines, which are usually made of copper, and remove the heating elements. Baseboard heat of this type has a removable front cover that allows access to the supply and return pipes. Be careful, however, not to damage the thin fins on the heating element. These fins are instrumental in the performance of the heating element. If they are damaged, the unit cannot perform properly.

If you need to keep the home warm with an operable heating system during the remodeling, you will have to solder caps on the supply and return pipes that you had cut off or connect the pipes with a loop of copper tubing. Even if you are doing a job during warm weather, you should cover the open ends of the pipes to prevent debris from falling into them. To remove the housing of the heating unit, you must remove the screws that secure it to the wall. Hot-water baseboard units have end-caps that are removable for access to the supplies and returns, as well as front access covers that may be removed to gain access to the heating elements.

When the time comes to reinstall hot-water heat, you must first mount the back section of the heating unit to the wall with screws. Plastic anchors should be used if you can not attach the screws to wall studs. Once the housing is in place, set the heating element on the brackets and remove any caps on the supply and return pipes. Solder the heating element back into place. You should use elbow fittings with air valves, since these fittings allow you to bleed out any air that may have accumulated in the system. The valves simply unscrew and a small rubber washer is removed. However, you should not take this step until you have turned on the water to the boiler and are ready to get water running through the heater. You should also be careful because the extremely hot water can burn you.

Now it is time to turn the water supply on to the boiler and test your joints. Open the inlet water valve to your heating system. Go to the bleed valves on the recently installed heating element and remove them in order to allow air to escape. When you get a good stream of water coming out of the bleed ells, replace the rubber washer and cap. Install the end-caps to cover the piping. Bleed the air out of all other heating elements in the house. This phase of your work is completed once you have steady water at all heating units.

I have covered the basics of the most common types of heating and air-conditioning systems. As you probably gathered from this discussion, these systems are rarely altered during the remodeling of a kitchen. Unless you are building an addition or adding substantial space to a kitchen, you will have to do little work with the HVAC system. If the HVAC system requires many changes or an upgrade, you should call in HVAC professionals to size the new requirements for the proposed heating and cooling needs. Adding a little extra demand on a system does not normally create a problem, but a complete kitchen or dining addition can place a substantial overload on an existing system. Under these circumstances, you may find it advantageous to use a new, independent system for the remodeled space. This system could take the form of electric baseboard heat or a single-package heat pump. Electric baseboard is the least expensive to install, but a heat pump offers the benefit of air conditioning and most likely a more cost-effective operating expense. Don't hesitate to talk with professionals if your remodeling plans involve major space expansion and HVAC additions.

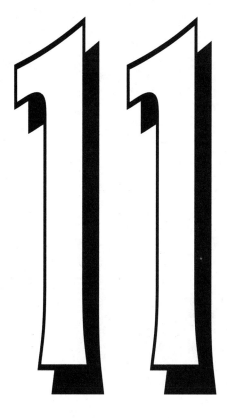

Lighting

Chapter 11

I F YOUR customer wants a bright, charming kitchen, you must let the light in with windows, doors, and skylights. Natural light is an ideal enhancement for any kitchen, and the choices available for maximizing lighting options have never been better. For example, there are skylights, garden windows, French doors, bay windows, casement windows, and awning windows. With so many options to choose from, you are sure to find something that suits the new kitchen you are creating.

Since so many large kitchens combine with dining and general-use areas, the possibilities for incorporating a lot of glass are nearly endless. For example, a contemporary kitchen might be set off with curved, solarium panels. A garden window adds charm and light to any kitchen. Awning windows let in a lot of light while maintaining maximum privacy. Casement windows are a good choice, since they open to allow optimum air flow and offer good security. Operable skylights fit the bill when a kitchen gets a little smoky or too hot. This chapter is going to give you a first-class tour of glass options and installation methods.

Many surveys have been done to determine what people want from a kitchen. Light always ranks high on the list of desirable features. In general, the more open and bright you can make a kitchen, the more people will like it. Of course, not everyone shares this opinion, but industry standards suggest that most home buyers love a bright, cheerful kitchen.

Types of windows

As you have already seen, many types of windows are available. Each style of window offers some special features and benefits (Fig. 11-1). Some windows are better choices for a particular job. Due to the number of options available, let's look at many of the various windows on an individual basis.

Figure 11-1

The woodwork in this kitchen is outstanding. The triple-panel window is ideal for natural lighting, and the framework blends well with the beams and cabinets. Hurd Millwork Company

Double-hung windows

Double-hung windows (Fig. 11-2) are the most common type of windows in homes today. These are windows in which a top half and bottom half move separately from each other. Generally, the bottom sash is pushed up, bypassing the top sash, to allow cool air to come in. Lowering the upper sash lets hot air out of a home. If only the bottom sash is designed to move, the window is a single-hung window. Double-hung windows are popular with real estate appraisers and the general public, but they are not always the best window to install (Fig. 11-3). For example, your customer might want a large window (Fig. 11-4) that is not available as double-hung unit. As you move through this chapter, you will find that various styles of windows all offer their own unique advantages.

Figure 11-2

Tilt-out double-hung windows make glass cleaning easier. Wenco Windows

Sliding windows

Sliding windows often conjure a thought of cheap aluminum windows that have condensation problems and often freeze in the winter and stick in the summer. Some sliders do suffer from these deficiencies, but there are a number of very good sliding windows available. Sliders can, in a way, be thought of as double-hung windows mounted on their sides. The main difference is that these windows allow the sashes to move back and forth on a track, rather than up and down. Also, good sliding windows often have removable sashes that allow easy cleaning.

Figure 11-3

Double-hung windows used in the creation of a walk-out bay window add to appearance and natural lighting, and the bay window adds floor space to the room. Pella Corporation

Casement windows

A casement window (Fig. 11-5) is one of my favorite types of windows. I like casement windows because they provide maximum air flow, good energy efficiency, and security. Unlike sliding windows or double-hung windows, where only half of the window space can be open at any given time, casement windows allow the entire window area to be open at once. If you enjoy cool breezes and outdoor aromas, casement windows are hard to beat.

Figure 11-4

This large garden window, featuring bent glass, creates a bright dining area. It is available in custom sizes for both remodeling and new construction.
Great Lakes Window, Inc.

Awning windows

Awning windows provide some unique qualities. Due to their design, awning windows can be left open in hard rain storms without any threat of drenching the interior of your home. Their design also makes them popular with people who desire good air flow and privacy at the same time. These windows open out from the bottom of their frame with the use of a crank. In addition, they can be installed high on a wall to provide privacy without making them difficult to open.

Figure 11-5

This full wall of casement windows provides for a stunning kitchen and dining area. Pella Corporation

Garden windows

Garden windows enhance any kitchen. The design of these windows allows plenty of light to enter a room and provides a sill that accommodates plants and decorations nicely. Since the sides and top of a garden window extend past the exterior wall of a home, it is natural for more light to enter through the window.

Garden windows are available in several configurations. Some have side and top panels that open, and others have operable glass only in the main window section. The sill construction also varies from manufacturer to manufacturer. If your customer will be setting plants in the window sill, you will do best to buy a window with a water-resistant sill.

Bow windows

Many people confuse bow windows with bay windows. There is an easy way to tell the two windows apart. Bay windows have only three panels of glass. Bow windows have four or more panels. The installation of a bow window is complicated, expensive, and requires some serious structural modifications. This job is not one that you will want to try to accomplish when you are pressed for time.

If you are doing extensive remodeling and wish to add a little space to an area, along with a lot of light, a bow window will work wonders. Investing the time, money, and energy necessary to install a bow window will reward homeowners with a finished job that gives the remodeled space an open, airy look.

Bay windows

Bay windows (Fig. 11-6) are not as complex to install as bow windows, but neither do they offer the same benefits. If your customer's primary goal is a large window, a bay window will do fine. When they are trying to achieve additional floor space, such as a dining nook, bay windows cannot compete with bow windows. Unlike a bow window, bay windows are available in prefabricated units that make installation of the window easier.

With all windows, you and your customer should consider energy efficiency. Will your customer want a double-pane window (Fig. 11-7) or a triple-pane window (Fig. 11-8)? Work out these details before you price a job.

Operable skylights

Operable skylights offer many benefits in a kitchen. They naturally allow a great deal of light to flood the floor space, and they provide a means of ventilation that is not possible with standard windows (Fig. 11-9). If someone is having a bad day at the stove and the kitchen is filling with smoke, an open skylight allows the air to clear out quickly.

Figure 11-6

This bay window provides abundant natural light and uses a stationary panel in the center. Side sections of glass could be double-hung or stationary with grids. Pella Corporation

Just think, an operable skylight can help homeowners eliminate those quick runs to cut off the smoke detector when the cooking gets out of hand.

Bubble skylights

Bubble skylights are inexpensive, are relatively easy to install, and provide substantial natural light. This type of skylight does not open. However, when you consider the low cost of the units, they are a bargain. I'll talk about what is involved in the installation of bubble skylights and other windows a little later in this chapter.

Figure 11-7

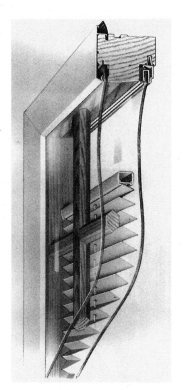

Double-pane windows with built-in blinds give customers something more than average for their remodeling dollars.
Pella Corporation

Types of doors

Just as there are many types of windows, there are also numerous types of door that can be included in remodeling projects. Depending on the location and layout of the kitchen, you might have no need for a door. However, if you are dealing with an expansive space, adding a double door and a deck could make a customer's kitchen even more enjoyable. The use of precut jamb kits (Fig. 11-10) and trim packages makes door installations easier, even on pocket doors (Fig. 11-11).

Figure 11-8

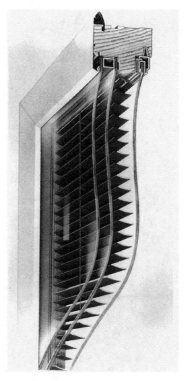

Triple-pane window with built-in blinds are popular in extreme climates. Pella Corporation

Standard entry doors

Standard entry doors are common in kitchen areas. When a kitchen location is such that it is convenient to a garage or driveway, it makes sense to have a door that allows access to the kitchen for unloading groceries. A door near a kitchen is also a good safety feature. Since fires sometimes start in kitchens, having a door close at hand for an emergency exit is smart thinking.

The replacement of a standard entry door is not a major job, but it can make an impressive difference in the look of a room. For example, assume that your customer has an existing entry door that

Figure 11-9

The skylights in this kitchen give plenty of natural lighting. Note the window seat/ daybed in the right of this photo. Timberlake Cabinet Company and American Woodmark Corporation

does not contain much glass. Can you imagine how the kitchen area would look with a new door that was full of glass? If customers have young children or large pets and are afraid to have glass near the floor, you could consider offering them a door that has a solid bottom half and a top half made of glass.

Sliding glass doors

Sliding glass doors were very popular at one time, but their appeal seems to have waned. Many people feel that sliding glass doors cheapen the appearance of a home. It is immaterial whether there is any truth to this feeling. The fact is that if people perceive a lower value, the worth of a home suffers.

Figure 11-10

Jamb kits, such as the one being installed here, can save contractors considerable time. L.E. Johnson Products, Inc.

Aside from public opinion, there are some drawbacks to sliding glass doors. Doors of lower quality often stick in their tracks, making them difficult to open. In cold climates the tracks sometimes freeze, making it impossible to use the doors. These factors are offset by the relatively low cost of average sliding glass doors and the amount of light they allow to enter a room.

Gliding glass doors

At first glance, gliding glass doors can appear to be sliding glass doors. The basic concept of how they look and work is very similar. Gliding glass doors, however, cost more and work better than sliders. Since the door panels are on gliders, they roll smoothly like a well-crafted kitchen drawer. If you like the look of a sliding glass door and want a door that is dependable and easy to operate, investigate gliders.

Figure 11-11

Pocket doors, such as this one, are ideal for kitchens where a swinging door would consume too much space. L.E. Johnson Products, Inc.

Double-hinged doors

Double-hinged doors are probably the most popular of all the various door types when it comes to a kitchen or dining area. These doors allow the installation of dead-bolt locks, can be purchased in many configurations, and are very energy efficient. They are not, however, cheap; good doors rarely are. For overall dependability and daily use, a quality double-hinged door is hard to beat.

French doors

French doors (Fig. 11-12) contain a lot of glass and add a good bit of elegance to the area they serve. They are, however, expensive. There is a significant benefit to a French door. If the unit is a true French door, both sides of the door can be opened simultaneously. This allows twice as much ventilation as can be achieved with other types of doors.

Figure 11-12

French swinging patio doors, like this one, can be used to exit a kitchen to an outside deck or a dining room. Wenco Patio Doors

Common door choices

Common door choices include the use of nine-lite units (Fig. 11-13) and six-panel, solid doors (Fig. 11-14). It is not uncommon for customers to want top-to-bottom glass in a door (Fig. 11-15). There are so many possibilities for doors that you have to spend a good amount of time with your customers during their decision-making process to make sure they will not be disappointed.

Figure 11-13

Nine-lite doors are popular in kitchens due to the light they allow in. Be aware, however, that many codes prohibit this type of door being used between living space and a garage. Benchmark Doors

Construction considerations

When you are evaluating windows and doors, there are certain construction considerations to be dealt with (Fig. 11-16). These considerations cover such aspects as the insulating value of glass used in the doors and windows, the type of frame construction used, and so forth. Let's take a few moments to run down a list of items to think about.

Insulated glass

Not all insulated glass is created equal. When you deal in window and door panes, you could be looking at single, double, or triple panes. Windows that have multiple panes are more energy efficient than

Figure 11-14

Six-panel doors provide good security and good looks. Benchmark Doors

those that don't. The air space created between the panes works as an insulator. However, not all double-pane windows have the same insulating qualities.

Most people are familiar with home insulation and R-values, but very few people know what a U-value is or what it means to them. When you are comparing windows, you must take a close look at the U-value. This is how you determine the energy rating of the window. Unlike R-values, where the higher the R-value the better the insulating quality, U-values are best when they are low. For example, a window with a U-value of four is good. A window with a U-value of six is not as good, and one with a U-value of two is better. Always compare U-values to determine the quality of a window.

Figure 11-15

Fifteen-lite doors are very popular in dining areas and are often used in kitchens with attached dining space. Benchmark Doors

Frame construction

The frame construction of a window can be very important. Windows with metal frames tend to condensate or sweat. This moisture can freeze in the winter and rot wooden structural members when the temperature is not freezing. Aluminum and vinyl-clad windows and doors eliminate any need for painting. Wood is a universal frame material, and it is generally considered to be one of the best choices available. This is not to say, however, that aluminum or vinyl are poor choices. The decision of what type of frame construction to purchase is a personal one.

Wooden frames are subject to rotting and insect infestation. These are two problems you will not encounter with aluminum and vinyl frames.

Figure 11-16

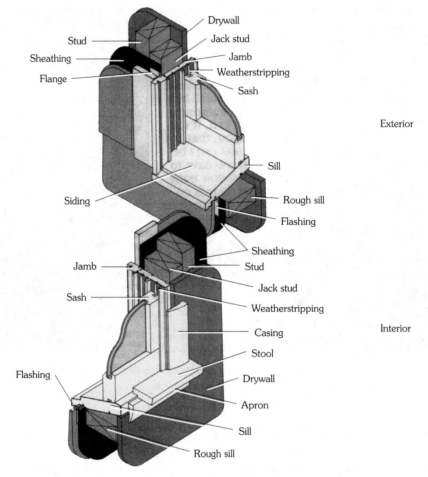

Cut section of exterior and interior window construction.
Anderson Windows, Inc.

The cost of aluminum and vinyl windows is generally more than that of windows with wood frames. If you are going to purchase an aluminum window, you should make sure the frame has a plastic or baked-enamel finish to retard corrosion. Wood windows that have metal channels for the sashes to move in are not as likely to swell and stick as are windows with wooden tracks. Before you purchase windows and doors, do a lot of homework. Compare the various types and brands to determine what will suit your customer's needs best.

Window and door sizes

Window and door sizes have a lot to do with how difficult it is to install them as replacements for existing windows and doors. If it is possible to obtain new products that require the same rough opening as your existing windows and doors, the retrofitting process will be much easier. With a little planning on your part, it should be possible to make replacing old windows and doors easy.

Installing new windows

Installing new windows can be extensive work. To do the job right, you will have to alter the exterior siding on the home and open the interior walls to reveal the existing window frames. If the rough openings for existing windows are not large enough to accommodate the new windows planned for installation, structural work will be required to enlarge the opening. A mistake during the swap-out could result in a costly lesson. Know what you're doing before you do it.

Windows that are in preset frames and mount flush in an exterior wall are the easiest to work with. A bow window is the most difficult type of window to install. Bay windows and garden windows fall in between the two extremes. If you plan to install a bow window, you should expect to build a foundation for the window to sit on. These windows are typically large and heavy. They cannot be supported well without a foundation. Garden windows and bay windows are usually one integral unit that can be installed on the side of a home. While either of these types of windows may require some outside support, the supports can be in the form of wooden members that extend from the underneath of the window and connect to the wall studs of the exterior wall. Flush-fitting windows do not require any external support, but all windows require a structural header to be installed over them. When you are replacing an existing window with a new window of an identical size, you will not have to alter the header. However, if the new window is larger than the one being replaced, you are in for some serious carpentry work.

To begin our exploration into the installation of replacement windows and into adding new windows where there have never been windows, let's start with flush-frame windows. These could be casement windows, awning windows, double-hung windows, sliding windows, or any other type of window that does not protrude past the exterior wall of the home. I'll start with replacing existing windows and then move onto the installation of new windows.

Replacing flush-fit windows

Replacing flush-fit windows with new windows that are the same size is not a big job. To do this, you must first remove the window trim. This can be done with a pry bar and a hammer. Start on the inside of the home. Remove the trim and the existing window sashes. Then go outside and remove the exterior window trim. Once the window jamb is exposed, the window can be removed. Now you have a framed rough opening to mount the new window into (Fig. 11-17). You may want a helper during this phase of the work.

With the old window out of the way, you can set the new window jamb into place. Make sure the new jamb is level both horizontally and vertically. Have some cedar shims on hand before you attempt to secure the new jamb. It may be necessary to shim portions of the window jamb in order to make the window level in all directions. Once the jamb is level, you should drive nails through the jamb and secure it to the rough opening. Begin by just tacking the nails into place. Don't drive them in tight until you have checked to see that the window operates properly.

After the window is installed permanently, it is time to trim it out. You can either cut your trim pieces from random stock or you can buy premade trim kits. These kits eliminate the need for cutting skills and enable the job to be done faster. Begin your trim work on the outside of the house. When the outside is trimmed, you can apply trim to the inside. When all the trim is in place, caulk the seams and fill the holes made by the nails. The nails should be countersunk to allow a filling compound to conceal them.

Figure 11-17

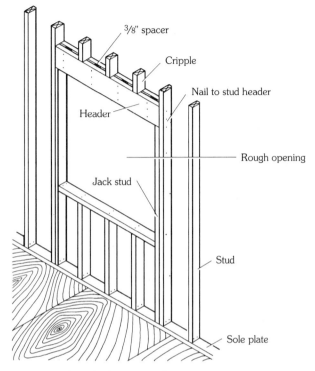

Framing details for a window. United States Government

Some windows are mounted with the use of a nailing flange. This is simply a thin piece of metal that surrounds the window frame and allows the window to be nailed or screwed directly to wall studs. If the old window you are replacing has this type of flange, it will be apparent once the outside trim is removed.

Installing new or larger windows

Installing new windows or installing windows that are larger than the units they are replacing requires more work. When you remove an existing window, you will see a header at the top of the rough opening. The header is one or two boards, possibly 2" × 6" or 2" × 8" boards, set above the opening. These headers support structural loads over the window. If you are cutting a new window into a wall where there has never been a window, you must install your own header. This work is not particularly difficult, but it is important.

Cutting a new window into an existing wall is not as difficult as it may seem. There are pitfalls that may be present, but anyone with basic carpentry skills can overcome most of these difficulties without breaking a sweat. The header I just mentioned, however, is crucial to the installation of a new window. The act of installing the header is not complicated, but it is mandatory, so let's discuss the process.

When you wish to add a window in an existing wall, you are going to have to work with the exterior finish of the home as well as the interior wall. The interior wall is easy—you will normally be dealing with drywall, which can be cut out with a sharp knife or a drywall saw. As with any hole you are cutting, it is usually best to start small and enlarge the hole as needed. Should you be taking the interior walls down to the bare studs anyway, your job will be a bit easier.

New windows are usually shipped with a set of instructions. These instructions recommend a size for the rough opening. The rough opening will be a bit larger than the window. To make this rough opening, you should start on the inside of the home.

Take a pencil and outline the area where you want to install the window. Make the outline the same size as the new window. This will allow you to visualize exactly where the window will fit and how it will look. When this is done, you should draw a second outline of the size required for the rough opening. Now you can cut away the interior wall covering with a keyhole saw to expose the wall studs.

Once the wall is opened up, you will see wall studs and probably some insulation. Remove the insulation. Now you are left with an open cavity that represents the rough opening of the window. Ultimately, you will have to expand the upward dimension of this hole to accommodate the work needed to install a header.

When you have the basic opening for the window open on the interior, you can focus your interests on the exterior wall. This work is a little more complex, so be prepared to take your time and to work diligently. Prior to cutting the inside opening, you should have checked to make sure there were no obstacles on the exterior wall that would prevent the installation of a new window. Obviously, you wouldn't want to install a window in a wall section that houses an electrical meter or some other nearly immovable object. Assuming that the outside wall is clear of obstacles, you can prepare to make a hole in the siding of the home.

How you proceed from this point depends, to some extent, on the type of siding you are working with. For the moment, assume that it is wood siding. Use a drill to make a hole in the wall. (The size of the bit is not terribly important in this step). Starting inside the home, drill a hole through the wall sheathing and siding. You can either drill the hole in the center of the wall cavity or at one of the corners of the opening. The purpose of this hole is to give you a reference point when you get outside.

After the hole is drilled, move outside and locate the hole. Using accurate measurements made from the inside opening, outline a proposed opening on the siding of the home. Once the shape of the rough opening is sketched out on the exterior wall, you can cut the opening out. If you are a little nervous about cutting in the wrong spot, you can drill holes at each corner of the inside opening to make sure your outline is where it should be. A mistake during these procedures is much easier to correct that a gaping hole in the side of a home.

When you are working with wood siding, you can cut the opening with most any type of wood-cutting saw. A reciprocating saw works very well, and some professionals like to use circular saws. You should cut the hole with a tool that you are comfortable with. When you are done cutting, the exterior hole should be nearly a mirror image of the inside hole. However, you're not done yet. You must still provide for a header, and you will probably have to add some wall studs in the area of the opening.

Headers for windows are installed above the rough openings. This requires opening up the hole for the window. The header will likely be made from boards with trade measurements of 2" x 8". If you cut above the rough opening, on the inside wall, by about 1 foot, you should have enough room to work. It is also routine to widen the interior rough opening by several inches on each side to accommodate the header.

Check with your local code enforcement office to see what size and what type of header is needed. Normally, two 2" × 8" boards, nailed together, are sufficient. Since wall studs are usually spaced 16 inches apart, on center, there is sure to be at least one wall stud that will have to be cut out of the window opening. The loss of vertical wall studs weakens the structural integrity of a wall, but a new header compensates for this loss. Go ahead and cut out wall studs that will interfere with your window placement. Before you start sawing, however, read the next few paragraphs so that you will understand at what point to cut the existing studs off.

When you frame an opening for a new window, several components must be included. Standard 2" × 4" studs are used to create a box that is slightly larger than the window unit. The bottom of this box sits on wall studs that have been cut to a proper length. The top of the box is usually set under a header with the use of very short pieces of 2" × 4" studs, called cripples. The sides of the box are typically nailed directly into wall studs.

To create a box for a window, many modifications may be necessary. The first step is cutting out wall studs that prohibit the window from fitting in the hole. These studs should be cut at a uniform height above the finished floor that will accommodate the bottom of the box of the window frame. Jack studs, studs that are nailed to other vertical studs, are installed to support the header. These jack studs are not full length. They are short enough to allow the header to sit on top of them. If a mistake has been made in calculating the width of a window opening, additional jack studs can be added to close in the opening.

The header is set on top of the jack studs and nailed into place. Nails connect the header to the full-length wall studs and the jack studs. Wall studs that were cut to accommodate the window bear down on the top of the header for support and are nailed in place. The sides of the box frame are nailed to the jack studs. Then, when necessary, short cripple studs are installed between the top of the box frame and the header. When this arrangement is complete, structural integrity is returned to the wall and a rough opening exists for a window unit.

Now you are ready to install the new window. If the window unit is equipped with a nailing flange, it will be installed from outside of the home. The window unit is set in the opening and the nailing flange should line up with studs that it can be screwed, or nailed, into. You must, however, make sure that the window unit is level in all directions prior to securing it into place.

Windows that do not have nailing flanges have wooden box frames. These frames are set into place and nailed to the side of the rough opening. Typically, shims made of cedar shingles are needed to level the window unit. Set the window unit in place and check it with a level. Slide shims under, over, and around the window frame as needed to plumb it. When the unit is level in all directions, nail it into place.

Trimming out new windows

Once a new window unit has been installed, you will be interested in trimming out the new window. The outside trim work is minimal if you cut your rough hole to a proper size. Many prehung windows, which are the easiest kind to work with, are shipped with trim kits or the trim kits are available separately. These kits make the trim work much easier to deal with.

Trim kits consist of pieces of wood that are installed to conceal the gaps between a window frame and the siding on a home. These pieces of wood are nailed into place. The nail heads should be countersunk with a nail punch. Then the holes made by the nails can be filled with a putty-type compound, sanded, and painted. Caulking should be installed along the edges of the trim material where it meets the siding. A clear, silicone caulking does a great job of weatherproofing the finished fit. Trim kits are also available for the interior portion of the window. The kits come with complete instructions for installation and all the parts needed to trim the window, except nails. Follow the manufacturer's recommendations during the installation. Basically, there will be a sill, a head jamb, and side jambs. These are simply finished pieces of wood trim that will conceal the window frame. Then casing material is installed over the wall covering to conceal cracks between the finished interior boxing and the rough boxing. Just as with the outside trim, the interior trim should be installed with countersunk nail heads to allow for a smooth finish job.

Installing new doors

Installing new doors is done with much the same procedure as is used for the installation of new windows, only the holes are much larger. When you buy a prehung door, the best kind to purchase, you will follow a procedure almost identical to the one just described for installing windows. There is one exception. Since windows don't extend down to floor level, there are short wall studs that support the bottom of a window frame. With a door, there are no studs left below the opening. The side and top framing for a door is the same as it is for a window, and the existing studs that would be left to support the underside of a window frame are removed completely for a door installation.

A good door (Fig. 11-18) will be shipped with instructions for installing it. You should always follow the manufacturer's recommendations for installation. One point cannot be stressed enough—windows and doors must be installed so that they are level in all directions or they will not function properly. Whether you are installing hardware (Fig. 11-19), building a door frame (Fig. 11-20), or doing rough framing (Fig. 11-21), you must pay attention to detail and make sure that all of your work is done to tight tolerances.

Installing skylights

Installing skylights is a bit different from framing in a window or a door. For one thing, the unit is installed in the roof of the home, but there are other differences. The type of skylight being installed determines the method of installation. Another factor in the installation of a skylight is the type of roof or ceiling configuration for the home. If a vaulted or cathedral ceiling exists, the installation will be easier than if there is an attic. Let's take some time now to discuss the different situations.

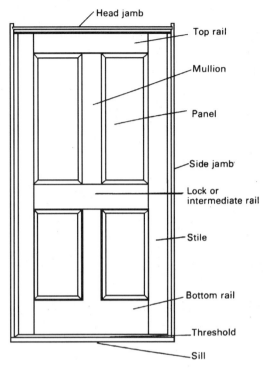

Head jamb

Top rail

Mullion

Panel

Side jamb

Lock or
intermediate rail

Stile

Bottom rail

Threshold

Sill

Details of a door. United States Government

Figure 11-18

If you have a vaulted or cathedral ceiling in the existing kitchen, installing a skylight will require a little less work than if attic space is over the ceiling. Since skylights are mounted in the roof of a home, it stands to reason that there must be no attic space between the skylight and the kitchen unless a light box is installed. I will talk about light boxes for attics as soon as this section is completed.

There are numerous types of skylights on the market. Bubble types are nonoperable and inexpensive. Some skylights open and have screens to prevent insect infestation. Of course, other types fall within these two extremes. All types of skylights produce abundant natural light, but the cost of the units vary greatly. The first step in installing a skylight is knowing what type your customer wants. If only extra light is desired, a bubble type will do the job. When a customer wants to vent a kitchen and increase airflow, an operable unit is in order.

Figure 11-19

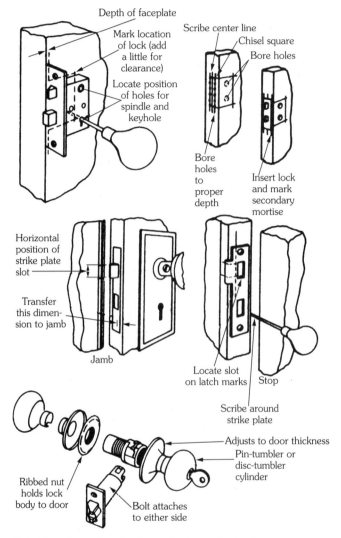

Specifications for the installation of a lock set.
United States Government

Each type of skylight may require a slightly different method of installation, so always follow the manufacturer's recommendations.

In the most simple installation possible, a skylight will have a nailing flange that attaches to the roof sheathing. This is usually the case with bubble-type units. A rough opening will be cut in the roof of the

Figure 11-20

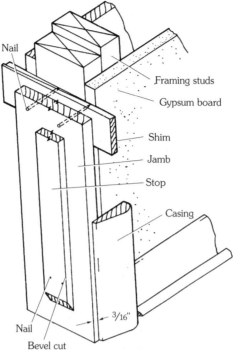

Nail

Framing studs

Gypsum board

Shim

Jamb

Stop

Casing

³/₁₆"

Nail

Bevel cut

Cut section of a door jamb. United States Government

home. This is best done with a reciprocating saw, but other types of wood-cutting saws can be used. The size of the opening is determined by the template supplied with the skylight.

Many skylights are small enough to fit between roof rafters. Since rafters are generally set on 24-inch centers, a skylight with small dimensions will not require any major structural modifications. However, even if you are installing a large skylight, the required modifications are simple enough for remodelers of modest skill levels to manage.

Let's assume that the skylight unit is large enough that one of the roof rafters must be cut. This may seem to be an imposing problem, but it really isn't. Let's assume you have laid the skylight template on the roof and cut out the roof shingles and sheathing. There is a rafter

Figure 11-21

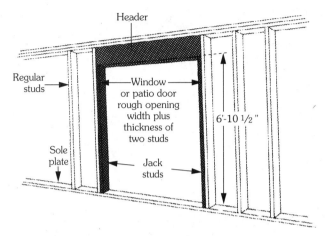

A rough opening for a patio door. Anderson Windows, Inc.

in your way. What should you do with it? Hack it off. I know this sounds a little extreme and rough cut, no pun intended, but you must do away with the rafter. Will the roof fall in? No, not if you follow the steps I'm about to recommend.

You're not going to just hack off a roof rafter and leave it hanging. Instead, you are going to install a header that gives you something to attach both the skylight and the severed rafter to. The rough opening you cut for the skylight can be cut from either side of the roof; however, the finish cut on the rafter that is in your way has to be made from inside the home.

Once you have a hole in the roof and the rafter section is cut out of the way of the skylight, you need to install a header. This header is just a piece of wood (sometimes two pieces nailed together) that spans the distance between the remaining, full-length rafters. Two headers are required, one for each end of the severed rafter.

Skylight headers are nailed at each end to rafters that have not been cut. They are positioned to butt up against the rafter, or rafters, that have been cut. The top and bottom of each header should be flush with the existing rafters. In other words, the lumber used to make a header should have the same dimensions as that used for the rafters.

Once the header is nailed into place, the end of the cut rafter can be attached to the side of the header. This can be done with nails, but special metal devices are available to make a better connection and support. These hangers have nailing flanges on each side so that the hanger can be secured to a flat surface, such as a header. The metal is formed to fit perfectly around a particular size of lumber. These brackets come in various sizes to accommodate different sizes of lumber. When this type of hanger is used, the cut rafter is supported completely. This does a better job than simply nailing the cut rafter to a header.

After both headers are installed, you will have created a box. This box should be just slightly larger than the skylight being installed. The instructions that come with skylights should tell you exactly what size to make the boxed opening. Now you are ready to install the skylight. Always follow the directions provided with the skylight.

I can't tell you exactly how your particular skylight should be installed, but I can give you a good idea of what is normally involved in such an installation. Bubble-type skylights generally have a nailing flange. Larger skylights are typically made with a curb stop or L-type brackets. With a bubble-type skylight, you simply set the unit on the box you've created and nail it into place. It is common practice to put either a foam sealant or a caulking compound under the nailing flange, between the skylight and the box, before securing the unit.

Once the skylight is in place, the roof can be repaired. If you cut the hole in the roof properly, this is simply a matter of allowing the shingles to lay back down over the nailing flange. When the hole that was cut for the skylight is too big to allow the shingles to just lay down and cover the flange, some flashing will have to be added. Roof flashing is sold in various colors (to match different roof colors), and it is normally sold in rolls. Again, I want to stress that you should follow the manufacturer's instructions in all installations.

Roof flashing, in the case of a bubble-type skylight, extends from the nailing flange to a point of termination under the surrounding shingles. Your goal is to install the flashing in such a way that water cannot leak through the roof. How this actually is done depends upon the type of skylight being installed.

The installation of curb-mounted skylights is a little different. These units require that a curb (raised box) be built on top of the roof. The exact dimensions of the curb are determined by the individual skylight. In any case, the curb is just a box that is nailed into place on top of the roof. Flashing is wrapped around the box and extended to a point under the shingles to waterproof the installation.

Once the curb is prepared properly, the skylight can be set into place. The skylight unit will have a recessed channel that is designed to fit over the top edges of the curb, on top of the flashing. Once the unit is in place, it can be secured through its mounting holes. This concludes your on-roof work, but you're not done yet.

When you move inside, you must create a finished look for the new skylight. With a vaulted or cathedral ceiling, this job is pretty simple. As you look up, you will see the rough framing that is holding the skylight in place. The purchase of a few wide trim boards will allow you to complete the interior part of your job. These trim boards can be nailed over the rough framing to provide a finished product.

If a kitchen has attic space above it, you have more work to do on the inside. Since the new skylight has a ceiling between it and the kitchen, you must create a light box. This is simply a boxed shaft that allows you to see the skylight from the kitchen. As simple as a light box seems, it can be a little tricky to build.

A plumb bob can be used to determine where a hole should be cut in the kitchen ceiling. By holding the string of the plumb bob in the center of the skylight and allowing the plumb bob to dangle just above the kitchen ceiling, you can pinpoint the location for your light shaft. Once your spot is marked, cut out the ceiling. The size of the hole should be the same as that of the skylight. If ceiling joists are in your way, cut them and head them off with the same techniques used to head off the rafters you cut for the skylight installation. Even if there are no joists to be cut, you will need to build a box like you did in the rafters for the skylight.

Now you should have a hole in the kitchen ceiling that lines up with the new skylight. However, you need to create a tunnel for the light to travel. This can be done with standard framing practices and drywall or sheets of plywood. Assuming you decide to use plywood, all you have to do is cut four pieces of plywood to create a box. The plywood is nailed to the inside of the box that houses the skylight and to the box in the ceiling joists.

If you decide to use drywall, frame your shaft with standard wall studs. The nailing surface of the studs should be flush with the inside edges of the two boxes you have built. This allows drywall to be installed on the studs in such a way that it will flow smoothly into the two boxes.

Adding and replacing windows and doors is not normally a complicated task. There are times, however, when circumstances turn this relatively simple job into a much more complicated task. Before you attempt this type of work, make sure you understand the principals involved. Read all literature supplied with your products and always follow the manufacturer's recommendations.

Flooring options

Chapter 12

THERE are many flooring options to consider when remodeling a kitchen. Sheet-vinyl flooring is simple to install, inexpensive, durable, and popular. Tile floors are more expensive than vinyl, but they enhance the appearance of a room considerably. Wide-plank wood or old bricks are a terrific choice for flooring if you are creating a rustic kitchen.

With so many options, how will you know what type of flooring to use? Much of the decision depends on your customers' personal tastes and lifestyles. This chapter introduces you to each type of flooring and gives you information on what to expect from the various types of floors. Additionally, you get a strong overview of what is involved with the installation of each type of flooring. If you will be doing the work yourself, installation methods could be an important factor in your decision about which type of material to use.

Existing flooring conditions

Existing flooring conditions can present some problems during remodeling. For example, if a dishwasher has been leaking slowly for a long period of time, you will need to repair or replace some subflooring before a new floor is installed. It might even be necessary to repair or replace floor joists that have deteriorated over time. These conditions can be a nasty surprise, but they don't have to ruin your job. Let's look at how you can cope with existing conditions that are not up to par.

Rotted subflooring

Rotted subflooring is sometimes a problem in kitchen remodeling. Dishwashers, kitchen sinks, and other sources of water can all contribute to the destruction of subflooring. This damage might not be evident until existing floor coverings are removed. Fortunately, the damage is usually confined to a small area and is fairly easy to correct. You should have a clause in the remodeling contract that addresses how unforeseen problems will be handled financially.

Subflooring that has been damaged by water is usually stained with a black color. If you suspect a floor is damaged but are not sure use a screwdriver to probe the wood. If the flat bit of the screwdriver can be easily be pushed into the floor using minimal force, the flooring should be replaced. Many floors have two layers, or more, of flooring between the finished floor covering and the floor joists. You should check the various levels individually for damage. If the top layer of subflooring (called the underlayment) is damaged, there is a good chance the subflooring below it has also suffered.

For the time being, let's assume that a section of flooring under the old dishwasher has rotted. In this example, you need remove only the damaged section of the existing subflooring. The first step in making the repair is to locate the floor joists by driving a long nail through the flooring and then going beneath the floor to locate the nail. The nail provides a reference point for measurements. This makes it possible to mark the joist locations on the subflooring in the kitchen. With the joist locations marked, you are ready to begin the repairs.

Use a circular or reciprocating saw to cut through the subflooring between the floor joists. Cut out the bad section until the hole is even with the joists, but don't cut through the joists. If the damaged section is large, you might have more than one hole between floor joists. Once the bad section is out, you must make a few precision cuts. Your goal is to cut out the subflooring where it rests on the floor joists. Find the middle of the top of the joist to use as your center line. If you do this right, you will have good subflooring covering one half of the floor joist and the other half of the joist will be exposed where subflooring was removed. This gives you a nailing surface that will allow new flooring to be installed flush with the existing flooring.

Now all you have to do is cut a section of plywood to fit into the opening you have created. The new subflooring must be of the same thickness of the existing subflooring. If there are more than two floor joists involved, only the two on each end of the span should be partially covered with existing subflooring. Any joists inside the span should be clear of all flooring, so that the new flooring can lay flat on them. The new section of plywood can be laid in the opening and nailed into place on the top halves of the floor joists at each end. If there are any joists in the middle of the opening, the plywood should also be nailed to them. This procedure eliminates your rotted flooring and provides an even surface for your new subflooring.

Damaged floor joists

Damaged floor joists are not commonly found during kitchen remodeling jobs, but they can occur. This problem may seem devastating, but there are a few simple ways to overcome the dilemma. Unless there are several bad joists, these simple repairs will suffice. However, if you open up a floor and find that a number of the joists are bad, you must plan on the time-consuming task of complete replacement.

Let's start with a situation where the top of a joist has rotted. The joist has a bad spot in it that runs for a length of 3 feet. In this case, there is no need to rip out the whole joist. You can simply nail a new section of floor joist onto the existing one. The new material should be of the same height as the joist being repaired. In terms of length, the repair joist should be at least 2 feet longer on each end than the damaged section. Since the damage in this case is 3 feet long, the repair joist will be at least 7 feet long.

Take the repair joist and position it along the side of the damaged joist. Make sure the top of the new joist is even with the tops of the other joists. When the repair joist is positioned properly, nail it into place. If you want to make the damaged joist even stronger, repeat the process on the other side of the joist. A double repair joist will provide plenty of strength to the damaged area.

If you have a joist that is rotted out for its entire length, you will have to alter the repair procedure. Instead of nailing repair joists onto the sides of the rotted joists, you are going to have to install a new joist right beside the old one. Measure the bad joist and obtain a new one with the same dimensions. All you have to do is slide the new joist into place beside the old one. You should remove subfloor to do this work, since the job is much easier when the subflooring is gone.

When the new joist is in place, it can be nailed to the band boards and sill plates. These types of repairs are not complicated, but the work can be heavy, and a second set of hands will be appreciated. Should you have extensive damage to a number of floor joists, you can use this same procedure to correct the problem. Now that you understand how to take care of the hidden surprises that may pop up, let's get on with your finished flooring options.

Sheet vinyl

Sheet-vinyl flooring (Fig. 12-1) is found in more kitchens than any other type of finished floor covering. This is due to many factors. Vinyl flooring is waterproof, which is a plus in a kitchen. It is also inexpensive, is available in an array of colors and patterns (Figs. 12-2 through 12-4), can be installed by many homeowners, and is easy to clean. I'm sure by now you can see clearly why it is so popular.

Figure 12-1

Here is an example of vinyl flooring that adds to the brightness and charm of a kitchen. Mannington Resilient Floors

Figure 12-2

Black and white tiles continue to be popular with some customers, as is shown in this photo. Mannington Resilient Floors

Is vinyl flooring a good option for your customer's kitchen? The answer to this question depends on your customer's personal feelings and tastes. A wide-plank wood floor gives a more rustic and realistic look than vinyl, but the benefits of vinyl flooring are numerous.

How difficult is it to install new vinyl flooring? When a kitchen has been gutted out completely, installing new vinyl flooring is pretty simple. If you will have to fit the flooring in around cabinets, island units, and other obstacles (Fig. 12-5), the process becomes a bit more trying. All in all, if you have plenty of patience, you should be able to accomplish the job by yourself in just a few hours. Most remodelers, however, sub this work out to a flooring contractor.

Before installing new vinyl, the existing floor must be prepared properly. This may entail considerable work. For vinyl to look good

Figure 12-3

The remodeler/designer has chosen to have the vinyl flooring extend from the kitchen into the dining area in this photo. While this practice is not common, it can be cost-effective and attractive.
Mannington Resilient Floors

(Fig. 12-6), it must be installed on a level surface. It is possible to install new vinyl over existing vinyl, but most professionals advise against this procedure. The old vinyl may be lumpy, and you can bet it has dirt and grease built up on it. These conditions are not favorable for a great-looking job (Fig. 12-7). Any existing floor covering should be removed or covered with underlayment before you install new vinyl flooring.

The first step in removing old vinyl is to remove all of the trim molding where the flooring meets walls and cabinets. This can be easily accomplished with a pry bar. Once the edges of the old flooring are visible, you may be able to lift the covering out of place in one piece. However, the flooring will more than likely be stuck to the subflooring. In this case you want to heat the flooring with a heat gun or a high-powered hair dryer. Again, most professional remodelers require their flooring contractors to take care of this type of work.

Figure 12-4

The corner accents used with this vinyl flooring give it a little more power than a plain floor would have. Congoleum Prestige "Paramount" sheet vinyl flooring

After the old flooring is out, scrape off all of the old adhesive from the subflooring. If you can't get the subflooring clean, you must either replace it or install layers of underlayment over it. Underlayment is a very thin wood that is usually sold in sheets like plywood and can be glued, nailed, or screwed to the subflooring.

If the subflooring is clean but exhibits damage such as cracks and depressions, you can use a filling compound to smooth out the surface. Your local flooring supplier can provide you with a brand of filling compound. Or your flooring contractor can provide and install the compound for you. This filling compound is placed in cracks and depressions and smoothed out with a putty knife. Once the compound dries, you are left with a smooth subflooring that is ready for vinyl.

Figure 12-5

Designs in vinyl flooring, as shown here, can tie it in quite nicely with wallpaper. Congoleum
Sensation "Inspiration" sheet vinyl flooring

When the prep work is done, it's time to install the sheet goods. Let me give you a few tips on installation in case you plan to do the work yourself. Before you begin your installation, you should roll the flooring up so that the finished side of it is facing out. The flooring should be stored for at least 24 hours in an area where the temperature will remain at least 65 degrees Fahrenheit.

An average kitchen can be floored without seams (Fig. 12-8), but large kitchens, those with dimensions in excess of 12 feet, may require seams. If you will have to seam your flooring, you will complete that step first. To make a seam, lay both pieces of vinyl in place with one overlapping the other. Make sure the pattern lines up and matches. You need something that is long and straight to help you cut the flooring—a typical wall stud will do fine. Lay the stud in place to guide your knife. (A razor knife works very well when cutting vinyl). After

Figure 12-6

Here is an example where vinyl flooring has been extended into additional living space. As you can see, this technique, while not often used, does well in the design of new living space. Congoleum Highlight "Americana" sheet vinyl flooring

making the cut, adhere both pieces of vinyl to the subflooring to make your seam.

Ask your flooring supplier to provide you with an adhesive that is recommended for your specific type of flooring. The adhesive is normally applied with a large, rectangular trowel. The trowel has serrated edges that are used to spread the adhesive. After sheet vinyl is laid on the adhesive, a roller of some type is used to press the vinyl into the adhesive and to remove air bubbles.

When you lay the flooring, make sure that you leave extra flooring that rolls up against the walls. You need this waste factor to ensure a good fit. Once the flooring is in place, you are ready to secure it.

Figure 12-7

Sheet-vinyl flooring can be used to achieve many looks, such as this down-home appearance. Congoleum Dimensions "Fame" sheet vinyl flooring

Some installers apply adhesive under the entire piece of vinyl, and others only use adhesive at seams and edges. Check with your manufacturer's recommendations for the proper procedure for your flooring.

At this point you should have the entire floor area covered with vinyl, and a few inches on the edges of the vinyl should be rolled up on the walls. Use your wall stud or a carpenter's framing square to push the flooring tight against the walls. When you can see that the vinyl is tight against the wall, use your razor knife to cut the vinyl where it meets the corner of the wall and floor. When you get to the corners, you will have to cut the apex of the folded vinyl. Keep the vinyl tight against all walls and secure each section as you cut it. To secure the vinyl, you can use adhesive or staples. If staples are used, they should

Figure 12-8

If you look closely at the vinyl flooring used in this kitchen, you will see that it mixes very well with the cabinets and drapes. Congoleum Dimensions "Fresco" sheet vinyl flooring

be spaced about 3 inches apart, kept very close to the wall, and covered with shoe molding for the finished product.

Continue to work your way around the room, following these directions. When you come to doorways or openings, allow enough flooring to be cut so that it will extend to a desired point within the opening, where it will be hidden under a metal trim strip. When you have finished the installation, you should allow the floor sit for a day before you set cabinets or heavy furniture on it. Vinyl often contracts after being installed, and heavy objects can stress the flooring if they are set on it too soon.

To finish off the vinyl job (Fig. 12-9), use metal strips to cover the edges of the vinyl in doorways. These threshold strips are held in

Figure 12-9

This kitchen is unusual in the fact that the cabinets have a wallpaper design on them. The woodgrain vinyl works nicely with this approach. Congoleum Carefree "Finger Block" vinyl tile flooring

place with small nails. The edges of the flooring at walls and cabinets can be concealed with wooden baseboard and shoe molding. If you wind up with a few small bubbles in your floor, you can remove them by poking a small hole in the vinyl with a straight pin.

Tile floors

Tile floors (Figs. 12-10 through 12-14) are considerably more challenging to install than vinyl floors. However, it is feasible for general remodelers to complete this task. The more work you can do yourself, the less you have to pay subcontractors.

Figure 12-10

Bright, large tile flooring will not work in every kitchen, but it can be used effectively, as shown here. Maytag Company

Ceramic and quarry tiles make beautiful floors, but they can be slippery when wet. Fragile objects that are dropped on these floors are likely to break. Also, heavy objects dropped on a tile floor can damage the flooring. Overall, tile floors give very good service for an extremely long time.

The key to a great tile job is proper planning. The act of installing the tile is not difficult at all (Fig. 12-15), but the layout is tricky. If you spend enough time planning your work and working your plan, you will wind up with a fantastic floor. Installing a tile floor is easiest if you do the work when the kitchen is stripped of its cabinets and appliances. Having a large open area to work in will improve your odds for success.

Figure 12-11

The tile flooring in this photo tends to draw a person into the kitchen.
Strategy in flooring can take many forms, and this is an effective one.
Maytag Company

Experienced professionals can lay a tile floor without dry-fitting the tiles. For an inexperienced installer, laying the tiles out on the floor before any adhesive is applied is a much better approach. Tiles should be laid by placing the first tile in the center of the space to be covered. Each subsequent tile will fan out from the center tile until the floor is covered. Depending on the style of tile being used, there may be patterns that are built as the tiles are laid into place. This too is easier for novices when the floor is not covered with adhesive.

To begin your installation, measure your room in both dimensions. If the room isn't shaped as one open rectangle, divide the floor areas up into individual rectangles. For example, an L-shaped kitchen would be made into two rectangles and a U-shaped kitchen would have three rectangular work areas. Once your work areas are defined, measure the

Figure 12-12

This photo shows the used of different types of tile used to make a stunning kitchen. Fieldstone Cabinetry Inc./Craig Buchanan

distances between the walls in both the width and depth dimensions. Find the center point of the work area and set the first tile into place on a dry subfloor. Your subfloor should be clean, sturdy, dry, and level.

As you lay in the practice tiles, you must keep in mind the width needed for joints and borders. When you are working with tiles that have a uniform shape, it is best to use commercial spacers in order to maintain an equal distance between the individual tiles. These spacers are made out of plastic and resemble little crosses. They are available from the same suppliers who sell tile.

After you have completed your dry run, you are ready to set the tiles permanently. Keep good mental or written notes on how you set the

Figure 12-13

Here is a kitchen with bright cabinets used to offset a dark floor. Fieldstone Cabinetry Inc./Masco Corporation

tile in the test run before you pick them up. After the tiles have been removed, spread adhesive over the subfloor in the immediate area where you will be working. Check with your tile supplier before you purchase any adhesive. Some adhesives work better than others with certain types of tiles. Your tile dealer will be able to recommend the proper adhesive for the type of tile you will be using. When applying the adhesive, follow the manufacturer's recommendations.

Just as you should follow the manufacturer's recommendations for applying adhesive, so should you follow its directions for installing your tile. In fact, some tile companies provide free how-to booklets that detail each step of setting their tile. While we are on the subject of freebies, many tile suppliers will loan purchasers of tile the use of free tile cutters. However, you may have to ask for the loaner.

Figure 12-14

Floor tiles are available in various sizes and shapes, as illustrated here. Latco Products

Once your adhesive is in place, you are ready to set the tile. You might want to use a chalk line to make marks on the adhesive. These lines will make it easier for you to line up your tiles. Retrace the steps you took in your practice run as you press the tiles into the adhesive. If necessary, a rubber mallet can be used to tap stubborn tiles into the glue. Make sure your spacers stay in place and that you maintain even gaps between the tiles.

Sooner or later you are going to have to cut some tiles. There are many ways to do this, but a professional tile-cutting tool is best. If your tile supplier will not loan you one of these tools, you can rent one at your local tool rental center. The provider of the tool will instruct you in its proper use. In addition to the primary cutting tool, a pair of nipping pliers will come in handy for nipping edges off of tiles as you work around corners and obstacles.

Once all of your tile is set in place, you must let it set for a prescribed amount of time. This time will be dictated by the type of tile and adhesive you are using, so check the manufacturer's recommendations. Once the tile has set up, you must remove the plastic spacers and prepare to grout the cracks.

Figure 12-15

Installing tile, as illustrated here, is a job that is often done on one's knees. Protect your future by wearing cushioned kneepads when doing this type of work. Dal-Tile

There are many types of grout material available, so you should ask for a professional supplier's recommendation. Some grout comes premixed, and others require mixing. Once you have the grout ready to apply, you simply smear it into all the seams between the tiles with a rubber-faced trowel. Don't worry about getting the grout on the tile—it will come off.

After all the cracks are filled with grout material, but before the grout has had time to set up, use a wet sponge to clean the tiles. This allows you to wipe off all excess grout before it dries. After you have used the sponge to clean the flooring, go over the tiles with an absorbent towel to remove any remaining grout. You must get it off before it hardens.

Now you will have to wait about 72 hours for the grout to set up. Some grout is faster to dry, some is slower. Be sure to follow the manufacturer's recommendations. When the grout material is dry, your floor is ready to use.

Should you choose to use individual vinyl tiles instead of ceramic tiles, you will find a few differences in the installation methods. For one thing, no gap is left between the tiles. Secondly, many inexperienced people use too much adhesive and have it squirt up through the seams as the tiles are set in place. If this happens, thin out the adhesive and clean off the tile with a solvent that is recommended by the tile manufacturer. Of course, vinyl tile is easier to cut than ceramic or quarry tile; it can be cut with a razor knife.

Brick floors

Brick floors in a kitchen are not very common, but this very fact makes them a potentially attractive option to consider. New bricks can be used. Or you may choose older bricks that have aged and weathered to provide a more rustic look. These older bricks are cheaper than new ones. In fact, sometimes they are free.

A brick floor is not for everyone. There are special considerations that must be addressed when brick is used. First of all, bricks are heavy, so the subflooring and support structures must be substantial enough to carry the weight of the bricks and mortar used to set them in. Unlike tile, bricks should be set in a mortar base. Also, the grouting used with bricks should be of a mortar type, rather than a typical grout material. One final consideration is the height of the bricks. Since the bricks are much thicker than tiles, the finished level of the kitchen floor will be elevated.

If you decide to go with bricks, you should prepare the subflooring just as you would for tile. The same layout procedures also apply. Any typical mortar mix can be used for setting a brick floor. The depth of the mortar may vary, but 1 inch is common. Mix your mortar in compliance with the instructions that were provided with it. Mix only a little at a time. A plastic mixing pan (these can be bought in hardware stores and general building supply outlets) is ideal for preparing mortar for brick floors.

Scoop mortar onto the subfloor with a shovel. Spread it out with a large trowel to obtain a uniform thickness. Start in the center of your work space and work outward, just as you would with tile. If you're using old bricks, they will not be consistent in size, and this may create some problems in your layout. However, with a good eye, you can avoid major discrepancies. Set the bricks into the mortar and tap them into place with the handle of your mason's trowel. Don't walk on the bricks until the mortar has set up; your steps will dislodge and shift the bricks.

After all the bricks are set and the mortar has dried, you are ready to fill in the gaps. Some people recommend filling the cracks as you go, and others suggest waiting until the mortar bed has dried. If you choose to wait until the mortar has dried, lay a large sheet of plywood over the bricks to work from. This will distribute your weight more evenly and help to avoid breaking bricks out of the bed. Mix up some more mortar and begin to chink it into the cracks with a triangular mason's trowel. A finishing tool can be used to crease the joint, or you can leave the joint flat by floating it out with the flat edge of your trowel. I should add that knee pads are a good idea when installing floors. They save a lot of wear and tear on your body parts.

After the brick job is done, let it set until the mortar has dried. Any excess mortar can be cleaned off with a wire brush or some muriatic acid. **WARNING:** Before you use the acid, put on some good eye protection. It is also wise to avoid contact between the acid and your skin by wearing gloves and long sleeves. To use an acid or a solvent, you should read and heed the manufacturer's instructions carefully.

Wood flooring

Wood flooring is not a common choice for a kitchen (Figs. 12-16 through 12-18). When you weigh the options for a wood floor, you must consider hard wood versus soft wood. Then there is the question

Figure 12-16

Brazilian cherry plank wood flooring makes an impressive statement in a home.
Kentucky Wood Floors, Louisville, Ky.

of whether to use planks, wide patterns, narrow patterns, or square wooden tiles. My personal preference leans toward wide-plank floors with peg holes, even though some soft-wood floors with worm marks make very attractive, rustic kitchen decor. The choice of which type of wood flooring (Figs. 12-19 and 12-20) to use is really a personal issue and should be left up to your customers.

The standard thickness for wood flooring is three-quarters of an inch. Width dimensions range, typically, from $1\frac{1}{2}$ inches to about $3\frac{1}{4}$ inches for strip floors and from 3 to 8 inches for planks (Fig. 12-21). Lengths are available as short as 9 inches, with longer lengths extending past 8 feet. If you choose wood tiles, they will vary from about 10 to 36 inches square.

There are many grades of wood flooring. The grade pertains to the quality and appearance of the wood. A wood graded as being clear is the best you can buy. Depending on the type of wood you will be working with (Fig. 12-22), the grading system varies to some extent.

▲

Figure 12-17

Plain oak bordeaux wood flooring has been used in this dining area, and it gives a feel of elegance. Kentucky Wood Floors, Louisville, Ky.

Talk with your supplier about your project and ask to see samples of various grades. This is the best way to get what you want.

When you take delivery of your wood flooring, inspect it all carefully. Make sure none of it is twisted or warped. If wood is not cared for properly when it is stored and transported, it can become damaged and difficult to work with. Insist on having only good wood to work with (Fig. 12-23).

Wood flooring can be installed directly over an existing vinyl floor or on a good subfloor. As with any type of flooring, you must make sure the base for the flooring is level and solid. While not mandatory, a 15-pound asphalt paper barrier should be laid over the subflooring before any wood flooring is installed. This will help to avoid moisture problems.

Figure 12-18

New traditional plank wood flooring provides a wealth of opportunities in dining rooms and kitchens.
Robbins Hardwood Flooring, Cincinnati, Oh.

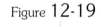

Figure 12-19

Contemporary maple wood flooring is not used often in kitchens, but it is an effective flooring that should be considered.
Robbins Hardwood Flooring, Cincinnati, Oh.

Figure 12-20

Notice the designs in this wood flooring. It gives a different appearance from traditional flooring.
Bruce Hardwood Floors, 1-800-722-4647:
Herringstrip™ Toast Color

Figure 12-21

Plank wood flooring is often thought of as being dark. As you can see here, that doesn't have to be true.
Bruce Hardwood Floors,
1-800-722-4647:
Caruth® Plank Creme Color

Figure 12-22

Rustic plank flooring, as shown here, is very effective in country kitchens. The Colonial Williamsburg Foundation and Lis King

Let's talk first about installing tongue-and-groove strip flooring. To do this job, you should go to a tool rental center and rent a floor nailer. Have the people at the rental center show you how to operate it properly. Basically, you hold the nailer at an angle, up against a piece of flooring, and hit the top of the tool with a mallet. This drives special barbed nails, called cleats, into the flooring at an angle. The nails are not visible once the flooring is installed, and the tool eliminates the need for predrilling each piece of wood for nailing by hand. Believe me, the rental fee is money well spent.

When you lay out your flooring, leave a small gap (about three-quarters of an inch) to allow for expansion of the wood. These gaps will be covered with decorative wood trim. Before the gaps are covered, however, they should be filled with cork strips.

Figure 12-23

A traditional strip wood flooring.
Robbins Hardwood Flooring, Cincinnati, Oh.

Start your first strip with the groove facing the wall. Remember to leave a gap around the borders of all walls. You will nail these starter pieces through the top of the wood, near the edge with the groove. This nailing is done with a conventional hammer and 8-penny nails. The nails will be hidden later with shoe mold. Before you start banging nails, drill holes in the flooring through which the nails will be inserted. If you just start hammering away, the wood is likely to split. Once you have a complete line of starter strips installed, you can move on with the rest of the flooring.

Don't continue by nailing flooring in haphazardly. Lay out several rows of flooring without nailing them. Move the flooring around as necessary to break up the seams. When you are pleased with the way your layout looks (Fig. 12-24), you can start nailing the floor in place. Line up the tongues with the grooves and press the strips into place.

Figure 12-24

Strip wood flooring in a light color doesn't darken a kitchen, and this is always desirable.
Timberlake Cabinet Company and American Woodmark Corporation

These strips will be blind nailed. This means that the nails will be driven in at an angle, so they cannot be seen as additional strips are installed. When you reach the other end of your room and are ready for the last row of strips, they will be installed just like the first starter row. If you have trouble getting the last row tight, use a pry bar to put tension on the ending strip while you nail it in place.

Working with plank flooring is a little different from installing strip flooring. You can still use the blind nailing method, but since there may not be a tongue-and-groove connection, you cannot hide the face nails in the starter strips with baseboard trim. The way to get around this is with the use of countersunk nails or screws and wood plugs. You can buy flooring that is provided with plugs, and this is the best bet for one-time do-it-yourselfers. You will definitely need to face nail the starter planks, and you may find that you want to continue a pattern of face nailing so that the plugs will add to the enhancement of the kitchens you offer your customers.

Some houses are built on concrete slabs. If you want to install wood flooring in a kitchen that sits on a slab, you will have to install a base for the flooring to be attached to. A popular way of doing this is the screed method (Fig. 12-25). To attach wood to concrete, you will find the job much easier when a powder-actuated nailing tool is used. By loading a powder cartridge (Fig. 12-26) into the tool (Fig. 12-27), you are able to drive special nails (Fig. 12-28) through the wood supports and into the concrete floor. It is possible, however, to simply install plywood on concrete to attach wood flooring (Fig. 12-29). Covering screw heads in plank flooring with hole covers (Fig. 12-30) is also popular. Having the right tools (Fig. 12- 31) and using them the right way (Figs. 12-32 through 12-34) are the keys to success.

Figure 12-25

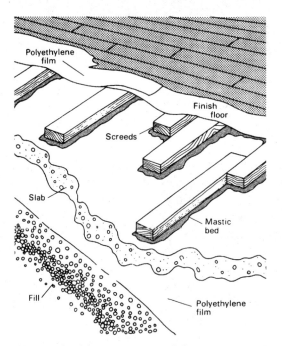

Houses build on concrete slabs require some preparation before installing a wood floor. One method of doing this involves the use of screeds, as shown here.
United States Government

Figure 12-26

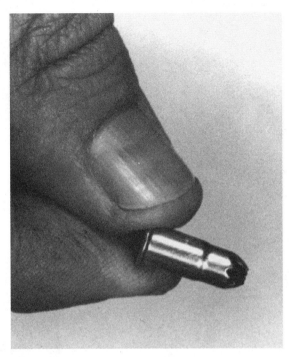

Cartridge for powder-actuated nailing tool.

The type of flooring chosen for your kitchen has much to do with the finished look, so let your customers take their time in making a buying decision. Further, be patient with your installation of the flooring. This job is too important to rush through.

Flooring installations are a phase of work that some remodeling contractors do very well. If you, or your crews, have the ability to install flooring, you can get more mileage out of the profits from each job you do. However, if you feel uncomfortable with the flooring process, find a reputable, dependable flooring contractor and sub the work out. Flooring is a big part of a job, so don't take a chance on ruining an otherwise good job with a slipshod flooring installation.

Figure 12-27

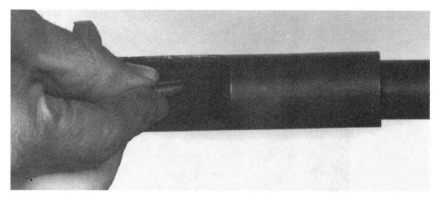

Powder-actuated nailing tool used to shoot fasteners into concrete.

Figure 12-28

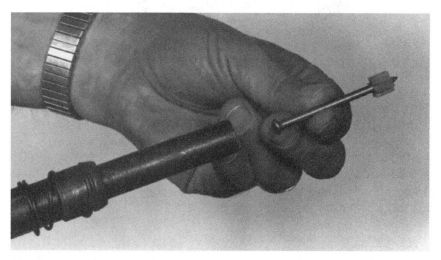

Nail for powder-actuated nailing tool.

Figure 12-29

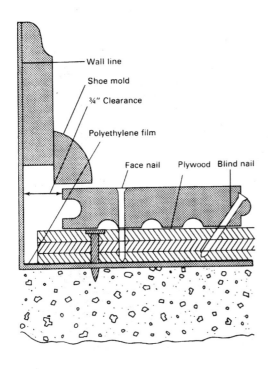

Wall line

Shoe mold

¾″ Clearance

Polyethylene film

Face nail   Plywood   Blind nail

*The correct method
of installing strip
oak flooring.*
United States Government

Figure 12-30

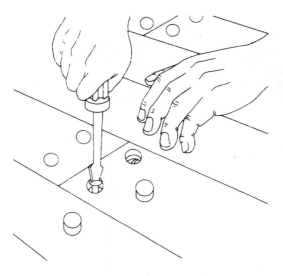

*Countersinking screw
heads in plank flooring
is simple when plugs
are used to cover
the fasteners.*
United States Government

Figure 12-31

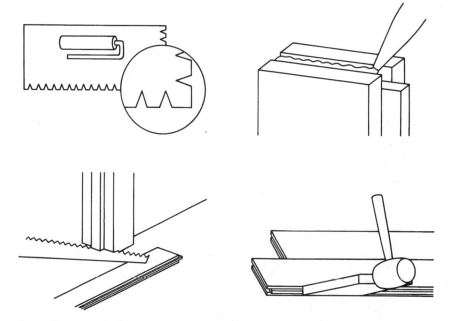

Installing wood flooring can involve many tools and methods, some of which are shown here. Robbins Hardwood Flooring, Cincinnati, Oh.

Figure 12-32

Adhesive pattern used when installing wood flooring. Robbins Hardwood Flooring, Cincinnati, Oh.

Figure 12-33

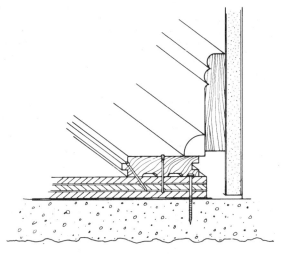

Nailing procedure for wood flooring.
Robbins Hardwood Flooring, Cincinnati, Oh.

Figure 12-34

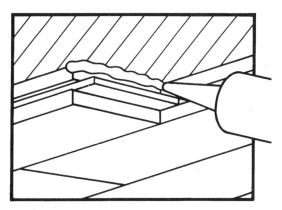

Installing wood flooring with adhesive.
Robbins Hardwood Flooring, Cincinnati, Oh.

Walls and ceilings

Chapter 13

CONTRACTORS often have questions about how to deal with the walls and ceilings of a kitchen. The solution to their problems might be as simple as learning how to work creatively with drywall. However, the situation may be complicated with many other elements, such as exposed beams, stenciling, and wallpaper.

Painted drywall is perfectly acceptable for the walls and ceilings of a kitchen. However, accents made with tile, wallpaper, stenciling, or even rough-cut boards can add a new dimension to the look of a kitchen. In this chapter, we are going to start with the basics of drywall and work our way into the many accent options.

When you remodel a kitchen, you may not have to install any drywall on the walls or ceilings. The existing material can usually be salvaged with minor repairs or touch-ups. However, if you gut the kitchen down to bare studs and ceiling joists, you will have to make major repairs to the walls and ceilings.

Drywall is by far the most common material used for walls and ceilings. You could opt for wood paneling, but paneling often darkens a room. Darker rooms often appear smaller and are less comfortable to be in. A light-colored room, especially a kitchen, is generally considered to be better than a dark one. To get started, let's assume you have removed all existing wall coverings and are left with bare studs and ceiling joists.

Hanging drywall

The only difficult aspect of hanging drywall is the weight of the material. Drywall can be attached to wall studs and joists with either drywall nails or screws. Most professionals use screws and electric screw guns to attach drywall. Whenever the material is secured to a wall or ceiling, the nail or screw must be installed so that a dimple is created around its head. Joint compound will be applied to this dimple in order to hide the fasteners.

Professionals use large boards of drywall (4' × 12') to minimize seams. However, you might be more comfortable with smaller panels, such as sheets. The bigger sheets are heavy and awkward, making them difficult to work with. Drywall can be installed either vertically or horizontally. Many professionals install the boards horizontally, but you can stand 4' × 8' sheets up vertically if it is easier for you.

Drywall can be cut with many tools, but the most common practice is to cut it with a razor knife. First the knife is used to score the drywall deeply (Fig. 13-1), then the unwanted piece of drywall is bent at the scored mark (Figs. 13-2 and 13-3), separating it from the desired piece. Having a set of saw horses on which you can rest the drywall during the measuring and cutting is advantageous. You also need a straightedge (Fig. 13-4) to keep your cuts on line; a straight wall stud will work well.

Figure 13-1

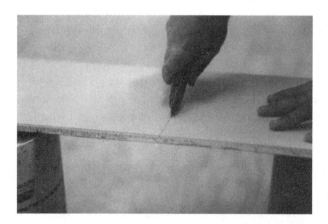

Cutting drywall with a razor knife is fast and easy.

Figure 13-2

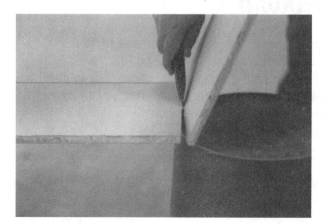

Once drywall has been scored with a razor knife, the board can be bent and broken easily.

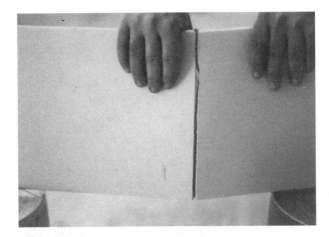

Figure 13-3

Snapping drywall after it has been scored with a knife.

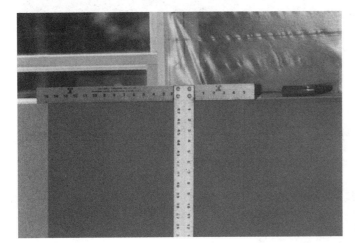

Figure 13-4

A T-square is used in cutting drywall to maintain straight cuts.

It is considered best to hang ceilings before hanging walls so that the drywall on the walls supports the edges of the ceiling. Hanging full sheets of drywall over your head is no easy matter if you are working alone. Full-time drywall pros use stilts (Fig. 13-5) to reach high spots. They are also equipped with a variety of trowels and tape holders (Fig. 13-6). Putty knives (Fig. 13-7) are used during the finishing process, but they are not needed when hanging drywall. To hang drywall, you need a razor knife or other cutting tool to cut the material with. You also need a hammer or a screw gun and possibly a ladder.

Figure 13-5

*Drywaller's stilt. A pair of
these makes taping drywall go
much faster.*

Figure 13-6

*Tools of the drywall trade: joint
compound, a roll of drywall tape,
and a trowel.*

Figure 13-7

A variety of widths in drywall knifes are needed to spread joint compound properly.

Hanging drywall alone is a tough job. However, some tricks of the trade can make the chore possible. You can use two stepladders and two short braces to hold a full sheet of drywall in place while you nail it to the ceiling joists. To do this, set the ladders up at an appropriate distance apart. Use ladders that nearly touch the ceiling joists. Climb one of the ladders and lift the edge of the drywall into place. The support brace will rest on top of the ladder and hold the drywall to the joists. Move to the other ladder and repeat the procedure. With the aid of a third ladder, you can nail the sheet to the joists.

Another trick for hanging ceilings alone involves the use of a couple of T-braces (Fig. 13-8). These braces are nothing more than wall studs nailed together to form a T-shape. The overall height of the brace should be just a few inches more than the distance from the floor to the ceiling. Use two ladders to get the drywall in position, then use the T-brace to lift the board to the ceiling and wedge it into place. This is a very effective way of hanging drywall when working alone.

Figure 13-8

A ceiling T-brace, like the one pictured, makes it possible for one person to hang drywall on ceilings.

When you install drywall, whether on ceilings or walls, butt each sheet tight against the previous one. Make the seams as tight as possible. Once all the drywall is hung, you are ready to tape with a special, nonadhesive, drywall tape and joint compound. The premixed joint compound comes in a bucket and is ready to use. Although outside corners on the walls will be covered with metal corner strips (Fig. 13-9), the inside corners will be taped.

To tape your seams, you first apply a coat of joint compound to the seam. Then you lay a piece of tape in the compound, along the seam, and seat the tape into place with a putty knife. The dimples that surround the nail heads throughout the installation are then filled with joint compound. A putty knife is used to apply and smooth out the compound. The metal corners installed on outside corners are perforated to allow joint compound to adhere to them. Simply cover the metal with a coat of joint compound and smooth it out with a putty knife. For inside corners, apply a coat of joint compound just as you did for the other seams. Take a piece of drywall tape and crease it down the middle. Place the creased tape into the inside corner and press it into the joint compound. When this is all done, you have to wait for the joint compound to dry for about a day.

Figure 13-9

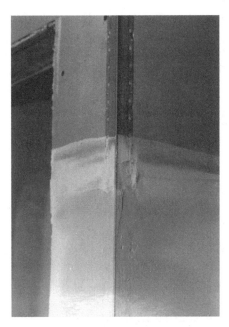

*Metal cornerbead should be
installed on all outside corners
when drywall is used.*

After the first coat of joint compound is dry, you have to apply
a second coat. This second coat should extend farther out on the
surface of the drywall than the first coat did. The total width of
the second coat should be somewhere around 6 inches. Feather
out the compound as it extends away from the seams. Wait for
the second coat to dry before going any further.

When the second coat of joint compound is dry, you must do some
sanding with a fine-grit sandpaper. This is a dusty job, so wear a
protective mask and make sure the dust won't infiltrate the rest of
your customer's home. Sand the joint compound lightly to smooth
it out and feather it. When you're done sanding, apply a third coat of
joint compound. This should be a wide, feathered coat that extends
for a total width of 10 to 12 inches. After this layer has dried, go over
the joint compound with a light sanding to smooth it out. This is your
finished coat, so make sure you are happy with the appearance.

Finishing drywall is something of a difficult art form. It is, however, a job that most people can manage if they work at it judiciously. To test the quality of your finish work, apply a coat of primer to the walls and ceiling. When the primer has dried, inspect your work. Check the work in both natural light during the day and artificial light at night. Seams that look good in one type of light can look bad in another type of light. If you find some rough spots, sand them out and prime them again. This inspection process is the best way to ensure a good job.

Painting

Painting is a job that almost everyone feels confident that they can complete successfully. In reality, professional-quality paint jobs are not as easy as they appear. One key to getting a professional-looking job is choosing the right primer and paint. Talk with a knowledgeable person in your local paint store to determine what will suit your needs best.

You should begin a paint job by painting a border all the way around the ceiling at the point where the ceiling meets the walls. In the trade, this is called cutting-in. As soon as you have the ceiling cut in, begin painting the ceiling. Rollers work very well for this part of the job and are available with extension handles that keep you off ladders. A lot of people roll paint on in even, long strokes that create long lines of paint. This method works, but if you begin by rolling out the paint in a zigzag pattern, you will not end up with a ceiling that looks like it was painted in a straight line. Instead, you will have a more fluid look that will appear to have been done professionally.

When you have finished painting the ceiling, you can move on to the walls. Cut in a border of paint with a brush around the edges of the walls. Then use a roller to fill in the center of the borders in a zigzag fashion. The end result should be impressive.

Your finished trim work can be painted before or after it is installed. It is usually easier to paint trim before you install it. Then all you have to do is fill the nail holes and do some touch-up painting. Also, since trim and walls are not usually painted the same color, this method helps you avoid overruns between the two paints.

Wallpapering

Wallpaper has come a long way in its development. Wallpaper is easier than ever before for amateurs to install. This is not to say it is a job you can do with your eyes shut, but it is a manageable task.

Prepasted wallpaper is the type most people choose to work with. If you follow this lead, you will not need an adhesive. However, you will need something to soak the wallpaper in. Normally, prepasted paper is rolled up with the pasted side out and soaked in tepid water for the period of time that is recommended by the manufacturer. Once the time limit has been met, the wallpaper is ready to install. If you choose a paper that is not prepasted, you will have to purchase an adhesive. There are several types of adhesive. My advice is to buy one that is recommended by the manufacturer of the wallpaper.

Proper wall preparation is very important to a successful wallpaper job. The walls must be smooth and free of cracks and holes. If you have installed new drywall in a kitchen, it should be sealed with an oil-based paint and brushed over with sizing prior to hanging the wallpaper. When you plan to cover a wall that is already painted with latex paint, you should apply a coat of primer-sealer before you hang the wallpaper. If you don't take these preliminary steps, your job might not turn out well. Then, if you ever decide to remove the wallpaper, you will have much more trouble in doing so.

One of the hardest parts about hanging wallpaper is keeping the pattern in proper alignment. As long as you pay attention to what you're doing, keeping the pattern lined up will not present too many problems. There are three basic types of matches: straight-across matches (Fig. 13-10), drop matches (Fig. 13-11), and random matches (Fig. 13-12). Look at your design and see if it runs horizontally or diagonally. The direction of your pattern will dictate how to align the paper.

Figure 13-10

*Straight
match for
wallcovering.*
Eisenhart Wallcoverings

Figure 13-11

*Drop
match for
wallcovering.*
Eisenhart Wallcoverings

Before cutting your wallpaper, remember to leave excess at both
the top and the bottom of each piece. A surplus of two inches is
considered normal (Fig. 13-13). Once the paper is hung, the excess
is trimmed off with a razor knife (Fig. 13-14). A butt joint is normally
used to join two pieces of wallpaper. For a butt joint, the edges of the
two joining pieces of paper are pushed together until a small ridge
is created (this is assuming that you are not working with vinyl
wallpaper). The little ridge will disappear as the paper shrinks. This
gives a perfect, tight seam. Inside corners are joined with overlapping

Figure 13-12

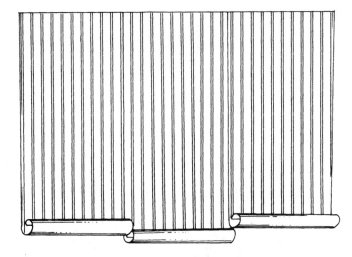

Random match for wallcovering. Eisenhart Wallcoverings

Figure 13-13

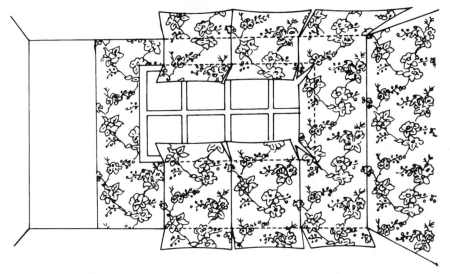

Applying wallcovering requires patience and precision, but it is a job most people can learn to do. Eisenhart Wallcoverings

seams (Fig. 13-15). The amount of overlap ranges from ¼" to ½". Hanging vinyl paper requires that you make your seams differently. For vinyl wallpaper, the two edges are overlapped and a straightedge and razor knife are used to cut through the overlap, leaving a tight seam, because vinyl paper does not adhere well to itself. However,

Figure 13-14

This illustration shows how to apply wallcovering around windows. The wallpaper is allowed to overlap the window and is then trimmed off. Eisenhart Wallcoverings

Figure 13-15

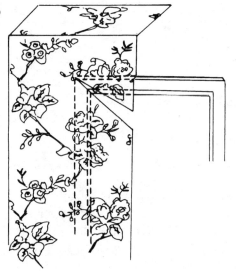

To trim wallcovering around windows, use a putty knife to put pressure on the wallpaper while cutting with a razor knife.
Eisenhart Wallcoverings

the inside corners made with vinyl paper are not cut, they are left overlapping each other and a vinyl-to-vinyl adhesive must be used.

Several questions may arise at the beginning of wallpaper application. Where should I start? How should the first piece be installed? Professionals normally start with the first piece of paper being applied along the edge of a door or window. The edge of the window or door makes a nice starting point, and as you work your way around the room, the meeting of the first and last strips of wallpaper will be inconspicuous.

Most kitchens don't present many obstacles for wallpapering. There will likely be a window, a cased opening, and a door. However, situations that require advanced papering skills are rare. As you hang wallpaper, use a wide brush to smooth the paper out (Fig. 13-16). Brush the paper both vertically and horizontally to attach it to the wall and to smooth out any bubbles. Wrinkles are removed by lifting the paper off the wall surface and reapplying it. Booking is a method used to ease the difficulties of working with the sticky paper. For this method, the sticky side of the paper is folded onto itself to make it more manageable.

To book (fold) a piece of pasted wallpaper, lay the paper with the design side down on a flat surface. Fold one end of the paper so that the edge meets the middle of the sticky side. Then repeat the process with the other edge. Your paper is now folded into thirds, and all the sticky part is concealed. This makes handling the paper easier. Once you've carried the paper to the installation location, you can unfold one of the edges and begin to hang the paper. Always start at the top of your work area and move downward. Once the first third of the paper is hung, you can continue to unfold the paper and secure it to the wall.

Dealing with windows, doors, electrical outlets (Figs. 13-17 and 13-18), and other obstructions in your path takes a little practice. Double-hung windows, doors, cased openings, and outlets are really not much trouble to work with. Basically, you just paper right over them, and then cut away the paper so that the seams are even with, or behind, the finished trim. In the case of electrical outlets, you should remove the cover plates before installing your paper. It is

Figure 13-16

Applying wallcovering around doors can be tricky. Let the wallpaper extend into the door opening and then trim it.
Eisenhart Wallcoverings

wise to cut off the electrical current to the outlets in your work area before removing the covers. The power should remain off until the paper around the outlet boxes has been cut and the cover plates replaced.

To keep your pattern lined up, you must keep the wallpaper hung evenly. This can be difficult when working in older homes or any home where the walls are not exactly plumb. Since many houses settle slightly out of plumb, you cannot even count on a new house being perfect. If you want your seams and pattern to work out exactly right, you need a chalk line and a plumb bob.

Figure 13-17

Cutting wallcovering for electrical outlets is simple. Use a putty knife to maintain pressure and a straight line while making the cut with a razor knife. Rough edges will be hidden by the cover plate for the outlet. Eisenhart Wallcoverings

Figure 13-18

Covering electrical switches with wall coverings requires that you leave tabs of the wallpaper to wrap behind the switch cover.
Eisenhart Wallcoverings

As you continue along the wall on which you are working, you will come to a point where the next piece of wallpaper to be hung will extend into the corner. Make your measurements from the adjoining seam along the flat wall and add ½" to the measurement. When you install the panel, the extra ½" will fill the corner and extend onto the adjoining flat wall. To measure from the last seam to the corner, take three measurements—one from the top, one from the bottom, and one from the middle. Now measure out from the corner onto the wall that has not yet been covered. Use the same measurements that you obtained in the previous step (excluding the ½" added for the corner). Mark each of the three measurements on the wall. Hang the plumb bob from the top mark with a chalk line. When you have a plumb line, snap the chalk line to mark the wall.

You now have a chalk line on the uncovered wall that should produce a reference mark for a seam. This seam will match the seam of the last strip of paper installed on the covered wall. Cut a piece of wallpaper and line it up with the chalk line, allow enough excess so that a ½" lip will overlap the edge of the existing wallpaper. By working to the chalk line, you should end up with a matched pattern.

When you go to purchase wallpaper, you are likely to discover that a multitude of hanging accessories are available. There will be wide-blade putty knives that are used to make tight seams where walls meet ceilings. You will also see a variety of rollers, water boxes, and cutters. Look over the tools and ask your local retailer for suggestions that may apply to the particular type of wallpaper you select. While some of the available accessories are more gimmicks than needs, many of the tools have specialized uses that can help you if your job has unusual angles or obstacles.

Installing false beams

False beams (Fig. 13-19) can convert a modern kitchen into a rustic one. While adding false beams may not have a structural purpose, you can choose from several options. Beams that are made from various composite light and easy-to-work-with materials are available. You can make your own hollow beams out of trim (Fig. 13-20). You do not need to use solid beams, and in fact, their weight could be a problem. Unless the beams will do more than create a decorative appearance, lightweight versions are best (Fig. 13-21).

If you buy preformed fake beams, all you have to do is install them with the provided instructions. Building your own wood beams from trim boards will give you the benefits of lightweight real-wood construction that is easy to stain or paint in the color of your choice. The size of the beams you build or buy depends on the size of your kitchen. Massive beams in a small kitchen are not a good idea.

Figure 13-19

Exposed beams, like these, can be made of solid timbers, but they can also be fabricated out of dimensional lumber. Timberlake Cabinet Company and American Woodmark Corporation

Figure 13-20

Exposed beams in patterns, such as the ones shown here, are usually built on site from dimensional lumber. Timberlake Cabinet Company and American Woodmark Corporation

Let's talk about how to build your own false beams. The first step is deciding what size you want. After that decision is made, you are ready for a trip to the lumber store. Choose flat, thin trim boards in a width that suits your needs. Plan on buying four boards for every

Figure 13-21

Vaulted ceilings and exposed beams go together nicely. Kitchens with tall ceilings often appear larger than they are. StarMark, Inc., 600 E. 48th St. N, Sioux Falls, SD 57104

beam you wish to create. The first board will be screwed to your ceiling joists. The second board will be laid flat on your floor. The two remaining boards will be stood up on their ends and attached to the board that is laying flat on the floor. You can use screws or nails for this part of the construction, but you should countersink the fasteners so that the holes can be filled with putty and painted or stained over.

As you look at your beam on the floor, the flat board will be installed between the two boards standing on their edges. When this is complete, you will need some help. Raise the prefab beam off the floor and up to the board you have attached to the ceiling joists. Let the two boards on your box surround the board on the ceiling. This will create a complete box. The side boards of the beam can be nailed or screwed into the sides of the board that is hanging on the ceiling. Once the boards are connected, you have a complete false beam. If the ends of your beam will be visible, you must cut a piece of trim board to fit into the end of the box. Any seams and nail holes can be filled with putty, sanded, and painted or stained.

Texturing

Texturing the walls and ceiling of a kitchen is not difficult, but the idea may not be a good one. Since kitchens commonly produce grease and grime, a textured wall or ceiling may not be a good choice. The rough texture has a tendency to trap grease and dirt, creating a hard-to-clean surface. This can be especially true when an island cooktop (Fig. 13-22) is being used. A smooth, washable surface is usually best in a kitchen.

If you decide to texture the walls or ceiling, you have many methods to choose from. You can buy paint that when applied will give a light texture. For a more defined texture, you can use joint compound (the same kind used to finish drywall) and a potato masher. To do this, you smear joint compound with a putty knife on the area to be textured. Then you push the potato masher into the compound and pull it out. With a little practice, you can develop a long or short texture, depending upon how you handle the potato masher. Another option involves spreading the joint compound with a putty knife using varying strokes to create a rough, wide-stroke texture.

Decorating with stencils

Stencils applied around the border of a kitchen where the walls meet the ceiling can produce fabulous results. Stencil kits are available in countless designs that range from pineapples to forest scenes. While stenciling can be done by hand, it can also be accomplished with the use of prepackaged, stick-on kits that are applied in much the same way that wallpaper is.

Figure 13-22

When kitchens are large enough, island cabinets and counters can be added to increase surface work area. This kitchen has taken advantage of an island cabinet to include a cooktop. Dura Supreme, Inc.

Wallpaper and stenciling are very popular in kitchens. The opportunities for these types of wallcoverings are nearly endless (Figs. 13-23 through 13-26). With enough shopping, your customers are sure to find styles and patterns to suit their taste.

Figure 13-23

Wallcoverings in kitchens are becoming more and more popular.
©Imperial Wallcoverings, Inc.

Figure 13-24

Wallcoverings used to join two rooms can complement each other without being identical.
©Imperial Wallcoverings, Inc.

Figure 13-25

Here is an example of splitting two types of wall coverings at chair-rail height. I would not have allowed the lower material to extend past the chair rail.
Eisenhart Wallcoverings

Figure 13-26

This photo shows that a small kitchen can be very user-friendly.
Dura Supreme, Inc.

Using tile

Tile can be used as a countertop (Fig. 13-27), backsplash (Figs. 13-28 and 13-29), accent, or complete wall covering (Fig. 13-30). The patterns and possibilities available with tile are almost endless. Tile is not inexpensive, but it is durable, attractive, and practical. It is cleaned easily, never needs painting, and is not too difficult to install.

Figure 13-27

Tiled kitchens can be quite colorful and full of designs, as shown here.
Rutt Custom Kitchens and Lis King

We talked about cutting and installing tile floors in the last chapter. Tile walls are a little different. The major difference in installation is the fact that you must plan your borders and trim tiles in advance. With a floor, you cover the entire subfloor and then trim down to the floor. When installing tile on a wall, you must allow for the fact that the edges of your tile must be finished trim pieces.

Figure 13-28

This small yet spacious kitchen is very efficient with good design and abundant cabinets. Rutt Custom Kitchens and Lis King

If you are installing tile only in a small area, such as a backsplash behind your range top, the job is very manageable. Doing an entire room is no more difficult, but it does take more planning and preparation, especially if your tiles will create patterns. Just as we discussed about wallpaper, your walls must be plumb for your patterns and grout joints to come out evenly. When the walls are not square, you can cheat in the corners and along the bottom row of tile to make up for minor discrepancies.

Before you buy tile, talk with a reputable and knowledgeable tile supplier. Get suggestions on which types of tile will best suit your needs. A tile that will do fine on the wall might not be a wise choice for use on a countertop.

Figure 13-29

The tiled walls and counters for this kitchen are in good taste and work well together. Schrock Handcrafted Cabinetry, Arthur, Ill.

A thin-set adhesive is the easiest to work with when installing tile. All you have to do is spread the adhesive with a toothed trowel to create a layer that is about $\frac{1}{16}$" deep. However, this procedure may vary with individual types of tiles, so always follow the manufacturer's recommendations.

A rubber mallet or a piece of board that has been covered with carpet and is tapped with a hammer can be used to seat tiles into the adhesive. Tapping the tiles into place might not be necessary for all jobs, but you should be prepared with some method for the seating of stubborn tiles. The grouting process for wall tile is the same as that described for tile floors in the last chapter.

Figure 13-30

The owner of this kitchen obviously likes tile. While I think the room here has been overdone, it does give a good visual indication of the possibilities that exist for tile work.
Rutt Custom Kitchens and Lis King

The creative use of decorative tiles can really give a kitchen a customized look. Accessories can also do much to enhance the overall appearance of a kitchen (Figs. 13-31 and 13-32). There are so many possibilities for walls and ceilings that an entire book could be devoted to the subject. Unfortunately, we do not have the space in this book to cover every option and angle. If you review the photographs in this book and let your creative juices flow, I'm sure you can come up will all sorts of unique ideas to personalize kitchens for your customers.

Figure 13-31

Hanging pot racks are enjoyed by many kitchen users. Latco Products

Figure 13-32

Counters and bars in kitchens can be used for eating, reading, or as added work space.

Cabinets, counters, and pantries

Chapter 14

CABINETS, counters, and pantries are all very important parts of a functional kitchen. These items, especially cabinets, are also a major portion of the total cost in a kitchen remodeling job. Considering the importance and expense of these items, you want to do your homework before you begin bidding for or installing the cabinets. This chapter is going to help you shorten the time needed for learning this aspect of kitchen remodeling.

There is a lot more to installing a set of cabinets or countertops than just buying them and screwing them into place. Without proper preparation, you are not likely to produce a quality job. When you consider the pantry space for a kitchen, you can either build a pantry from scratch or install a prefab unit. Both options have their advantages. Since cabinets are the single largest, most expensive element of most new kitchens, I'll start the discussion with them.

Refacing cabinets

Cosmetic improvements are possible without the high cost of purchasing new cabinets. If the existing cabinets are sound and in good working order, you might want to consider simply giving them a facelift (Fig. 14-1). A fresh look can be created by replacing the cabinet doors and hardware and installing new end and accessory panels.

Refacing existing cabinets has become a common practice. Homeowners can do the work themselves, or they may hire specialists, like yourself, to complete the work for them. In either case, the cost of refacing is much lower than the cost of replacing all of the cabinets in a kitchen. In fact, homeowners may spend only about one-third of the cost of new cabinets to make existing cabinets look new again (Fig. 14-2).

When you investigate the idea of giving old cabinets (Fig. 14-3) a new look, you will find that there are numerous possibilities and a wide range in the cost of various options. The best-looking changes (Fig. 14-4) will not be cheap, but they will be considerably less than the cost of buying new cabinets. If your customers are on tight

Figure 14-1

A tired old kitchen before remodeling. Quality Doors—1-800-950-3667 (DOOR)

·budgets, you can use cabinets doors that are not the same high quality as actual wood but will still give the cabinets an acceptable look. This inexpensive method utilizes adhesive paper that has a wood-grain look to it. Due to the vast differences in quality and cost, you should look into refacing options (Figs. 14-5 through 14-8) on your local level and make sure you explain carefully to your customers exactly what they will be getting.

Installing new cabinets

The process of installing new cabinets should begin during the rough-in work of the remodeling job. Check all walls and floors to see that they are plumb and level. Finding a wall that is out of plumb or a floor that is not level adds some work to your remodeling project, but it is

Figure 14-2

The same kitchen as shown in Fig. 14-1 after a facelift. Quality Doors—1-800-950-3667

far better to discover the problem early in the job rather than after the bulk of your work is done.

If you find a wall that is out of plumb during the rough-in stage of a remodeling job, you can shim out the studs while you are still in the middle of the dirty work. Finding this same problem at the time you are hanging cabinets might mean tearing out the new walls in order to fix the problem. During the rough-in stage, a wall can be furred out with wood strips to compensate for minor inconsistencies. When the floor is your problem, you might need to place a few cedar shims under the base cabinets. If the floor problem is extreme, you might have to correct it with new underlayment and some filling compound. In either case, correcting the problems during the rough-in is no big deal.

There are vast differences in the quality of various cabinets. Your customer's budget and tastes will dictate the style and quality of cabinet you provide. However, let me give you a few hints of what to look for in a good cabinet.

Figure 14-3

Tired old cabinet facing on a hutch.
Quality Doors—1-800-950-3667 (DOOR)

First you need to decide what material the cabinets will be comprised of. Particleboard is a common material in kitchen cabinets. Good particleboard cabinets are covered with a wood venéer. This type of cabinet will be priced in the low to mid-range of cost comparisons. While moisture can create problems with these cabinets, they are usually fine for average installations.

Top-of-the-line cabinets are made with plywood that is covered with a quality veneer. These all-wood cabinets are in the middle to high price range. They are sturdy, give years of dependable service, and are a pleasure to use.

Figure 14-4

Same cabinetry as shown in Fig. 14-3 after refacing. Quality Doors—1-800-950-3667 (DOOR)

Custom-made cabinets are also an option. However, these cabinets are expensive and can take months to be delivered to your job. If you want custom cabinets, allow plenty of time in your production schedule.

Base cabinets with drawers should be equipped with metal tracks and drawer glides (Fig. 14-9) that move the drawers smoothly. If you are shopping where cabinets are on display, you can work the drawers and doors to see that they function to your satisfaction. Good cabinets have drawers that can be worked with one finger and doors that latch securely. You might want to check what type of joints were

Figure 14-5

Step one in door replacement. Quality Doors—
1-800-950-3667 (DOOR)

Figure 14-6

Step two in a cabinet facelift. Quality Doors—
1-800-950-3667 (DOOR)

Figure 14-7

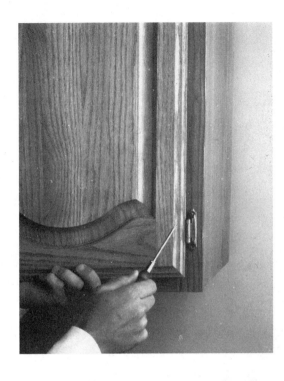

*Step three—adding the
new face to your cabinets.*
Quality Doors—1-800-950-3667 (DOOR)

Figure 14-8

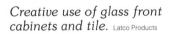

*Creative use of glass front
cabinets and tile.* Latco Products

Figure 14-9

Recycling bins and organizing units with metal tracks and glides. Rutt Custom Kitchens and Lis King

used in the drawers. Dove-tail joints are much better than butt joints. Also, inspect the hinges on cabinet doors to see that they work well and are sturdy enough to stand up to daily use and occasional abuse. Another simple test is to try wiggling the base cabinets. If the cabinets are well built, you won't be able to get much movement out of them.

Installing base cabinets

Installing base cabinets is pretty easy. Professionals debate whether base cabinets should be installed before or after wall cabinets. The people who believe that base cabinets should be installed first claim that by installing base cabinets first, you can use them to support props for the wall cabinets. Of course this is true, but I disagree with the advice of putting base cabinets in first.

When base cabinets are installed before wall cabinets, two things are likely to happen. The base cabinets will definitely be in your way as you work above them with wall cabinets. There is a good chance that something will happen during the hanging of wall cabinets to damage the base cabinets. As for the props, you can use wall studs that span from the bottoms of wall cabinets to the kitchen floor for support. There is no law that says wall cabinets must be installed first, but I believe you will find that your job will go better if they are.

There are two basic types of base cabinets, those that have backs and those that don't. If you are working with cabinets that do not have backs, you will have to install cleats on the wall behind the cabinets. A cleat is a wood ledger, usually made with a 1" × 2" board. The ledger is attached to wall studs along the back of all base cabinets. The top of the cleat must be level with the top of the cabinets. You see, the countertop that covers the base cabinets will depend upon this cleat for support. Make sure the cleat and the front, top edge of the base cabinets are level with each other. If your cabinets have backs in them, you won't need to install a ledger strip.

When you install base cabinets, you should start in a corner and work your way around the walls. The cabinets should be set in place and checked with a level. Add shims if necessary. When you are content with your layout, it is time to connect the base cabinets to each other. C-clamps are a handy item to have when doing this. Use two C-clamps to hold side-by-side cabinets together tightly. Double check the tops of the cabinets to be sure they are still level. When everything is positioned correctly, either screw or bolt the cabinets together. If you are using bolts, you will have to drill holes through the cabinets. The screws or bolts should be installed near the top edges of the cabinets, but you should avoid getting too close to the edge because it might split. If you stay an inch or so below the top, you should be fine.

Continue attaching base cabinets together until they are all mated with each other. Go back and check the tops of the cabinets to confirm that they have remained level. At this point, you must attach the cabinets to the wall studs. It is best to do this with screws. When your installation is complete, check one more time to see that all the tops are level.

Hanging wall cabinets

Hanging wall cabinets is done in about the same way that you install base cabinets. However, the work is a little more awkward, since the work is over your head and there is nothing to rest the cabinets on. It is possible to hang wall cabinets by yourself, but the job will be easier and faster if you have some help. When you are working alone, you must hang one cabinet at a time. If you have enough muscle standing by, you can put the wall cabinets together on the kitchen floor and raise them into place on the wall as one unit.

A standard kitchen will have the top of its wall cabinets at about 84 inches above the kitchen floor. There is no rule that says you must hang your cabinets at this height, but it is a common reference point. To begin your installation, choose the height you want to maintain. Mark the location and draw a straight line across the wall with a pencil. This line provides a constant reference of where to hang the cabinets.

Gather some wall studs to use as temporary supports for the cabinets. If you are going to put the cabinets together on the floor, you can use your C-clamps and the same basic procedures described for base cabinets. The cabinets must be matched horizontally and vertically to maintain an even line when hung. Once the cabinets are attached to each other, get your helper(s) to lift them into place. Place supports under the cabinets. Make sure your temporary supports are solid and will not allow the cabinets to fall.When the cabinets are propped in place, check them with a level. Make adjustments as needed and screw the cabinets to the wall studs. You will notice strips of wood on the inside of your cabinets. These are the mounting strips where screws are normally inserted to hold the cabinets against the wall. Depending on the type of cabinets you are using, you might have to add some filler strips for the final installation. These are simply pieces of wood that match the cabinets exactly and that hide any gaps between the cabinets and side walls. Adding some custom door and drawer pulls can really bring out the personality of a cabinet (Figs. 14-10 through 14-13). Now you are ready for your countertop.

Figure 14-10

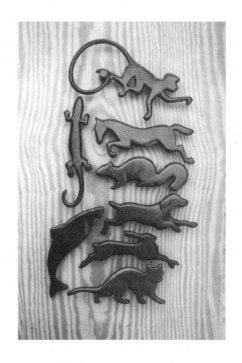

Animal cabinet pulls. Chris Collicott, 115½ N. LaBrea Ave., Los Angeles, CA 90038, (213) 876-5112)

Figure 14-11

Squirrel drawer pull. Chris Collicott, 115½ N. LaBrea Ave., Los Angeles, CA 90038, (213) 876-5112

Figure 14-12

Animal cabinet and drawer pulls. Chris Collicott, 115½ N. LaBrea Ave., Los Angeles, CA 90038, (213) 876-5112

Figure 14-13

Animal cabinet pulls. Chris Collicott, 115½ N. LaBrea Ave., Los Angeles, CA 90038, (213) 876-5112

Installing countertops

Countertops can be bought premade, or you can make one yourself. If you are going to use tile, you will have to make your own top. Most kitchens are equipped with preformed counters. This is the fastest, easiest, and least expensive way to get a quality countertop. Since few contractors make their own countertops anymore, I will assume that you are buying your counter from a building supplier.

The measurements for a counter are crucial. For this reason, the counter should not be ordered until after the base cabinets have been installed. If the counter measurements are wrong and the counter doesn't fit, the supplier is not likely to accept its return. In other words, a missed measurement usually results in the purchase of a second counter. If you measure for the counter yourself, be very careful. Most suppliers are happy to send a representative out to measure for the top. This is your safest bet. By letting the supplier gather measurements, you shift the burden of responsibility to someone else. Standard counters don't take too long to order, but talk to your supplier in advance and be prepared to wait a while for the top to be made up.

When your new counter arrives, installing the counter can be tricky. Plan on having some help available for lifting and positioning the counter. Set the counter on the base cabinets and check its fit closely. Small gaps between the backsplash and the back wall can be filled with caulking, so don't worry about them. Unless your wall is way out of plumb, the counter should fit snugly in place.

With the counter sitting in place, you are ready to attach it to the cabinets. The length of the screws you use for this part of the job is of great importance. Screws that are too long will come right through the top of the counter and ruin it. If you look inside your base cabinets, you should see little triangular pieces of wood in each corner. These braces are the mounting blocks where you will screw the cabinets to the counter. It is best to drill pilot holes through the blocks so that your screws will not split them. In tight spots, it is sometimes easier to get the screws in if the pilot holes are drilled on a slight angle. The most important thing to keep in mind is avoiding a disaster by not running your drill bit or screws through the top of the counter.

Selecting pantries

Pantries are a convenient addition to any style of kitchen. You have two basic options when it comes to pantries: You can buy them premade or you can build them yourself. If you plan to build your own pantry, you will have to frame it during the rough-in portion of your job. Premade pantries can be purchased and installed at the same time that you are installing your kitchen cabinets.

Framing a pantry is not a big job. You can nail the framing in place in just a few hours. If your customer wants a large pantry, it would be best to make the pantry yourself. On the other hand, if your customers are not stocking food, store-bought pantries equipped with an organizer will do just fine.

One advantage to a commercially available pantry is that it will match the kitchen cabinets exactly. Also, these units take up very little space and can be used for everything from holding cans of food to brooms. If your customer wants more space than what a single unit will provide, you can buy more than one pantry and install them either side by side or on opposite walls. For these reasons, I prefer to buy prefab pantries.

Whether you buy a pantry or build one, you should seriously consider the optional organizer accessories that are available for use in them. Homeowners love these little devices. Organizers allow people to maximize the storage capacity while enjoying easy access to all of the items.

You and your customer should work out all details of what products will be used on your job before any work is started. This is how it is supposed to work. However, customers often change their minds about what they want before a job is finished. They often add accessories or change their minds about some other aspect of the job. You have to be prepared for this situation. Show your customers a wide selection of what is available before you have them commit to a particular type of cabinet or accessory (Figs. 14-14 through 14-19).

Figure 14-14

Decorative yet functional cabinetry can make even a small kitchen very efficient. StarMark, Inc., 600 E. 48th Street, N Sioux Falls, SD 57104

Figure 14-15

Open-style cabinets, like this one, are popular for holding china.
StarMark, Inc., 600 E. 48th Street, N Sioux Falls, SD 57104

Figure 14-16

Hickory cabinets add warmth to a kitchen. StarMark, Inc., 600 E. 48th Street, N Sioux Falls, SD 57104

Figure 14-17

Maple corner cabinets are light in color and take advantage of all available space. StarMark, Inc., 600 E. 48th Street, N Sioux Falls, SD 57104

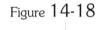

Figure 14-18

Maple sink base cabinet. StarMark, Inc., 600 E. 48th Street, N Sioux Falls, SD 57104

Figure 14-19

*Decorative range hoods are showing up
more and more often in newer kitchens.*
StarMark, Inc., 600 E. 48th Street, N Sioux Falls, SD 57104

Another aspect of kitchen cabinets to consider is how user-friendly they really are. The right designs and accessories can make an average cabinet a pleasure to work with. For example, doors that have racks (Fig 14-20) increase storage capacity. Thinking ahead can make a kitchen much more desirable. You can install recycling centers (Fig. 14-21A, B, and C). Also, pull-out sections (Fig. 14-22) in pantries make gaining access to foods and supplies easy.

Installing cabinets, counters, and pantries is not difficult work. You can save quite a bit of money by doing the work yourself instead of subcontracting the work out to others. As long as you are willing to take your time and pay attention to what you're doing, this is one phase of a job that can pay off handsomely.

Figure 14-20

Spice rack with adjustable shelves. Rutt Custom Kitchens and Lis King

Figure 14-21A

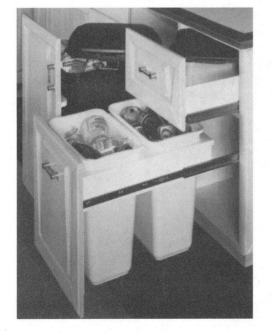

Kitchen organizers are popular for recycling.
Rutt Custom Kitchens and Lis King

Figure 14-21 (continues)

Figure 14-21B

Figure 14-21C

Figure 14-22

A pull-out pantry organizer makes working in a kitchen much more enjoyable. Wellborn Cabinet, Inc.

15

Fireplaces and wood stoves

Chapter 15

FIREPLACES and wood stoves can be valuable additions to kitchens. A stove or fireplace can add a lot of ambiance to a room. I'm not suggesting that your customers have to hang old cast-iron pots over the glowing embers of a fireplace to heat up their beans, but there is something magical about the aroma of wood smoke and the flickering of flames. For these reasons, many homeowners will be attracted to your suggestions for fireplaces and wood stoves in their remodeled rooms.

If customers have young children or a kitchen with cramped quarters, a wood stove probably is not a good idea. The risk of getting burned can be serious. However, if a spacious kitchen and dining area run parallel to each other, surely room can be found for a small stove that will not present a safety hazard.

Fireplaces are a bit more difficult to add to kitchens than to many other rooms of the house, but the task is manageable. You could choose a conventional masonry fireplace (Fig. 15-1), or you might opt for a prefabricated metal fireplace. I had a metal fireplace in the bedroom of one of my homes, and I didn't like it. The unit worked fine, but it just didn't meet my expectations of a fireplace. The firebox was shallow, making the unit seem artificial. You might keep this bit of my experience in mind as you are talking to your customers about fireplace options.

Prefab units vs. masonry fireplaces

What's involved with installing a fireplace in an existing kitchen? Well, first of all, unless you are an experienced mason, you should not attempt to build your own fireplaces. You can install a prefab unit on your own, but leave the building of a fireplace to a professional. A masonry fireplace needs to have a footing poured. This is a matter of digging a hole to allow concrete to be poured below the frostline in the ground. Although it is possible to do this under an existing floor that has solid ground located underneath, it is much easier to dig the

Figure 15-1

Brick fireplace. Latco Products

footing on the outside of the home and have the fireplace built into one of the exterior walls.

There is no point in going into a lot of detail about what is involved with the construction of a masonry fireplace since it is not a job for which average general contractors are prepared. If your customer wants a large fireplace, talk to local masons for pricing and construction requirements. As long as you are aware of whether it is possible and feasible to add one to a home, you are fulfilling your obligation to the customer.

Installation

Prefab units (Fig. 15-2) are relatively easy to work with, as they do not require a concrete footing. These units can sit on either an existing floor or a wood frame. Their chimneys can be made of triple-wall stove pipe that is rated for minimum clearance from combustibles. The whole unit, fireplace and chimney included, can be installed in less than one day.

Figure 15-2

See-through gas fireplace. Majestic Fireplaces, Huntington, Ind.

When a prefab unit is installed, the edges are generally concealed with wood framing and standard wall coverings. The installation is quick and simple. The costs for prefab units vary, but they are all affordable, costing less than half as much as a masonry fireplace. I mentioned earlier that I had not been pleased with the one prefab fireplace that I'd owned. However, I should note that not all prefab units are like the one I had. There are good prefab fireplaces available that come close to imitating a masonry fireplace.

When you buy a prefab unit, it will come with installation instructions. You should read and follow the instructions carefully. Some units require more open air space between combustibles than others. Due to fire and safety concerns, you should install the unit exactly as the manufacturer recommends. Although I will give you an overview of what to expect, don't use my instructions to install a fireplace; use only the manufacturer's recommendations.

A prefab fireplace will have its chimney connection built right into its top. The normal procedure is to first place the fireplace in the location of choice. Remember to comply with local code requirements and the manufacturer's recommendations. The next step is to attach the chimney. The most logical way to create a chimney for this type of add-on fireplace is to use triple-wall, steel chimney pipe. The pipe is very expensive on a per-foot basis, but it still works out to be the most cost-effective means of venting a prefab fireplace.

You have a few different options with installing the chimney. You can run it straight up, passing through the ceiling and attic, and out of the roof. Or you may choose to use an elbow to run the chimney out of the home's exterior wall and up the side of the house. Side venting (Fig. 15-3), corner venting (Fig. 15-4), and rear venting (Fig. 15-5) are all possible options. All of these ways are effective. The method you choose depends on your preference and the structural conditions of the home. For example, if there is additional living space above the kitchen ceiling, it is logical to use the elbow. If there is only attic space above the fireplace location, going straight up is more feasible and will even cost less.

Figure 15-3

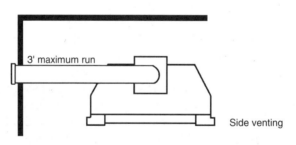

Side-venting fireplace. Vermont Castings, Inc.

Figure 15-4

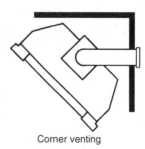

Corner-venting fireplace. Vermont Castings, Inc.

Figure 15-5

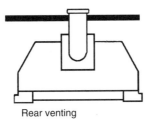

Rear venting

Rear-venting fireplace.
Vermont Castings, Inc.

If you decide to run the chimney out of the side wall of the house, you must purchase a special mounting adapter. This device is called a wall bracket. With the use of special spacers and a thimble, you may put the chimney through the wall with the wall bracket configured so that the pipe rises vertically. It is common to frame-in this type of exposed chimney and to conceal it with siding that matches the siding on the home.

If the chimney is to go straight up through the ceiling joists, a special ceiling collar should be purchased. This device fits between either the ceiling joists or the headed-off space in the ceiling. It allows the chimney to rise without coming into contact with any wood. There are adapters available for any occasions in which the chimney must penetrate roofs, joists, walls, and/or similar combustible materials.

After the chimney is positioned through the roof, a cap must be installed on its end. This not only prevents rain from running down the pipe, but also often utilizes some screening to prevent sparks from blowing from the chimney's top. Additionally, there are code requirements on how high the chimney must extend above the roof (Fig. 15-6) and how far the pipe must be from combustibles. Check your local code requirements on these issues.

If you are installing a wood stove near a combustible wall, it might be necessary to install a heat shield between the wall and the stove. Again, there are code requirements that dictate how close the stove can be to the wall and what types of heat shields are acceptable. Be sure to check with your local authorities.

Figure 15-6

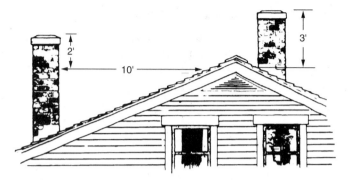

Typical chimney extension. Be sure to check local code requirements. Vermont Castings, Inc.

As you shop for your customer's wood stove, you will discover that there are several makes and models from which to choose. Some are modern, air-tight stoves that consist of a plain exterior. These stoves are extremely functional, but they might not put enough pizzazz in a kitchen. An enameled stove or a stove with an etched scene of a forest and wild animals might be more to your customer's liking. Some models are equipped with glass fronts so that you can watch the fire in your stove. It is also possible to buy a stove that is equipped with screens to cover the door opening when the fire door is open. Wood stoves come in a wide variety of sizes, shapes, and colors, so there are plenty from which to choose.

This brings us to the end of our discussion on kitchen remodeling. You now possess a host of ideas to ponder and present to your customers. Kitchen remodeling is a very popular area of construction and home repair. Many customers are looking to create their image of the ideal kitchen. They will come to you with many ideas and suggestions. Although they could accomplish some of this work themselves, they will look to you as a magician. It will be your job as a knowledgeable and experienced contractor to aid them in the understanding of what is possible and desirable as opposed to what may in the long run be impossible or impractical. If you present your potential customers with enough options, you're sure to become known for your work as a kitchen remodeler. Once you've achieved this status, work should be plentiful and financially rewarding for you.

Throughout this book, I have attempted to impart to you the knowledge and skills that I have gained over years of experience. My goal was to speed up your learning process. I hope that I have spared you some of the less pleasant experiences that usually find their way into beginners' jobs. However, when obstacles appear, don't be disheartened; every professional contractor has had his or her share of battles. I wish you the best of luck with your remodeling career.

Glossary

ABS pipe A type of plastic pipe frequently used in plumbing. ABS is an abbreviation for acrylonitrile butadiene styrene. It is black in color and is most frequently used in the form of schedule-40 pipe.

adjustable rate loan A loan with a flexible interest rate tied to a common reference index. This index can be a Treasury Bill rate, the Federal Reserve discount rate, or some other agreed upon index. These loans typically start at a lower interest rate and escalate over a period of five years. After five years, most of these loans stay at a fixed rate for the remainder of the loan.

air gap The most common use of this term in remodeling is in reference to the device connected to a dishwasher drain. These devices protect a dishwasher from the risk of back siphoning contaminated water from the drainage system into the dishwasher.

annual appreciation rate The rate at which real estate values increase each year.

appraiser An individual whose profession is to determine the value of real estate. Appraisers may be certified. However, in many states appraisers are not required to pass stringent licensing requirements.

architectural plans Blueprints designed and drawn by an architect.

bait-and-switch scam A frequently used unethical marketing ploy to make people respond to advertising. The advertising entices an individual to come to the advertiser, but the advertised price or product is not available. Then the advertiser attempts to sell the consumer a different product or a similar product at a higher price.

balloon payment A single lump-sum payment frequently associated with real estate loans. These payments are generally due and payable in full after an agreed-upon time.

band board The piece of lumber that runs the perimeter of a building and is attached to the floor joists. This wooden member is normally the size of the attached floor joists. The band board is placed on the outside wall end of the floor joists. A band board provides a common place for all floor joists to attach and maintains stability and proper alignment.

baseboard trim A decorative trim placed around the perimeter of interior partitions. Baseboard trim is used where the floor covering meets the wall to create a finished and attractive appearance.

bid phases The different phases or aspects of work to be performed and priced. Examples include plumbing, heating, electrical, roofing, and all other individual forms of remodeling or construction.

bids Prices given by contractors and suppliers for labor and material to be supplied for a job.

block number One of the elements needed for a legal description of real estate property in areas segregated into blocks.

blueprints The common name of working plans that are printed in blue ink and show all aspects of the construction methods to be used in building and remodeling.

boiler A type of heating system usually designed to provide hot-water heat from baseboard radiation.

bow window A window that projects outward beyond the siding of a home and is supported by its own foundation or support beams. Bow windows are sometimes referred to as a bay windows.

breezeway A covered, and sometimes enclosed, walkway from one part of a house to another. Breezeways are commonly used to connect a garage to a house when direct connection isn't feasible or desirable.

BTU British thermal unit; an industry standard in the measurement of the amount of heat needed for an area. One BTU equals the amount of heat required to raise one pound of water one degree in temperature.

builder grade A product of average quality used in production-built housing.

call-back A warranty service call. A call-back is a form of service call where the contractor is not paid for the services rendered due to the nature of the problem.

cantilever A building practice in which the wooden frame structure extends beyond the foundation. Cantilevers are created when the floor joists overhang the foundation.

cardboard-style cabinets Inexpensive production cabinets of low quality.

carpet pad The support, generally foam, between the carpet and subfloor or underlayment.

casement window A window with hinges on the outside and a mechanical crank that is used to open and close the window. These windows open outwardly and are typically very energy efficient.

caulking A compound used to fill cracks and provide a satisfactory finish.

ceiling joists Structural members providing support for a second-story floor and a nailing surface for a lower story's ceiling.

ceramic tile A product used for floors, countertops, wall coverings, and tub or shower surrounds. The most common ceramic tiles are approximately 4" square and comprise a pottery-type material.

certificate of occupancy Certificates issued by the local codes enforcement office when all building code requirements are met. Certificates of occupancy state the legal inhabitants of a dwelling or business property.

chair rail A wooden member of finished trim quality that is placed horizontally at a point along the walls where chairs would be likely to come into contact with the wall. Chair rails serve some practical purpose, but they are most frequently used as decorative trim in formal dining rooms.

change order A written agreement allowing a change from previously agreed-to plans. Change orders detail the nature of the change and all pertinent facts affected by the change.

china lavatory A bathroom wash basin made of vitreous china. These lavatories provide a clean, nonporous service for a wash basin and usually have a shiny finish.

circuit breaker The modern equivalent to the old-style electrical fuses. These devices add protection from overloaded electrical circuits by shutting down the circuit if it is producing a dangerous electrical current.

close-coupled faucet Also referred to as a 4-inch center faucet. These faucets are produced as an integral, one-piece unit. The handles and the spout of the faucets are molded from the same material, producing a faucet with all working parts molded together.

closed sale A consummated or settled sale. A closed sale is a completed transfer of the property being sold.

closing costs Expenses incurred in order to settle a loan transaction. They can include legal fees, appraisal fees, survey fees, insurance, and other related expenses.

clouded title A title is clouded when it has unanswered questions or liens about or against the title. Clouded titles can make the transfer of the property to another owner very difficult.

code enforcement officer An authorized representative of the building code enforcement office. A code enforcement officer is the individual responsible for the approval or denial of code inspections and issuing a certificate of occupancy.

commercial grade carpet Normally a close weaved and very durable carpet, suitable for heavy traffic and abuse. This carpet is designed for easy cleaning and handling the most demanding traffic without undue wear.

comparable sales book Generally produced by multiple listing services, these books reflect a history of all closed sales for the last quarter of a given year. These books are used to determine appraised values of the subject properties.

comparable sales sheet A form used to compile information on real estate activity in an area. A comparable sales sheet allow an accurate appraisal of a property to be made.

competitive-grade fixture An inexpensive fixture normally found in tract housing or starter homes.

completion certificate A document signed by the customer acknowledging that all work is complete and satisfactory.

compression fitting A type of fitting used to make a plumbing connection. A compression fitting typically uses a brass body and nut with a ferrule to compress over the pipe, preventing water from leaking.

concrete apron The section of concrete where a garage floor joins the driveway. Aprons allow for a smooth transition from a lower driveway to an elevated garage floor.

contract deposit A financial deposit given when a contract is signed and before work is started.

cornice A horizontal molding usually projecting from the top of an exterior wall to provide better water drainage.

cosmetic improvements Improvements with no structural significance, performed as an aesthetic enhancement to the property.

cost approach An appraisal technique used to determine a property value and based on the cost to build the structure.

cost estimate sheet A form designed to accurately project the cost of a proposed improvement.

cost increase cap A limit place on the price increase of a future purchase.

craftsperson A word used to describe a person working in a trade who is experienced and proficient in the trade.

crawl space The space beneath a house between the first-story floor joists and the ground. A crawl space is surrounded by a foundation.

crown molding A decorative wood trim placed at the top of an interior wall where the wall meets the ceiling.

curb appeal A term used in real estate sales referring to the exterior appearance of a property.

cut sheets Illustrated fact sheets providing detailed information on a product.

daylight basement A basement with windows that allow natural light to flow into the basement.

decking The materials used to build an exterior deck or interior flooring systems.

deed description A legal description of a property as it is referred to in the registered deed.

demo work Other wise known as demolition work. Demo work is the process of dismantling or destroying existing conditions.

demographic studies Statistical studies of the population. These studies can include specifics such as age, sex, income, and other highly detailed information.

denial notice A notice of rejection or turn-down for a requested service, such as a loan.

direct market evaluation approach An appraisal technique used to determine property value by comparing the subject property to other similar properties. All pertinent features of the subject property are compared to similar properties, and financial adjustments are made for the differences to establish a value on the subject property.

discretionary income Income not committed to a particular expense. Discretionary income is the amount of money an individual has to spend on anything he or she wishes.

dormer A projection built from the slope of a roof allowing additional room height and the opportunity to install windows.

downtime A period of nonproductive or lost time.

drain A pipe carrying water or waterborne waste to a main drainage system.

drywall A type of wall covering made of gypsum.

drywall mud The substance used to hide seams and nail or screw heads in the finished walls of a home.

DWV system Drain, waste, and vent system. The DWV system is the plumbing system used in a home for the drainage and venting of plumbing fixtures.

8-inch-center faucet A faucet designed to have its two handles spaced on an 8" center. These faucets comprise separate elements for each handle and the spout, which are connected beneath the fixture's surface to allow the faucet to operate.

18-inch toilet A special toilet designed for physically restricted individuals. The seat of these toilets is higher than that of a standard toilet, allowing easier use without as much demand for physical strength.

electric heat Electric baseboard heating units attached permanently to the interior wall of a home. Electric heat can utilize other forms of heating equipment such as a wall-mounted blower unit. Electrical current provides the source for producing heat.

electrical service The size and capacity of a home's circuit breaker or fuse box. Older homes were equipped with 60-amp electrical services. Modern homes have 100-amp or 200-amp electrical services as a standard service.

elevations Illustrations on the blueprints. Examples are drawings of the front of a house, the side of the house, and the rear of the house.

estimated job cost The projected cost required to complete a job.

exclusions Phrases or sentences within a contract that release a party from responsibility for certain acts or circumstances.

exterior framing The material or labor used in the construction of exterior walls and roof structures.

exterior improvements Improvements made outside of a dwelling. Examples are garages, landscaping, exterior painting, and roofing.

exterior wall sheathing The exterior wallcovering placed between the exterior wall studs and the exterior siding.

fair market value The estimated value of a property quoted to the buying public in the real estate market.

fiberboard A composite sheet made from pressed materials bonded together for use as a wall sheathing.

fill-in job A job with no committed completion time. These jobs are often completed at discounted prices, because they allow flexibility for the contractor.

finished basement A basement that has been completed into finished living space. The walls, ceiling, and floor are all completed to an acceptable finished standard. The basement is also provided with heat, electrical outlets, lights, and switches.

fixed rate loan A loan with an interest rate that does not fluctuate at any point in the life of the loan.

flashed The attachment of articles to houses or roofs and the penetration of roofs by pipes. When these conditions exist, they are flashed to seal the area from water infiltration. Plumbing pipes exiting through a roof are flashed with neoprene or some other material to prevent water leaks around the pipes. Where decks or bow windows are attached to a house, they are flashed with lightweight metal to prevent water damage behind the point of attachment.

floor joist A structural member or board used to support the floor of a house. Floor joists span between foundation walls and girders at regular intervals to provide strength and support to the finished floor.

fluorescent light A lamp or tube producing light by radiant energy. Fluorescent lights contain tubes that are coated with a fluorescent substance that gives off light when mercury vapor comes into contact with electrons.

footing A support, usually concrete, under a foundation that provides a larger base than the foundation on which to distribute weight. Footings are placed on solid surfaces and reduce settling and shifting of foundations.

forced hot air furnace A type of heating system producing warm air heat and forcing the warm air through ducts, through the use of a blower, into the heated area.

form contract Standard or generic forms, available at office-supply stores and stationery vendors, that are intended for use as legal contracts when the blank spaces are filled in.

foundation The base of a structure. Foundations are used to support the entire structure.

4-inch-center faucet Otherwise known as a close-coupled faucet. These faucets are produced as an integral, one-piece unit. The handles and the spout are molded from the same material, producing a faucet with all working parts molded together.

framing The process of building the frame structure of a home on which siding, sheathing, and wall coverings will be applied.

fumigation The process of exposing an area to fumes to rid it of existing vermin or insects.

functional obsolescence The absence of common desirable features in the design, layout, or construction of a home. A kitchen without cabinets or a modern sink would be considered a form of functional obsolescence.

general contractor The contractor responsible for the entire job. The general contractor coordinates subcontractors in individual aspects of the job.

grace period The period of time a commitment may go unkept before enforcement action is taken.

greenhouse style window A bow window unit designed to extend beyond the exterior wall of a house and made mostly of glass. This type of window is meant to allow additional lighting and provide a feeling of openness.

ground fault interceptor outlet An electrical outlet, used primarily in bathrooms and kitchens, with a safety feature to protect against electrical shock.

grout The substance used to fill cracks between tile during the installation process.

hard costs Expenses easily identified and directly related to a job. Examples of hard costs include the cost of labor and materials for the construction process.

heat lamp, fan combination An electrical fixture commonly placed in the ceiling of bathrooms. This unit combines an exhaust fan with a heat lamp and provides warmth along with the removal of moisture.

heat pump A device used for heating and cooling a home. Heat pumps are an effective heating and cooling unit in moderate climates and are being improved for use in extremely cold climates. They are energy efficient and do not require a flue or a chimney.

HVAC Heating, ventilation, and air-conditioning.

in the field Being out of the office and on the job.

incandescent light A light that uses a filament, contained in a vacuum, to produce light when the filament is heated by electrical current.

insulated foam sheathing A type of sheathing made from compressed foam and covered by a foil or other substance. Insulated foam sheathing can be used as a wall sheathing with increased insulating value.

interior partitions The walls located within a home that divide the living area into different sections or rooms.

interior remodeling Altering the condition of areas within the home.

interior trim Any decorative wood trim used within the home. Examples are baseboard trim, window casing, chair rail, crown molding, and door casings.

job juggling The practice of moving among multiple jobs during the same time frame. This practice is frequently used to describe the ineffective work habits of a company that has taken on too much work or has a slow cash flow.

joint compound Also know as drywall mud. Joint compound is the substance used to hide seams and nail or screw heads in the finished walls of a home.

joists Supporting structural members, usually made of wood, that allow the support of floors and ceilings.

liability insurance Insurance obtained to protect the insured against damage or injury claims and lawsuits.

lien rights The right of contractors and suppliers to lien a property where services or products are provided but not paid for.

lien waiver A document used to protect property from mechanic and materialman liens. These documents are signed by the vendor upon payment to acknowledge the payment and to release their lien right against the property, the products, or services rendered for a customer.

line drawing A simple plan drawn with single lines indicating the area's perimeters and divisions into sections and rooms.

liner feet A unit of measure representing the distance between two points in a straight line.

load-bearing walls Walls supporting the structural members of a building.

loan company Companies specializing in making loans, but not offering the services of a full-service bank or savings and loan association.

lot number A number assigned to a particular piece of property on zoning or subdivision maps.

lowboy toilet A one-piece toilet with a low profile. These toilets have an integrated tank that does not rise as high above the bowl as a standard toilet.

market analysis A study of real estate market conditions used to establish an estimated fair market value for the sale of a home.

market evaluation Market analysis. A market evaluation is a study of real estate market conditions used to establish an estimated fair market value for the sale of a home.

marketability The feasibility of selling a house on the current real estate market. Marketability is determined by the features and benefits of a home.

material The products and goods used in building and remodeling.

material legend An area on blueprints describing in great detail the types of materials to be used in the construction or remodeling of the proposed project.

materialman's lien A recorded security instrument placed on the title of a property to secure an interest in the property until a legal dispute can be resolved. These liens are placed when a supplier has supplied material for a property and has been refused full payment. Liens create a cloud on the title and make transferring ownership of the property very difficult.

mechanic's lien A recorded security instrument placed on the title of a property to secure an interest in the property until a legal dispute can be resolved. These liens are placed when a contractor has supplied labor for a property and has been refused full payment. Liens create a cloud on the title and make transferring ownership of the property very difficult.

metes and bounds The oldest method of describing the boundaries of a property. In this method the boundaries are described in detail using natural or artificial monuments and by explaining the direction and distance the property lines run.

miter box A small box that is designed to allow a saw blade to pass through the box and cut wood that is laid in the box. Slits guide the saw along a specific angle when the wood is cut. Miter boxes are used for cutting angles on finish trim boards.

mortar A mixture of lime or cement used between bricks, blocks, and stones to hold them in place.

mortgage A pledge or document securing a lender's investment and accompanying the note for the loan.

mortgage broker A liaison between a borrower and a lender. A mortgage broker is an individual who attempts to procure financing for a client for a fee.

multiple listing service A service provided to real estate brokers that include a listing of all real estate for sale by the members of the service. Multiple listing books provide information on all homes that are for sale and that have been sold during a given time by the participating members in the real estate profession.

nonconforming A house or improvement that is not similar to surrounding properties in age, size, use, or style. An example would be a one-level ranch-style house in a neighborhood comprising two story colonial-style homes.

nonstructural changes Changes not affecting the structural integrating of building. Examples are replacing kitchen cabinets, installing new carpet, and painting.

oak veneer vanity A vanity constructed of plywood or particleboard that is covered with an exterior finish of oak.

one-piece toilet A modern style toilet with the tank and the bowl molded as a single element. A one-piece toilet has a sleek appearance and an easy-to-clean surface. Standard toilets have the tank and the bowl as two separate pieces that are joined together with brass bolts and nuts.

open-end billing Working on a time-and-material basis and billing for all labor and material involved in a job. In open-end billing, no limit is place on the total amount to be billed.

outlet plate The cover placed over and screwed to the center of an electrical outlet.

outside wall Any wall with one side meeting outside air space.

overbuilding The practice of investing money in a home that is unlikely to be recovered, due to surrounding properties. An example would be adding three bedrooms to a home, for a total of six bedrooms, when surrounding houses only have three bedrooms.

particleboard A composite of wood chips bonded and pressed together to create a sheet that can be used for subflooring or sheathing.

pedestal sink A prestigious style of bathroom sink that has a china bowl hung on the wall and supported by a china pedestal. The pedestal adds support to the bowl and hides the plumbing connected to the sink and faucet.

permits Documents issued by the code enforcement office that allow work to be legally performed.

plans scale A defined and constant unit of measure for blueprints and drawings. An example is standard blueprints that use a scale in which each quarter of an inch on the blueprints equals one foot in the actual building.

plumbing stack A pipe that rises vertically through a building to carry waste and water to the building sewer or to vent plumbing fixtures when it penetrates the roof of the building.

plywood A wood product comprising multiple layers of veneer joined with an adhesive. Plywood usually has three layers, but the number of layers is always an odd number. Typically, the grain of each veneer is joined at 90° angles.

point-up The procedure used to repair or replenish the mortar between bricks, blocks, stone, and tile.

points Also known as discount points, they are fees paid to a lender that increase the yield of a loan being offered by the lender.

polybutylene pipe A modern type of flexible, plastic pipe used for the distribution of potable water in building.

potable water Water meeting the requirements to be considered safe for drinking, cooking, and domestic purposes.

powder room A room containing a toilet and a lavatory but not a bathtub or shower. Also known as a half bath.

prefab truss system A manufactured roof system that eliminates the need to stick-build a rafter roof. Trusses require no on-site cutting or building.

prepayment penalty A penalty charged by a lender when a loan is paid in full before its maturity date. Prepayment penalties ensure the lender of receiving the full yield of a loan, regardless of when it is paid off.

pressure balance control A type of plumbing faucet. These faucets are considered a safety feature because they prevent the user from being scalded by hot water when there is a fluctuation in the cold-water pressure.

preventive improvements Improvements designed to reduce costly repairs and replacements through routine maintenance.

prime for paint The process of preparing a surface to receive paint.

production schedule The agenda for events to be performed in the construction and remodeling process.

progress payments Periodic payments made as work progresses into defined stages, such as rough-in and final.

punch-out The process of correcting deficiencies and making minor adjustments at the end of the job.

PVC pipe Polyvinyl chloride, a type of plastic pipe used in plumbing. PVC pipe is frequently used for drains and vents. It is also occasionally used for cold-water piping.

quotes Firm prices given by contractors and suppliers for labor and material.

rafter cuts The angles cut on rafter boards when stick-building a roofing system.

rafters Structural members, usually made of wood, that support the roof of a building.

registry of deeds A place where deeds are recorded and are available for public inspection.

rehab Reconstruction or restoration of an existing, run-down building.

remodeling The practice of altering existing conditions and adding new space to existing structures.

retainage A hold-back of money owed to a contractor for an agreed-upon period of time. Retainage protects the consumer from defective material or workmanship.

rigid copper tubing Frequently called copper pipe. Rigid copper tubing is a common material used in the potable water distribution system of residences. It typically comes in rigid lengths of 10 or 20 feet and can be cut as needed.

rimmed lavatory A drop-in style lavatory with a steel rim surrounding the lavatory bowl to hold the bowl in place.

rip-out The removal of existing items to allow the installation of new items. An example would be the removal of an old bathtub and surrounding tile to allow for the installation of a new tub and tile.

roof sheathing The material secured to the rafters or trusses to allow the installation of a finished roof. Plywood and particleboard are frequently used as roof sheathing.

roofing felt A black paper-like product applied between the roof sheathing and the shingles. Roofing felt reduces the effects of extreme temperatures and moisture levels.

rough plumbing The pipes and fittings of a plumbing system, not including fixtures.

rough-in The installation of material prior to enclosing the stud walls. The bulk of plumbing, heating, and electrical systems must be installed before the wall coverings are applied. This is considered rough-in work.

rough-in draw A progress payment made when the rough-in work is complete.

round front toilet A toilet with a rounded bowl. Most residential toilets have round fronts.

schedule-40 A rating for the thickness and strength of a pipe. Schedule-40 is the standard weight of plastic pipe used for residential drainage and vent plumbing systems.

seal for paint A sealing agent applied to stains before painting is begun. This process prevents the stain from bleeding through the new paint.

secondary market Markets in which banks and other lenders sell their real estate loans. The original lenders normally continue to service these loans for a fee but are able to recycle their available lending funds by selling the loans to the secondary market. The secondary market comprises individual investors, corporations, and organizations.

section of property A legal description of a property. The section of a property is typically referred to on zoning and subdivision maps.

selling up Selling a customer additional services and products.

setback requirement Zoning regulations in which a certain amount of unobstructed space must exist between properties. With setback requirements, owning the land does not mean you can build on all of it. These requirements establish a rule about the necessary distance between a structure and each property line.

sheathing The material applied to exterior studs and rafters to allow the installation of finished siding and roofing.

sheet-vinyl flooring Also known as resilient sheet goods. These floor coverings are available in widths of 6, 9, and 12 feet. Sheet-vinyl flooring is a common and well-accepted floor covering for kitchens and bathrooms.

shims Small pieces of tapered wood used to level construction and remodeling materials, such as doors, cabinets, and windows.

shower head arm outlet The female adapter located approximately 6 feet, 6 inches above the finished bathroom floor, in the center of the shower area.

sill The board placed on top of the foundation and beneath the floor joists.

site conditions The conditions of a construction site. Examples would be level, sloping, rocky, and wet.

site work The preparation of a site for construction.

skylight A glass panel located in the roof. A skylight allows natural light to fill a space below it.

slab Usually a flat, interior-reinforced concrete floor area.

soft costs Expenses incurred in a project that are not directly related to construction or remodeling in the strictest sense. Examples are loan fees, surveys, legal fees, and professional fees.

spa A bathing tub with whirlpool jets that is filled with a garden hose. Spas are designed to hold and heat water indefinitely with the use of chemicals and an independent water heater.

specifications A compilation of the services and products to be used in the completion of a project. Specifications can be addressed individually in a contract or may take the form of a separate collection of documents.

square feet A unit of measure frequently used by contractors. To obtain the square footage of an area, you must multiply the length of two perpendicular walls together. In a space with 90° corners, this procedure will give you the total square footage of the area.

square-foot method An appraisal technique where a value is assigned for each square foot of space contained in a building. This method is reasonably accurate with standard new construction procedures but is rarely accurate or used in remodeling.

square yards A unit of measure most commonly used in floor coverings. To obtain square yardage, you must take the square footage of an area and divide it by nine.

standard-grade fixture A builder-grade fixture. A standard-grade fixture is a product of average quality that is normally found in production-built housing.

stick-build To build a structure on-site with conventional construction methods.

storage ceiling joists Ceiling joists rated to carry an additional weight load for storage above the ceiling.

strip lights Multiple incandescent lights mounted on a metal or wood strip. Common applications include three or four lights mounted on an oak strip for use in bathrooms.

structural members Structural members normally consist of wood and support a portion of the building. Examples are floor joists, rafters, and ceiling joists.

structural plans Plans or blueprints detailing the materials to be used and the placement of these materials for structural additions or changes.

structural integrity The strength of a structure to remain in its planned position without fail.

structural work Work involving the structural integrity of a building. Examples are adding a dormer addition, expanding an existing structure, or relocating load-bearing walls.

studs The vertical wooden members of a wall. Studs are placed at regular intervals to allow support and a nailing surface for wall coverings and exterior siding.

subfloor Generally either plywood or particleboard sheets attached to floor joists under the finished floor covering.

subcontractor A contractor working under the supervision of a general contractor. Examples are plumbers, electricians, or HVAC contractors.

subs An abbreviation for subcontractors.

substitution clause A common clause in contracts allowing a supplier or contractor to substitute a similar product in place of the specified product. These clauses should only be allowed when they are heavily detailed and clearly define the products substitutions will be made with.

suppliers The companies supplying materials that are used in construction and remodeling.

support columns Vertical columns used for structural support. An example could be the columns found in basements or garages that support the main girder.

T & M Time and material. T & M is a form of billing for all labor and material supplied and has no preset limit to the billed amount.

take-off An estimate of the materials and labor required to do a job. Take-offs are generally associated more with material than labor.

tankless coil An internal part of a hot-water boiler heating system. A tankless coil is also referred to as a domestic coil. The coil provides a source of potable hot water by heating water as the water passes through a copper coil located beneath the boiler's jacket.

taped drywall Drywall that has been hung and taped. The tape is applied with the use of joint compound to hide the seams where sheets of drywall meet.

temperature-controlled foundation vents Modern foundation vents that sense the temperature and respond by opening or closing automatically. These vents allow for better foundation ventilation throughout the year.

templates A trade term with multiple definitions. The first definition is a plastic stencil kit allowing draftsmen to draw consistent symbols of items for blueprints. Examples are toilets, doors, electrical switches, and sinks. The second use of the word is to describe a guide. These guides are used for cutting countertops in order to allow the installation of kitchen sinks and other related work.

tented fumigation The process of enveloping an entire house in a tent to allow a total fumigation of all the home's wood-related products. This process is used to remove certain wood-boring insects.

threshold A trim piece that connects two flooring areas. A threshold is usually made of wood, metal, vinyl, or marble. It serves as trim for the seam between two different materials, such as a vinyl bathroom floor and the hall carpet.

time-and-material basis Basically the same as open-billing. Time-and-material basis is a method of billing for all labor and material supplied without a set limit to the billed amount.

title search A function frequently preformed by attorneys to certify that a title is clear of liens or other clouds preventing a satisfactory real estate closing.

toilet bowl The part of a toilet where the seat is attached.

toilet tank The part of a toilet that holds the handle. A toilet tank is a reservoir tank that holds up to 5 gallons of water and allows the toilet to be flushed.

tongue-and-groove paneling A type of paneling or siding with a groove on one side and a projection on the other. The projection is placed inside the groove of adjoining panels to form an attractive finished seam.

tract housing Production or subdivision housing. The term refers to houses built on a tract of land.

tradespeople People working within a trade.

trigger points The key words or actions that result in a potential buyer agreeing to make a purchase.

trim Any object, normally wood, used to provide a finished look to a product or installation.

12-inch-rough toilet A standard toilet where the center of the drain pipe is located 12 inches from the finished wall behind the toilet.

two-piece toilet A combination of a toilet tank and bowl that are connected by brass bolts and nuts in order to form an operational toilet.

type "K" copper tubing Copper tubing that is marked with a green stripe and has a thicker wall than type "M" or type "L" copper. Type "K" is the preferred choice in copper tubing for underground installations. However, this tubing sees little use in above-ground, residential applications.

type "L" copper tubing Copper tubing that is marked with a blue stripe and is approved for use underground. Type "L" copper tubing has a thicker sidewall than type "M" copper. This tubing is becoming the most frequently used copper in residential water distribution systems.

type "M" copper tubing Copper tubing that is marked with a red stripe and is frequently used for piping residential hot-water heating systems. Until recently, it was a common carrier of potable water to plumbing fixtures. However, it is not approved in most locations for underground use; code revisions are phasing out type "M" as a potable water distribution pipe and requiring type "L".

underlayment A smooth sheet of wood applied between the subfloor and the finished floor. Underlayment is most commonly used when vinyl-sheet goods are to be installed. This material provides a smooth even surface for the vinyl to rest on.

unfinished basement A basement with a concrete floor and unfinished walls and ceiling. In an unfinished basement, there are minimal electrical outlets and little or no heat.

valance A short curtain that forms a border between a window and the ceiling or a short trim board connecting the top of kitchen cabinets to the ceiling.

vanity A base cabinet for a bathroom lavatory or sink.

vent pipe A part of the plumbing system designed to allow the free circulation of air within the plumbing drain and vent system.

vented exhaust fan Fans used to remove fumes, odors, gases, and moisture from a kitchen or bathroom and disperse them on the outside of the house.

vinyl siding A type of exterior siding requiring little-to-no maintenance and having a life expectancy of 20 years. The color of the siding is a part of the molded vinyl and will not fade or wear off under normal conditions.

wainscotting The procedure of installing wood on the lower portion of a wall, joined by chair rail, to meet the upper wall, which is finished with paint or wallpaper.

walk-in closet A closet large enough to walk into and store or remove clothing.

walk-out basement A basement with a door on ground level allowing ingress and egress directly between the basement and the outside of the house.

wallcovering Anything covering a wall, usually consisting of paint, wallpaper, drywall, wood, siding, and plaster.

wall-hung lavatory A bathroom lavatory designed to hang on the wall with no other support.

washer outlet box A metal or plastic box designed to be recessed in an interior partition that allows the connection of washing machine water hoses and provides an indirect waste for the washing machine discharge hose.

water-distribution pipes The pipes carrying potable water to the plumbing fixtures.

water-saver toilet A toilet using 3 gallons of water or less each time the toilet is flushed.

whirlpool A bathing tub with whirlpool jets. These tubs are equipped with faucets and sanitary plumbing drains. They are designed to be filled and drained each time they are used.

whirlpool jets The devices found in whirlpool tubs and spas that cause jets of water to circulate the standing water contained in the bathing units.

workers' compensation insurance Insurance that protects workers who are injured while performing their professional duties.

working plans Any set of plans that adequately allow tradespeople to perform their duties in a satisfactory manner.

Index

About the author

Chase Powers is a familiar name in the building and remodeling industry. He is a licensed general contractor with extensive experience in both building and remodeling on a residential and light-commercial level. His work has included all types of remodeling, including attic and basement conversions, room additions, cosmetic changeovers, and many more nonstructural as well as structural changes. Kitchen and bathroom remodeling have long been his specialties. Among his other accomplishments, he has conducted home remodeling seminars across the East Coast.